BUREAUCRATS, PETTY BOURGEOIS AND TOWNSMEN:

An Observation on Status Identification in Kota Bharu

Halim Hj. Salleh

Monash Paper on Southeast Asia — No. 8
1981

CENTRE OF SOUTHEAST ASIAN STUDIES
MONASH UNIVERSITY

ISBN 0 86746 109 8

Printed by Aristoc Press Pty. Ltd.
Glen Waverley.

PREFACE

This is a revised version of a Master of Arts thesis submitted to the Department of Anthropology and Sociology, Monash University, Victoria, Australia in 1976. Except for the introduction which is mainly the result of almost four years of associating Social Anthropology with problems of development in Malaysia, a great deal of the original ideas and arguments have been retained. The main observation presented in this work must however, be seen in the light of this new introduction, rather than be judged against it.

A short note about the choice of the Kampung in Kota Bharu town as the fieldwork area may be in order. It originated from one of the earliest concentrations of population in the town, that is the 'fort' which in the earlier times characterised the residential pattern of the indigenous town. It is situated in what is commonly known as the older part of Kota Bharu, in which case the area in its vicinity is marked by long established capitalistic enterprises like for instance the renowned Kelantan Match Factory. These two factors are therefore particularly important as a background framework from which the historical changes in the class structure consequent to the penetration of capital may be analysed. In addition, it is only within the context of the contrast between the past and the present patterns of social life in the specific historical continuity that we may see such changes as meaningful.

Whenever Malay words are used in the text, they are either italicised with the English equivalents in brackets, for example *jemaah* (prayers), or where the English meaning is clear, the Malay words have been included in the brackets and italicised. Malay concepts are explained in the footnotes that appear at the end of each chapter and wherever possible their English equivalents are subsequently used. Otherwise Malay concepts (italicised) shall be subsequently used.

I would like to thank Professor M.G. Swift, the original thesis supervisor at Monash University whose suggestion also gave me the necessary confidence to revise the thesis into the present form. I am also grateful to Dr David Chandler, Research Director, Centre of Southeast Asian Studies, Monash University who has not only read and suggested some revision, but also put up with my delays. I am grateful to Lois Osborn of the Faculty of Arts Office for typesetting the monograph.

To repeat what was originally stated in the thesis, I owe a great deal to the people and friends in the Kampung observed, and to my teachers at Monash University. The usual disclaimers, however, apply.

H.S.

PREFACE

This is a revised version of a Master of Arts thesis submitted to the Department of Anthropology and Sociology, Monash University, Victoria, Australia in 1976. Except for the introduction which is mainly the result of almost four years of teaching Social Anthropology with problems of development in Malaysia, the content of the original ideas and arguments have been retained. The many observations presented in this work must however be seen in the light of the new introduction rather than be judged against it.

A short note about the choice of the Kampung in Kota Bharu town as the fieldwork area may be in order. It originated from one of the earliest concentrations of population in the town, that is the 'Fort' which in the earlier times characterised the residential pattern of the indigenous towns. It is situated in what is commonly known as the older part of Kota Bharu, in which case the area in its vicinity is marked by long established capitalistic enterprises like for instance the [illegible] Kelantan Match Factory. These two factors are therefore particularly important as a background framework from which the historical changes in the class structure consequent to the penetration of capital may be analysed. In addition, it is only within the context of the contrast between the past and the present patterns of social life in the area as historical continuity that we may see such changes as meaningful.

Whenever Malay words are used in the text, they are either italicised with the English equivalents in brackets, for example *kampung* (village), or where the English meaning is clear the Malay words have been included in the brackets and italicised. Malay concepts are explained in the footnotes that appear at the end of each chapter and wherever possible their English equivalents are subsequently used. Otherwise Malay concepts (italicised) shall be subsequently used.

I would like to thank Professor W.C. Geddes, the original thesis supervisor at Monash University whose suggestion also gave me the necessary confidence to revise the thesis into the present form. I am also grateful to Dr. David Chandler, Research Director, Centre of Southeast Asian Studies, Monash University who has not only read and suggested some revision, but also put up with my delays. I am grateful to Lois Osborn of the Faculty of Arts, Office for typesetting the monograph.

To repeat what was originally stated in the thesis, I owe a great deal to the people and friends in the Kampung observed, and to my teachers at Monash University. The usual disclaimers, however, apply.

H.S.

CONTENTS

LIST OF MAPS

LIST OF TABLES

INTRODUCTION

This is the account of an observation on social relations among the Malays in a residential section I have called Kampung Bendahara in Kota Bharu town, the State capital of Kelantan. Recognizing the importance of historical perspective in the observation, it becomes imperative that this exercise focuses largely on the problems related to changes in, or the process of reproduction of the structure of social relations consequent to the penetration and subsequent dominance of capital in the State.

I do not claim that the fictitious Kampung Bendahara is representative or typical of the residential wards of the town. Kota Bharu as a whole had a total population of 55,124 in 1970, in an area of 4.4 square miles. Physically, the area had increased to 44.65 square miles by 1978 and the population had grown to more than 70,000 people. This makes the area under observation only a small dot of the town, but the residents do emphatically designate their eight acre residential area as their Kampung, i.e. a complete socio-cultural unit which I shall refer as the local social formation bearing the characteristics of a kampung as the word is understood in the Malay language. It has a total of 321 people consisting of 123 adults, 52 youths and 146 children organised in 68 households of bureaucrats, petty-bourgeois, proletariat and semi-proletariat clustering around a small prayer house (*madrasah*). Being part of the town, it has some of the necessary albeit publicly accessible amenities like tarred access roads, electricity, water supply, sewerage and rubbish disposal services. Many people still make use of the river on the eastern fringe of the Kampung for the supply of non-drinking water for washing, bathing and processing batik cloth. The river is also used to dispose waste products, including human waste. In so far as the micro-anthropological study is significant therefore, the dynamics of social relations in the Kampung exposes some of the complexities involved in conceptualising social change in Malaysia today.

Obviously the quest for social change in Kelantan in the tradition of western social science began and expanded at the same rate as the rise of penetration and dominance of capital in the State itself. The slow beginning of capital penetration was accounted for generally by Graham (1908). The subsequent increase and dominance of capital in the State was followed by a more penetrating analysis of the problem, though the main focus was on the fishermen of Perupok (Firth: 1966) The latter study marks the beginning of the present era of systematic analysis of social change effected on Kelantan social formation by mature western social science. In any case it has set off a train of interest in the subject among foreign and local scholars as well as organisations (Appendix 8). To some extent, this new interest which invariably takes the form of fieldwork research projects has become a nuisance to the people of Kelantan.[1] Similarly, the scholarly content of such projects may to a large extent be questionable.

However, save for the work of Kessler (1978) and Syed Husin Ali (1978), it seems that studies on Kelantan are, to a varying degree caught up in the futile search to determine the extent to which the fishermen or peasants have become capitalists. For instance, while Firth (1966) himself recognised the 'structural' aspects of the economy of the fishermen, he was still worried about the fact that the fishermen were not accumulating sufficient capital to increase production in the manner of capitalist business enterprises. More remarkable is the case of Downs who observed in 1967 that the peasants were less controlled by the belief in supernatural forces, thus facilitating monetization and commercialization of the economy, 'specialization associated with modern economic changes' and 'introduction and adptation of new ideas and practices' (1967, 168–183 *passim*). Possibly, the most exemplary case in this regard is worth quoting in full. Nash states that:

> Malaysia is poised on the edge of full modernisation, its chief problem being the orderly induction of most of the Malay peasantry into a modern economic sector with all the implications of modernity: increased occupational differentiation: class structures based largely on economic performance and education: reduced familial networks: and loss some sense of community in return for spatial and social mobility. The peasantry in Kelantan exhibits in an extreme form the social and cultural problems involved in this sort of economic shift. (1974, 148).

Therefore, he continues:

> The peasants in these circumstances, cannot merely have his life incrementally improved. He must be transformed into a farmer, into a worker or into some other modern occupational categories. (*op. cit.*, 149)

The fact that this modernist approach is to a large extent dominant in the study of Malaysian and generally, the Third World development and modernisation may explain the above emphasis (cf. Amin 1974, 5–10). Referring to South East Asia for instance, Geertz (1965) is so strongly dominated by the approach that the problems of change which define the present state of social affairs in the Third World become, in his eyes, the problems of transition. One may well ask: transition to what? Even though the tradition remains unexpressed, to some degree, Evers (1973) is similarly caught up in it when he would not commit himself to a definite theoretical conclusion in introducing a discourse on issues in South East Asian 'modernisation'. If anything, this widespread inconclusiveness is symptomatic of the extreme poverty inherent in the approach of the modernists. While to some extent the approach may amount to a teleological exercise, there is the tendency among the modernists to reduce the problems of social change to problems asociated with psychology, refurbishing the colonial manipulation of images and characteristics of the indigenous population. Speaking about the Malays for instance, Tham Seong Chee states very neatly that

> The fact that economic development continues to be a major concern of the Malays after such a long period is suggestive of the absence of the total restructuring of values and ideas including ideals relating to the cognitive framework of the Malays. (1977, 285).

This of course has been vigorously demonstrated to be no more than a 'myth' created by the dominant colonial class to serve the needs and requirements of the colonial interest (Syed Hussein Alatas, 1977).

These distortions in the current state of conceptualising social change created by the imperialist social science may be explained by the nature of capital penetration itself. In many ways, this school of social scientists has been aware that regardless of its many guises, it has never been the aim of capital to develop the fishermen or peasants in Malaysia or in any other Third World country into capitalists. It would only defeat the fundamental and original aim of capital to plunder and destroy the natural economy around the globe in order to export capital and to achieve 'super profits' and thus maintain the 'rate of profits' from declining, especially in times of hardship and strong competition within the European economy (Mandel 1962, 448–458). It is therefore senseless to conceive a situation where capital goes all the way out to create capitalists, i.e. their own competitors, either in the colonies or in the present Third World, to undermine their own position and accumulation. Indeed, it is suicidal for capital to 'develop' and 'modernise' others exactly into their own image. On the contrary, it is in fact vital that the pre-capitalist society or the Third World be dominated and oriented in any conceivable way either directly through violence and destruction, or indirectly through 'modernisation' and 'development', so long as they are transformed to serve the needs and the requirements of capital and its expansion. This is because, the original state of pre-capitalist society is not only useless for purposes of capital accumulation but more importantly because it forms what Marx calls the 'anti-capitalistic cancer':

> We have seen that the expropriation of the mass of people from the soil

> forms the basis of the capitalistic mode of production. The essence of a free colony, on the contrary, consists in this — that the bulk of the soil is still public property and every settler on it therefore can turn part of it into private property and individual means of production, without hindering the later settlers in the same operation. This is the secret of both the prosperity of the colonies and their inveterate vice — opposition to the establishment of capital'' (Marx 1967, 768). ''So long, therefore, as the labourer can accumulate for himself — and this he can do so long as he remains possessor of his means of production — capitalistic production and capitalistic mode of production are impossible (*loc cit.,*).

It is this fundamental logic of law of value or development of capital extended onto the international scale that Luxemburg emphasises:

> A natural economy thus confronts the requirements of capitalism at every turn with rigid barriers. Capitalism must therefore always and everywhere fight a battle of annihilation against every form of natural economy that it encounters . . . (1951, 369).

Regardless of the controversy and debate to determine the main driving forces which destroy the natural economy of the present pre-capitalist society (cf. Bukharin 1972), one may rest assured that the development of capital from the beginning (merchant capital) up to and until the present dominance of monopoly and finance capital in the world economy was driven by the primary concern for 'profits', especially 'super profits' (cf. Rydbers, Johnsson, Elmquist and Langemar 1974; Lenin 1970). In this regard, Bukharin rightly asserts that regardless of whether imperialism involves 'export of capital' or the use of cheap labour, the former '. . . is not done because it absolutely cannot be applied at home, but *because it can be employed at a higher rate of profit* in a foreign country', (1972, 245), and the latter may be exploited '*at the highest rate of exploitation*' (*op. cit.,* 249).

This primary interest in capitalist profit and therefore capital accumulation and expansion thus makes the question of capitalisation of the Third World only a secondary consideration, if at all. Rather, capital will seek the most economical way to maximise surplus production and surplus value such that the transformation of the local social relations to anything close to capitalist relations of production must be done only if it is beneficial to the requirements for capital expansion (cf. Bradby 1975, 149). In fact, it is significant to note that the ''backwardness'', ''underdevelopment'', or the maintenance of pre-capitalist relations of production in the Third World today appear to be a result of a deliberate capitalist design rather than a residual and transitional condition awaiting transformation into capitalism. Indeed it '. . . is an inherent condition of the process of accumulation in the central countries'

(Laclau 1971, 35). It is in this light that we may see the development of private property in land in Malaya as being dictated by foreign capital which entrenched and forced the indigenous population into simple reproduction within the pre-capitalist relations characterised by poverty and backwardness (cf. Wong 1975; and Lim 1977).

It is of course difficult to ascertain the exact nature of the confrontation between indigenous and the capitalist economies (cf. Banaji 1972; Foster-Carter 1978), but in the case of Malaysia, we may suggest that the fishermen or peasants are changed, 'developed' or 'modernised' individually or collectively only to the extent that they become useful for capital to accumulate and expand. What this means is that the incomplete nature of capitalisation of the indigenous Malay mode of production does not and will never completely change the Kelantan fishermen and peasants class as a whole into 'modern' entrepreneurs and workers in the way the process is conceived by the modernists. The confrontation between capitalist and indigenous modes of production in Kelantan with the dominance of the former tends to absorb some individuals and groups of people into capitalist relations of production more than others. This means that there are only certain individuals and groups of people in Kelantan who are transformed to approximation of the entrepreneurs and workers of the capitalist mode of production. Others remain dominated to a large extent by the dictates of the indigenous mode of production. To suggest that the latter group is untouched by capital is of course ridiculous. The mere fact of being subservient to capital forces the indigenous modes of production to operate to the success of the former. It is this complexity of the confrontation that is described by Taylor as the 'uneven subsumption of non-capitalist division of labour under increasingly dominant capitalist relations of production' within the context of the corresponding 'dislocation between and within instances of social formation' (1979, 215; 216).

Given the foregoing discussion, it is now necessary to suggest that the approach to the issues of social change in Kelantan has to be oriented away from problems of becoming 'modern' to problems associated with the manner in which the people have been manipulated, exploited and mutilated to serve the reproductive requirements of capital, including the international variety.

I cannot claim to have studied social change in Kelantan exhaustively in the current exercise. Also, I may have underrepresented some aspects. But assuming that the changes in the structure in social relations is an important aspect of social change, the current observation seeks to establish that given the specific nature of incomplete capitalisation of the indigenous Malay mode of production inherent in the process of imperialist expansion, the problem of change in social relations in the local social formation under observation may appear as problems of relation between two different modes of production, i.e. the indigenous and the capitalist modes. Indeed, it may be suggested that it is the articulation between these two modes that defines and structures the relations between classes and the reproduction of such relations in the Kampung under observation.

In order to do so I contend that the social relations in the indigenous Kota Bharu social formation was underpinned by the notion of '*daulat*' (royalness), an ideological construct which legitimises the centralisation and concentration of power, wealth and prestige, and the associated patterns of behaviour and way of life exclusive to the ruling class. The relations of production then distinguished people into two main classes, the *daulat* and the commoners, with the former distinguished into a hierarchy of positions expressed by their birth titles of the '*Tengku*' at the top most, followed by the '*Nik*' and '*Wan*' subclasses. The hierarchy within the ruling class signifies the relative closeness and accessibility of the subclasses to the absolute monopolist of power, wealth and prestige, that is the *sultan*. It may also be conceived that the '*Nik*' and '*Wan*' subclasses were in fact the executives who extracted the produce from the commoner classes for the ruling class as a whole. The commoner class, on the other hand, consisted mainly of the peasants, poor artisans, petty traders, slaves of the courts of the ruling class and other town dwellers who were all living at the whims and fancy of the ruling class.

With the increasing dominance of capital in the State, especially in the last two decades, the social relations in the town appear to have changed dramatically. In some cases, the royalness is no more indicative of the specific position within the productive system of the town or simply reduced to a mere formality, and in some other cases, the monopoly of power, wealth and prestige by the '*daulat*' class is now broken by some commoners. More important however, there is now a strong tendency for the objective class position within the local social formation to be highly distorted. It is no longer real in an objective class sense. It is rather highly subjective and regarded by the people concerned as mere social (status) groups in which a person may be included or otherwise depending on whether one is able to mobilize the necessary economic and the non-economic (religiousness and wealth) resources or a combination of both. One may enter these groups by way of life style. The notion of class as it is now conceived, therefore, need not coincide as before within the indigenous social formation with the objective class position of an individual. At any rate the basis of class structure in the local social formation now seems to have veered away from the simple notion of '*daulat*'. Given such a situation, I would argue that when capital preserves and defends the subservient indigenous mode of production as in Kota Bharu, the classes and the class relations it generates become highly distorted; while the new productive system introduces the new classes, the non-economic instance (especially religiousness in the present case) of the indigenous mode of production negates the reality of such classes and its relations. Consequently, 'classes', ideological and highly subjective in nature, become no more than loose groupings of people from various classes. In short, the consciousness of class and class relations in the town of Kota Bharu have been tranquillized, obviously for the benefit of the dominant capital to accumulate and expand.

This is what seemed to be the case in 1975 when the fieldwork was conducted. I started out with the idea that a particular type of expressive social relationship distinguishes, separates and brings together individuals and groups of persons in daily life (Simmel 1950, 309; Weber 1972, 63). This may be regarded as the vehicle through which the class position of a person is reminded, reaffirmed and confirmed in daily life, thus, theoretically conceived provide continuity to social relations of the town. This is at least true with the indigenous social relations.

My observation distinguishes people into what I have come to call the 'feasting circle', the 'individualists' and the 'raft-users'. As I have suggested above, these categories of people are not classes defined by their objective position within the productive system of the town. In addition, the people observed tried to deny the operation of the new class relations by idealising indigenous social relations, while at the same time emphasising the importance of religiousness in such relations. In other words, they try to construct a system of social relations in which they can find and understand their respective position in an increasingly alien productive system, thus distorting their conception of classes and class relations. It is within this complex relation between the indigenous social relations and the dominant capitalist ones that the present problem of class structure is presented.

Universiti Sains Malaysia, Halim Hj. Salleh
Batu Uban, Pulau Pinang.
December, 1981.

Footnotes

1. This is at least expressed by the people in the Pasir Mas and Tumpat region when the writer was conducting a research project on Local Industries in Kelantan in 1978 and again in 1979.

dividuals. At any rate the basis of class structure in the local social formation now seems to have veered away from the simple notion of 'status'. Given such a situation, I would argue that when capital preserves and defends the subservient indigenous mode of production as in Kota Bharu, the classes and the class relations it generates become highly distorted, while the new productive system introduces the new classes, the non-economic instances (especially religiousness in the present case) of the indigenous mode of production negates the reality of such classes and its relations. Consequently, 'classes', ideological and highly subjective in nature, become no more than loose groupings of people from various classes. In short, the consciousness of class and class relations in the town of Kota Bharu have been tranquilized, obviously for the benefit of the dominant capital to accumulate and expand.

This is what seemed to be the case in 1975 when the fieldwork was conducted. I started out with the idea that a particular type of expressive social relationship distinguishes, separates and brings together individuals and groups of persons in daily life (Simmel 1950:309; Weber 1947:65). These may be regarded as the vehicle through which the class position of a person is reminded, reaffirmed and confirmed in daily life, thus theoretically conceived opposite contrary to social relations of the town. This is at least true with the indigenous social relations.

My observation distinguishes people into what I have come to call the 'feasting circle', the 'individualists' and the 'rent-lords'. As I have suggested above, these are categories of people and not classes defined by their objective position within the productive system of the town. In addition, the people observed tried to deny the operation of the new class relations by idealising indigenous social relations, while at the same time emphasising the importance of religiousness in such relations. In other words, they try to construct a system of social relations in which they can find and understand their respective position in an increasingly alien productive system, thus distorting their conception of classes and class relations. It is within this complex relation between the indigenous social relations and the dominant capitalist ones that the present problem of class structure is presented.

Universiti Sains Malaysia — Halim Hj. Salleh
Batu Uban, Pulau Pinang
December, 1981.

Footnotes

1. This fear is expressed by the people in the Pasir Mas and Tumpat region when the writer was conducting a research project on Local Industries in Kelantan in 1978 and again in 1979.

CHAPTER ONE

THE INDIGENOUS SOCIAL FORMATION: THE OLD KOTA BHARU

The one hundred and thirty-first anniversary of Kota Bharu town was celebrated in July, 1975, commemorating its founding in 1844 by the Sultan of Kelantan, Sultan Mohamad II. Ever since then it has guarded and protected Kelantan in various confrontations, before finally succumbing to forces of colonialism and capitalism.

Kota Bharu as the capital-town of Kelantan on the east bank of Sungai Kelantan is not, however, the oldest settlement in the State. As early as the seventeenth century the Kelantan plain was extensively settled in the forms of conglomerations around 'fort of rulers' (*kota raja*).[1] In the eighteenth and nineteenth centuries the settlements spread out to the banks of rivers and at river mouths.[2] Their origin, though somewhat mythical, lies in the initial movements of the deity Che Siti Wan Kembang from her royal seat at Gunung Ayam to the flat alluvial land in the Kelantan plain. Subsequently, this was followed by the nomadic movements of her successors in their zeal for opening up the country. Thus, repeatedly the whole array of court officials, members of the royal households, indispensable specialists (*bomoh* and *nujum*), and few loyal subjects were mobilised, while at the same time leaving behind the old 'fort' under the charge of some trusted member of the royal household. Through the ages, the 'fort' broke down into clusters of Malay villages.[3]

Kota Bharu town in particular however, has its beginning in the form of clusters of villages (namely Kampung Che' Bu, present Kampung Sireh and Kubang Garong, the present Padang Garong) which were in existence prior to the reign of Long Tunus, the founder of the present royal house (Sa'ad Shukri *op. cit.*, 58, 61) who, after a successful usurpation of the throne, established the royal capital at Kampung Che' Bu in the 1780's. Subsequently it came to be known as Kota Istana Galoh Pengkalan Leser, presently the site of Istana Kota Lama. A Chinese visitor who roamed the 'South Seas' between 1783 and 1797 described it in the following manner:

> The King lived at the port. This port was where the morning market was held and where the ocean vessels were anchored. A circle of bamboo clusters had been planted to make a stockade and planks were added to

strengthen it. There was only one gate and the people lived outside the circle of bamboo'' (Wang Gungwu 1960, 31–32).

After the death of Long Yunus which was followed by a war of succession, Long Muhamad, the successor who took the title of Sultan Mohamad I, moved the royal capital in 1816, to Kota Istana Kebun Menseta or Kota Saba about two miles downstream. Oral reports emphasise that the settlement was the Kampung Kota Sultan situated directly in front of the present Jabatan Kastam (cf., map 4). This was where trading with foreigners was conducted, where taxes from river and coastal traders were collected and where a daily market was located. Though torn by civil war, it was presumably the town and the market where 'mainly foodstuffs were sold by women' as visited by Abdullah Munshi on Friday, April the thirteenth, 1838 (cf. Skinner 1965; cf. Skinner 1966, 24–33; cf. Kassim Ahmad 1960, 75–76).

However, it was not until 1844, after a civil war[4] that Sultan Mohamad II built a palace called 'kota bharu' (new fort) which laid the foundation for an urban conglomeration as it is today. Possible explanations for such movements of royal capitals (save for the erosion of the river bank in the present case) are unconvincing and scanty.[5] However, the fact remains that Kota Bharu was established in 1844 as the royal capital town of Kelantan.

Indigenous Town Growth

The foregoing establishes two characteristics of nineteenth century Kota Bharu. First, the town owes its origin to the indigenous Malay enterprise that centered around the court, and second, town social life was directly related to the stability of the royal house. Thus civil wars among the immediate successors to the throne represent not so much conflicting claims to the rights to rule as reflected in the non-evolution of a formal rule of succession; rather they represent the desire to compete for what the ideological legitimacy which permitted incumbents to tax river and coastal trades, foreign visitors and, eventually to monopolize trade itself. For instance:

> The rajah of that place it appears, has the good sense to patronise a more liberal system of trade than is usually countenanced by his compeers along the coast, and not to act on the principles of rigorous monopoly'', in contrast to the usual case ''where the rajah himself is the principal trader and almost always a monopolist (Editor, *Singapore Free Press* quoted by Skinner 1965, 24).

Heavy taxes were imposed on traders. These included taxes on goods, on boats (these varied from 200 to 300 silver coins according to their size), and foreigners, who were compelled to pay one silver coin on arrival and another with every subsequent year of stay (Tweedie *op. cit.*, 218). Chinese gold miners were even taxed a tahil of gold on leaving the country (*ibid*). The fact to be recognized here, then, is that nineteenth century Kota Bharu was a strong commercial post which stood 'confessedly unrivalled' especially in the gold dust trade (Skinner 1965, 24). This then emphasises the involvement, as well as the control of the trade by the Sultan. The often quoted visit of Abdullah to Kelantan was in fact with the sole intention of rescuing valuable trading boats which were stranded there during the 1839 civil war.[6]

The influence of trade logically initiated the development of a monetary system. Clifford for instance found in 1895 what was apparently a long established system of money in the form of coins (*pitis* — a term which persists today), complete with a system of denomination and rates of exchange.[7] Apart from the inscription on the money which is undoubtedly Kelantanese, the use of so many forms and shapes of money (in the form of gold, silver and tin coins of various shapes and sizes, indicating the stages of evolution of the money under different Sultans) was extensive and extended to the South as far as Besut (Clifford *op cit.*, 134). Even as late as 1906, the Sultan issued the money to be expended on state activities (Sa'ad Shukri *op. cit.*, 105). Kota Bharu is, therefore, an offshoot of a lucrative trading post where accumulation of wealth in terms of money was the main concern.[8] Moreover the system of punishment provides further evidence of this claim. In cases of guilt, punishment was always in term of fines, and ". . . this was based on the wealth of the guilty person or his family" and which doubled with every day the fine was delayed (Wang Gung Wu *op. cit.*, 33).

Thus to confer Kota Bharu the status of 'Traditional settlement' as a logical growth of a peasant economic system (Zaharah Hj. Mahmood 1970), somewhat in the tradition of 'total power' vested in the Sultan, is not only misleading, but represents an over-emphasis on agriculture associated with problems explicable in terms of ownership of land. The question of control of land, that all land belonged to the ruler ('*tanah raja*') (cf. Graham 1908, 93), is only a recent phenomenon created by colonialist-capitalists. The state had no records of ownership of land prior to 1881 when the village headmen were almost wholly autonomous.[9] It is highly probable, therefore, that as far as Kelantan is concerned, a system of total power in the sense of central authority at Kota Bharu controlling all the land in the state is inapplicable. As a corollary, the independence of the headmen is more than a historical reality. The fact that intensification of the land administration in the form of 'grant' systemised during the reign of Sultan Mohammad II (in 1896) is a clear indication of an effort to preserve the disintegrating state that is torn by centrifugal forces stemming from such independence of the headmen. In fact the weakness of central power was remarkably widespread in early settlements of Southeast Asia as a whole. But the rights to absolute control and ownership of land were often claimed by the ruling class and this is later formalised by colonial governments (Wertheim 1973).[10]

Nineteenth century Kota Bharu was thus not the nineteenth century Kelantan. Tracing the Sultanate at Kota Bharu in order to reconstruct the Kelantan social formation of the period, is to some extent an injustice to the people of Kota Bharu town and to people of Kelantan as a whole. However, to view Kota Bharu formation as completely closed is equally a misrepresentation. For Kota Bharu in the nineteenth century was a social formation where a royal aristocracy directly dominated the subjects (*ra'ayat*) within the town, mainly as a result of direct exploitative relations between the two classes: direct control by the ruling class over land in the vicinity, some estates in the hinter-land, and river and sea trade, while the productive activity and trading in the town was left in the hands of the dominated subjects and foreigner-Chinese. Such was the mode of production underlying the town's social formation. To some extent nineteenth century Kota Bharu was a combination of the 'kraton town' (divorced of its systematic exploitation of a 'whole country') and the 'harbour principality', without its economic dependence on trade alone.[11]

The significance of the control of trade activities however, declined towards the end of the nineteenth century. This was due partly to the more intensive penetration of British interests[12] in the area, and partly to the increasingly disadvantageous position of the town as a centre of trade.[13] As a result the Sultan turned to reorganising the control of the state through intensive administration, instituting various forms of exploitation on the population. For instance together with minor rules regulating proper dress for the town population, padi tax, coconut tax, durian tax, sireh and tobacco tax were for the first time directly imposed on the people (*ra'ayat*). A separate tax, partially for the collection of '*Bunga Emas*' for the Siamese king, in the form of 'poll tax' (*chukai kepala*) was exacted. Similarly export and import duties were either increased or strengthened.[14]

All these were complemented by the new bureaucratic structure of the time where the ruling class or nobles, residing at Kota Bharu, controlled, by way of taxation, different areas of the state through their representatives at the local level who were known as '*To 'Kweng'*.

Severe taxation over the populace then shows that Kota Bharu in the late nineteenth century was changing more towards Van Leur's kraton town where the Sultan and the nobilities began to rely exclusively on the exploitation of the subjects (*ra'ayat*) for affluence. For instance, Graham noted that prior to 1904:

> . . . the treasury consisted of two or three clerks at His Highness' palace, who received the revenue, made a — usually inaccurate — note of it, and passed it into the interior of the palace, when it never again emerged unless . . . to pay long standing accounts for jewellery and similar luxuries (*op. cit.,* 112).

Understandably, in 1900, the uncles and the relatives of the Sultan not only shared the revenue, but:

> . . . they abrogated to themselves the right to use corvee labour when they pleased, to exercise the power of courts of Justice and to imprison for indefinite period, by mere verbal order any person who might displease them . . . (and) they succeeded in attaching to themselves many thousands of the inhabitants of the state, who paying the tax through them were taught to consider their allegiance to the head of state or ruler secondary . . . to their overlord. The uncles also accumulated large estates in land by equivocal means . . . and they protected numbers of evil doers from whose unconcealed crimes they derived pecuniary and other benefits'' (Nik Mohamad Nik Mohd. Selleh, *op. cit.,* 32)

We may suggest, therefore, that Kota Bharu by the beginning of the twentieth century was a town in the service of the dominantly powerful and wealthy ruling class spearheaded by the Sultanate; it was, in short, a royal town.

Kota Bharu Town in the Late 19th and Early 20th Centuries

The physical characteristics of Kota Bharu in the late nineteenth century and the early twentieth century were often recorded in the form of sketches in European travellers' diaries. For instance, F.F. Laidlaw (1953) on approaching the town from the river described it as "a line of straggling buildings spread along the south bank''. He also recorded that the town's drainage system consisted only of one ditch running to the river, while the principal buildings consisted of the '*istana*' (palace) and the residences of the aristocrats, and the town's business quarter consisted of Chinese shops made of bricks and a big atap-roofed open market where daily transactions of items both locally produced and imported were carried out using both the '*pitis*' and straits dollars (Laidlae *op. cit.,* 149, 156).

In 1900, Graham depicts a town of 10,000 people in the following manner:

> ... a semicircle of a mile radius, the *misjid* or mosque standing in the middle of the arch ... the town is well laid out with metalled roads which divide the area into many rectangular blocks. The principal building is the palace of the H.H. the raja standing in the enclosure of from 5 to 6 acres ... (*op. cit.,* 27)

This is reconstructed by an informant in the form of a map (map 3).[15]

Within the town, the aristocrats or the ruling class were reported to live in their respective 'forts' (*kota*) surrounded by bamboo fences with gardens, palm and fruit trees, and with gates elaborately carved — an item of particular attraction to Skeat (1953). However, the town was also described by Annandale as one which:

> ... totally lacks a clean and tidy look ... much more barbarous than Patani ... its streets far more malodorous than those of any other Malay town ... (and where) ... filth is allowed to accumulate beneath their dwellings (100, 515).

Presumably, this description fits the area inhabited by the town's artisans, traders and carpenters, in short, the subjects (*ra'ayat*).

Generally speaking, Kota Bharu town was then a 'fort' (*kota*) settlement with the ruling class living in personal 'forts' wielding absolute power over their servicemen and followers. This is highlighted by the 'fort' of the Sultan which is commonly known as '*Dalam Kubu*', whose area was the biggest of all the 'forts' (5 to 6 acres) and where the followers were the most numerous (oral reports estimate their number at 1000 people). Outside the fort, the subjects congregated mainly in the northern area of Kampong Kubang Pasu (see map 3).

Indigenous Social Formation: The *Daulat* Model

In order to see the nature of social relations predominant in the indigenous town of Kota Bharu, let us now probe the history of the kampung in which the fieldwork for the present study was carried out.

The kampung had its origin in the 'fort' of Tengku Bendahara (a title given by the Sultan) which was erected in the late 1800's in an area given by the Sultan after the former's help in securing the latter's throne during a war of succession. With the establishment of the 'fort' he (Tengku Bendahara) was also given supremacy over the land east of Sungai Keladi as far as the river mouth (Sungai Kelantan). The 'fort' was enclosed within a bamboo (*buloh duri*) fence running almost along the present boundaries of the kampung and with a massive gate at the front (the carvings on which are now placed on the kampung's prayer house).

Living in the "palace" within the enclosure of his 'fort', he was surrounded by his warriors (*hulubalang*) and their families, his immediate kinsmen, his personal servants (*bidari*) and he was served by his craftsmen and specialists (*bomoh* and *nujum*) who lived outside the 'fort'. His 'fort' then formed a conglomeration of about fifty families made up of his personal followers (*orang dalam kota*) — royal persons (*raja*) and some common (*keluaran*) people who, in one way or another, were in his service.

Tengku Bandahara ruled autocratically: his feelings and discretion became the law in the area under his control, and his punishments included the death penalty, which was supposed to be in the hands of the Sultan at '*Dalam Kubu*' alone. He ruled his territory with an iron hand. The writer was told that thieves had their hands cut off and on one occasion a man was buried alive for supposedly committing adultery with one of the Tengku's mistresses. Food and property were confiscated and redistributed as he saw fit, though he derived his own supplies and wealth mainly from taxation on his subjects and his rice (*padi*) estates in Bachok and Pasir Puteh districts.

He demanded absolute loyalty from his subjects, both inside and outside the 'fort', though the latter (besides the poll tax) were less affected as distance from the 'fort' increased. His general behaviour was described as cruel (*zalim*) by many who were acquainted with the 'royal' group. He was however endowed with super-natural characteristics like '*kebal*' (literally, 'strong'). Stories are told of his strength in lifting two sacred cannons which others, including the Europeans, were unable to lift. He named them *Sri Kuning* and *Sri Hijau,* which later were said to give birth to two baby cannons. He also possessed a spirit (*jin*) which even today is said to destroy food and crockery if a feast (*kenduri*) is held without prior acknowledgement to it. His words were also described as effective, or as residents term it '*masin mulut*'. In short, he is described as '*keramat*' (having supernatural qualities).

To consolidate his power, he was served by seven warriors who were loyal, well-trained and courageous men of skill similar if not equal to their master. It is claimed that during a civil war, these warriors defeated an army of 400 strong. Acting in association with the Tengku Bendahara, they enjoyed, though to a lesser degree than the Tengku, the freedom to roam around the villages under their control confiscating both property and women at will.[16]

Residents of the Kampung explain these recollections of the power and the personal habits of Tengku Bendahara as expressions of his '*daulat*' (royalness), which legitimised his personal laws and behaviour, giving him the right to rule freely. Loyalty of his subjects, fear and respect among his immediate 'fort' population were directly based on his '*daulat*'.

The '*daulat*' is prescriptive in nature, and is associated with sacredness and divinity conferred on persons of royal descent. It is also associated with high morals (*darjat*), refined manners, speech and expressions which differentiated the royal person from the average common people. As such, 'power and status' as well as freedom in exercising personal wants and desires were regarded as the rights of royal blooded persons.

The question of '*daulat*' is often related to superior royal origin in the form of a mythical deity (Che' Siti Wan Kembang) thus conferring 'supra-human' characteristics on the descendants. These were manifested by the males in the forms of personal strength, bravery and vicious behaviour, (like Tengku Bendahara above) and by the females in the forms of beauty, refined behaviour and general sophistication.

Taken as a group, the royal persons conferred with '*daulat*' (*raja ber-daulat*) then possessed high morals (*darjat*) and consequently high status which distinguished them from the common people.[17] As implied earlier, the '*daulat*' people related to the commoners as dominant and powerful rulers who controlled all the wealth (real or nominal) in the state. To further distinguish the '*daulat*' people and the commoners living in the Kota Bharu town in the early twentieth century, the following economic and non-economic considerations are also relevant.

The most important consideration is probably the use of one's labour. While the commoners were employed in labour-intensive employment like weaving, pottery, carpentary, petty-trading and operating bullock and hand carts to transport goods within the town, the '*daulat*' people abstain from any exertion. It is in fact a taboo for '*daulat*' people to be involved in labourious tasks or manual employment. Even the collection of taxes and dues were carried out by personal followers and warriors (nobilities).

Indeed, the '*daulat*' people are to remain separate and removed from common people. Under the circumstances their friendship and to some extent marriage are limited and confined to the same class, though the people involved may not possess the same degree of '*daulat*', i.e. their relative closeness to the ruling royal house may differ.

The '*daulat*' people also used specific and exclusive terms of address, expressions and vocabularies which differed from the language of the commoners. This is commonly known as the language of the royal persons (*bahasa raja*) which, in contrast to Kelantan (dialect) Malay, is more refined and sophisticated.[18] In cases of *daulat* people-commoner contacts, the latter faced royal wrath (*murka*) and punishment unless such terms of address and expressions were observed, while at the same time subservient self-references like '*patek*' or '*te 'ku*' must be used to designate the lower status of the commoner. The '*daulat*' people however may use such derogatory and coarse terms of address like '*kamu*' (you) in addressing commoners.

Unlike the commoners, '*daulat*' people were forbidden to consume a type of bamboo shoot (*rebung buloh bentong*) and a kind of sword fish from the sea (*ikan kachang*). These foodstuffs were taboo because their association with the ancestral origin of the '*daulat*' people and the curse laid upon such foods by their ancestors.[19]

Though the '*daulat*' people were allowed to wear any kind and form of clothing, they had the sole monopoly of wearing yellow (royal) clothing. This is fact was observed by '*daulat*' people and commoners alike up until the Japanese occupation. In fact, Graham noted that "*anak raja* or the better class youth is nothing but dressy . . . a long Arab coat, even though now old, worn and musty" signified religiousness, and high status. Similarly, ladies of 'high degree' dressed in high quality materials and "on more occasions would wear '*kebaya*' " (*loc. cit.*, 23–24, 25).

All these distinguished the '*daulat*' people from the commoners in the town of Kota Bharu. To some extent such differentiation extended to include even the skin complexion. As noted by Graham, the complexion of the skin "varies from olive in the upper class to dark brown in the peasantry" (Graham *op. cit.*, 25). Given such a situation we may argue that the division of labour and generally, the productive system of the town distinguished and separate people into two classes, i.e. the '*daulat*' and commoner classes or the ruling and the subject classes respectively where the commoners were not only followers of the '*daulat*' people but also producers exploited by the latter for affluence and power.

Such a clear cut dualistic conception of 'ruling class and a subject class' is however too simplistic. The ruling class in the first place was not a homogeneous group staffed by members of the royal household, for the history of the ruling class in Kota Bharu is synonymous with the accounts of wars of succession. The 'subjects' being excluded from such activities of the royal houses were also to a large extent unaffected by the rules and policies of any one ruler. The immediate impact of such rules fell on the nobles and other contenders to the throne who, given the opportunity to achieve positions of power, would ammass support to undermine the position of the ruler. As such the execution of laws and rules to strengthen the position of the ruling house had to be entrusted to the loyal commoners, who, paradoxically, had to be respected and feared by the ra'ayat. The logical consequence of such a precarious situation was the growth of the 'royal executives', and the whole array of one-step removed royal persons or *Nik* families, which since time immemorial had been closely associated with the ruling house. They were as powerful as the royal persons but not sacred enough to rule in their own right.[20] A mechanism then evolved through which the position of a particular ruler was secured as far as the threats from the contenders were concerned, while at the same time the legitimacy of the ruling class was maintained by conferring on the 'royal executives' the title of '*Nik*', which theoretically speaking carried a status just below that of members of royal households but above that of the commoners. Though the origin of the *Nik* family is little known (Nik Mohamad Bin Nik Mohd. Salleh, *op. cit.*, 103, n. 3), the fact that the *Niks* (who were neither commoners nor royal) were in the service of, and close by kinship links to the royal houses, is sufficient evidence to believe that they carried the '*daulat*', though in a lesser degree.

Further, the fact that the 'royal executives' were drawn from a commoner group meant that the ruling class as a whole was conferred with '*daulat*' but in varying degrees. '*Daulat*' then is a concept which makes the classes in present day Kota Bharu more meaningful. Firstly, we have the division into people conferred with '*daulat*' and those without it, and secondly there is the division because people of high '*daulat*' and those of low '*daulat*' within the '*daulat*' class itself. The '*daulat*' bound the low '*daulat*' sub-class to the high '*daulat*' sub-class but at the same time prevented the former from overriding the latter because low '*daulat*' sub-class often emerged as the stronger and more powerful of the two.

Secondly, viewing the concept of '*daulat*' as such rendered the notion of endogamy of the ruling class open to question. For the *Nik* families to be incorporated and to become an integral part of the '*daulat*' class, marriage between a female royal person and a male commoner was necessary. By ruling class tradition, the issue of such marriages were the *Nik*. Further marriages of a female *Nik* to a commoner would give the offspring the status of lesser (second step removed) royal persons or the '*Wan*'. In the nineteenth century the ruling class of Kelantan was then not as rigid as its counterpart on the west coast. The penetration by commoner warriors and officials, and to some extent by Arab merchants into the '*daulat*' class, thus subdividing the ruling class into high and low '*daulat*' sub-classes, establishes the fact that the ruling royal households were to a large extent hypogamous. Criteria for such class mobility include among others, proof of skills, courage, wealth, and strength in warfare.

Kota Bharu formulation, then, may be viewed beyond its immediate, simplistic division of '*daulat*' and commoner classes. Rather they should be seen in the perspective of the '*daulat* model' where classes were distinguished and hierarchised on the basis of power, wealth and '*daulat*'. This is represented by the sacred and divine ruler and the royal households at the top, the lesser '*daulat*' *Nik* and *Wan* subclasses in the upper and lower middle rung respectively and the commoner classs, at the bottom, largely manipulated and exploited by the *Niks* and *Wans* to produce, serve and obey the sacred ruler and the royal persons. To put it in other terms, these classes may be seen as arranged in a series of decreasing '*daulat*' from the ruler to the commoners, but with the commoners distinctly removed, separated and dominated by those involved in the activities of ruling.

Thus, overt personal freedom and enjoyment expressed in the form of unconstrained gratification of personal desires while at the same time observing restrictions on manual work, was a way of life exclusive to the people conferred with '*daulat*' (high or low). Such a way of life then differentiated the '*daulat*' people from the commoners who more often emphasised submission, hard physical work and to some extent righteousness and a clean life. Town life, then, logically centred around the 'gossip of the courts, tales of brave deeds, the learned discussions or the rough sports ..." (Clifford 1897, *op. cit.,* 29) which by and large determined the social relations within Kota Bharu social formation of the period.

Footnotes

1. Kota Jelasin at the present Kampong Kota, Kota Mahligai in the present Mukim of Melor, Kota Bukit Marak and Kota Jembal at Kuala Kemasin are examples of these settlements (cf. Map 2; Sa'ad Shukri 1971, 32–48).

2. Good examples would be Kota Kubang Labu across the river from the present Kota Bharu and Kota Pasir Mas (Sa'ad Shukri *op. cit.,* 53–62).

3. As an illustration, Mukim Melor came into being after the breakdown of Kota Mahligai which was entrusted to Raja Abdul Rahim when Putri Sa'adong moved to Kota Bukit Marak (Sa'ad Shukri *op. cit.,* 47).

4. The predominance of civil wars in nineteenth century Kelantan was probably due to the lack of formal rules of succession to the throne (cf. Nik Mohamad Nik Mohd. Salleh 1974, 6, 30–31; Tweedie 1923, 27). According to Heine-Geldern however, the remnants of belief in Hinduism is a significant determinant in such case (1942, 26–27).

5. Gullick suggests that it was habitual for a successor to 'find some other abode' (1958, 63). However, Winstedt gives importance to the ideological foundation embedded in the Hindu conception of king which emphasises that place of the dead predecessor be vacated for 'resting place for spirits' (1947, 130–31).

6. Abdullah valued the cargo at 40 or 50 thousand dollars whereas the editor of Singapore Free Press valued it at 50 or 60 thousand dollars (Skinner 1965, 25; Kassim Ahmad *op. cit.,* 21).

7. To reorganise what was originally presented by Clifford (1938, 134), its denominational system may be shown as follows:

5 *keping*	=	1 *lada kecil*
2 *lada kecil*	=	1 *lada besar*
2 *lada besar*	=	1 *keneri*
2 *keneri*	=	1 *jembir*
4 *keneri*	=	1 *kupang*
4 *kupang*	=	1 *amas*
2 *amas*	=	1 *ringgit tua*

Clifford further indicated that the smallest unit of the money the *keping* (locally pronounced as *kepeng*) was equal to 0.274 Straits cents, and the largest unit, the *ringgit tua* was equal in value to one Straits dollar.

8. Similar conclusion is also made by Malacca (cf. Dakers 1939).

9. Even though the administrative apparatus under the Siamese Adviser were very much bureaucratised under the noble Chiefs and To' Kweng system (Graham *op. cit.,* 109–113), the central monarchical control over the peasantry was somewhat meagre if not wholly nominal. This has been especially the case in earlier period of the nineteenth century where "... the authority outside the capital is said to have been exercised for all practical purposes largely by the Imam of the village surau" (Roff 1974, 104). It is perhaps this relative freedom of local Chiefs and the peasantry generally that Swift refers to the indigenous political system of Malaya as a system of 'inefficient authoritarianism' (1960, 90–94).

10. It may be noted that the notion of land ownership prior to British colonialism in Malaya as a whole was free of monarchical control, "... the attribution of superior ownership in land to a Malay ruler was, indeed, a total fiction. It was, as one may add, a sheer imposition of the English concept of land tenure" (Wong 1975, 18).

11. Van Leur states that "the chief role of the cities was that of being royal seats — kraton town, thus — in which levies in kind were brought together from the whole country and royal storehouses in which the levies were stocked and from which the host of officials, the army and the royal household were provided". (1955, 56–57). He also describes the 'harbour principality' as a town where "a sultanate with a small area of land and living from trade" (*op. cit.,* 77).

12. This is the outcome of the competition between British and Siamese business interests in the area especially with regards to mining and trade (cf. Roberts 1973, 59, Appendix B, C, D; cf. Emerson 1964, 98–99; cf. Tregoning 1967, 47).

13. For instance Allen reports that "the town has failed to move seawards with the land" (1953, 53–54; cf. Fowler 1923, 46–47).

14. As shown by Leslie R. Robert (*op. cit.,* 1973, 37–42 *passim*), every steamer entering Kelantan was subjected to \$25–\$35 tax according to their respective size in addition to their anchorage tax. Every ox and buffalo exported was taxed up to \$2/=. Opium trade cost \$2000/= per month. Padi tax was 5% of the produce, payable in cash and kind, and except for royal persons, the poll tax was \$1/= per year.

15. Similar version of the map is produced by the informant, Haji Husin Latiffi, in Pengasoh, Bil. 407, June, 1975.

16. It is recorded by Clifford that such pattern of behaviour was typical of those in the courts of Sultans known as *budak raja* (1897, 186–187).

17. For the present purpose, I would use the term '*daulat*' people to refer to the class of royal persons and the term 'commoners' to refer to the average common people or the '*keluaran*' people as they are known today.

18. For instance, to name a few, the '*dualat*' people used terms of address like '*kita*', '*bonda*', '*ku*' and '*Nik*' instead of the commoners' '*ambo*' '*emak*' and '*mu*', and they used specific expressions like '*bersiram*', 'santap', '*ta'cerap*' instead of commoners' '*mandi*', '*makan*' and '*ta'tahu*'. For the present purposes, I would use the term 'court language' to refer to this language of the royal persons.

19.. These taboos are connected with a belief that one of the princes who founded the royal lineage in Kelantan originated from a particular type of bamboo bush (*buluh bentong*). As such the shoot of the bamboo is forbidden for consumption. Similarly, the taboo on the fish is related to a belief that once upon a time, a prince who was shipwrecked at sea was brought to land by the sword fish. Out of gratitude, the prince consequently vowed not to eat the kind of fish, and likewise forbade his descendants to consume it.

20. For instance only the *Niks* were entrusted by all Sultans to carry and present the '*Bunga Emas*' to the Kings of Siam (Ismail Bakti 1960), and the most powerful and influential people after the Sultan seems to be people from the *Nik* sub-class (Nik Mohamad Bin Nik Mohd. Salleh, *op. cit.,*).

CHAPTER TWO

CAPITALISM IN KOTA BHARU: THE CREATION OF TOWN WARDS

The indigenous mode of production of Kota Bharu town — the main feature of which was the segregation of classes on the '*daulat* model' — revolved around the court and 'forts' of royal persons. Underlying this mode, we noted, was the dominance and exploitation of commoners by the '*daulat*' class. This occurred in a context where authority was based on punishment, including the application of physical force, an ideological instance where sacredness and divinity or '*daulat*' of royal persons were feared, revered and unquestioned, and an economic instance characterised by petty and long distance trading, and petty commodity production among the commoner class. The ruling class remained parasitic and unproductive.

The early twentieth century, however, saw the introduction of the forces of Western capitalism. This affected the physical and social character of the town dramatically.

Bureaucracy and Commerce

It is often argued that the process of change in Kelantan was initiated by the Duff Development Company, the carrier of the British capitalist flag that penetrated Kelantan in 1902. This initial stage has been the subject of several previous inquiries so that it does not require further elaboration here. (Crawford 1970; Robert 1972; Nik Mohamad Bin Nik Mohd. Salleh *op. cit.*).

However, to emphasise the role of the Duff Company, and similarly to attribute to Graham, the first British Adviser to the state who introduced many bureaucratic changes, the responsibility for the dominance of capital in the state, is unfruitful if not totally misleading. This is because the penetration of capital from Europe into the state was also largely attributable to the way of life of the ruling class. With their decreasing control over indigenous trade and commercial activities, but traditionally uninvolved in any other income-giving activities, the ruling class extended their traditional preoccupation with collecting taxes to impose taxation over crops, produce and even over individual commoners. As noted earlier, the bureaucratic revolution culminating in the system of

'*To'Kweng*' and the reorganisation of the land administration in 1896 were evidently indigenous efforts by the ruling class to maintain control over the state in the context of rivalry between the Siamese and the British which led in the long run to British control over the state. It is the combination of these two interests, the maintenance of indigenous social relations and the introduction of capital and capitalist relations which shapes and structures the nature of subsequent development in the state. The condition of the state was more than ready for a vigorous act of, to use Barrington Moore term, 'massive violence' (1966, 29) to be taken up by Graham and the subsequent British advisers. The ease of capitalist penetration, therefore, was founded on the inclination and policy of the ruling class to remain affluent and unproductive.

The subsequent reorganization of the bureaucracy especially that of land — with generous concessions given to the ruling class in the form of tax-free land — by the colonial governments, was an answer to the prayers of the ruling class who, relieved of any difficulties in direct administration, found comfort in new and varied, if slightly lower bureaucratic positions created by the colonial government. In 1939, for example, when the government departments came under full British control, there were only eighteen British officers holding key positions; the day to day administration of keeping 'simple records and accounts' was handled by the members of the traditional ruling class who seemed to enjoy the immediate tangible benefits of 'definite political allowances and salaries' (Peppys 1960).[1] Though there were a few commoners in the bureaucracy, almost all the lower bureaucratic positions were held by the members of the ruling class. There are at least three main reasons accounting for such a development: a) there was a lack of European staff generally (Peppys *op. cit.*), b) non-Kelantan Malay (*orang luar*) proved to be unpopular with the general population, and c) the opening of a Malay school in Kota Bharu provided a training ground for "... clerkships in government offices" (Graham *op. cit.,* 116) which at the same time opened the bureaucracy to a few commoners people (cf. Khoo Kay Kim 1974, 191-3). On the whole however, recruitment into the bureaucracy was operated in such a way that the indigenous power structure was least disturbed. Therefore the immediate domination process in terms of taxation had to be carried out by people who have some traits of '*daulat*' i.e. the *Tengku, Nik* and *Wan* or the people appointed by the Sultan. The process then without doubt rests on the manipulation of the indigenous ideology of legitimacy and status prerogatives.

This is further seen in the large-scale commercial enterprises (including mining and planting) where ownership was in the hands of Europeans or outsiders, save for the two aristocrat-owned rubber estates (Graham *op. cit.,* Appendix F). This is because the majority of the aristocrats and the ruling class, especially the most powerful aristocrats who were now directly incorporated into the highest decision making body, the state council (Graham *op. cit.,* Appendix A), were content to enjoy the meagre returns from the taxes and small proportions of the profit from such commercial ventures. To put it in other terms, the ruling class opened up the way for capital to dominate by being content in their traditional roles of passing out rules, signing agreements, giving out certain permissions and collecting taxes, which within the indigenous structure accorded them high status. This is symbolised in the position of the Sultan whose power, by this stage, became almost nominal. The common interpretation of the introduction of capital by the British, i.e. the concept of 'least disruption of Malay custom and tradition' may also be seen here as a way of covering up the bureaucracy and power institution rather than as one that emphasised only 'custom and religion'. This is how capital penetrated the Kelantan indigenous mode of production and established Kota Bharu as its centre. The ruling class, given overt power through the new bureaucracy, maintained their distinctiveness in relation to the commoners while at the same time allowing the Europeans and the outsider-Chinese the chance to exploit whatever trading and commercial opportunities existed in the state. Moreover, the ruling class were then able to come close to, if not be at par with the Europeans in terms of status, thus preserving their traditionally dominant position. In short, the recruitment and rewards systems of the colonial government maintained the privileges of the ruling class in a slightly altered form. In other terms, the British systematised the inherently repressive tendencies of the ruling class.

The introduction of western capitalist interests therefore went hand in hand with the ruling class's concern for the preservation of their status. Together they transformed the character of Kota Bharu. Instead of rings for bull-fights, ram-fights, cock-fights and huts for '*wayang kulit*', '*mak yong*' and '*peteri*' (cf. Skeat *op. cit.,* 115), the town came to contain tennis courts, football fields, a jail house, a police station, school, Chinese shops, Company warehouses like Bousted Co. and a bank. In other words, both the forms of entertainment and the townscape in Kota Bharu changed.[2] What is important is that this change was only comprehensible to the ruling class, who alone derived much benefit and pleasure from them. Peppys for instance noted that the ruling class "were friendly and turned up regularly at the weekly tennis parties at the Residency" (Peppys *op. cit.,* 36).

The whole town was in fact developed more in the manner suitable for the enjoyment of the few Europeans and the ruling class. As an administrative centre it served only as "... a country market town ... (which) can never be a market town ... (and where) little change has taken place in the growth of the town in the last 15 years during which we have seen two booms ... " (Reid 1932, 2). Therefore, a few light industries grew up. Among the earliest were the match factory (1933), Hing Bing and a few other sawmills which altogether employed more than 400 workers (cf. Appendix 4). Regardless, the Malay population of the town grew rapidly:

Table 1
POPULATION OF KOTA BHARU 1911 — 1970

Year	*No. of Malays*	*Total Town Pop.*	*%of Malay*
1911	—	12,548	88.2
1921	10,456	13,089	78.9
1931	11,430	15,490	73.8
1947	14,517	22,863	63.5
1957	23,306	38,106	61.1
1970	37,294	55,052	67.7

In 1921, 10% of Malays in Kelantan lived in the town, making it the third highest concentration of Malay urban population in British Malaya after Brunei and Trengganu, where the towns were densely populated and "resemble the larger town of Java ... ". (Population Census 1921, 43). In 1970, 10.3% of the Kelantanese were still within the area administered by the Town Board (Lembaga Bandaran) and to include the area 'showing evidence of house patterns and house lots' surrounding the town boundary an additional 14,704 people may be included (Statistics Department, 15). The increase of the Malay population in the town, though characterised by a marked fall in their percentage, was largely due to inflow of outside of Kelantan Malays and people from rural areas.[3] For instance, applications for jobs in Kelantan government departments from outside Malays became a problem to the administration (B.A. office, 8.9.1931) on top of the fact that the place was being 'overrun by Chinese clerks and Tamil clerks' (B.A. file 29.8.1931).

However, it was the policy of the British colonialists to employ only the Kelantan Malays in the bureaucracy. The Kelantan Public Works Department and several other departments for example depended solely on the Kelantan Malays for its manual labourers (B.A. file 183/31; 162/31). Presumably there were ample opportunities for the town's commoners to be employed in the government services, especially in the labouring and menial sections in the service.

Such development also meant a wider choice of employment for the town population as a whole. For instance, the general increase of the town's population naturally meant greater demand for a variety of services. This then led to the proliferation of the bazaar market sellers, trishaw pedallers, and small roadside eating stall operators, many of whom operated without the license from the Town Board. For instance, as early as 1931 shopkeepers, stall operators and bazaar market sellers started the tradition of picking strategic positions in the town to conduct their trade (Memo. K168/1931). Further, the Town Board Report for the year 1949 states (among other things) that:

> . . . the producers bring a variety of articles to the market and sell direct to the consumers and as one seller brings a variety of articles (one woman brings one or two fowls, some vegetables and some fruits and sits and sells wherever she likes) for sale arrangement for stalls for sale of specified articles only is to a certain extent defeated. The Kepala Bakul people prefer to squat on the floor and sell their things rather than to keep their articles on raised stalls." (p. 9)

The petty traders in Kota Bharu then operated within the framework of 'free enterprise' in the real sense of the word, but at the level and in activities where they do not pose a competition to capital to accumulate. This is the way in which capital allowed the commoner class to participate in the development and growth of capital, and more important, it gave them the illusion of possible prosperity and affluence attributable to the new bureaucracy and the capitalist mode of production. Directly they provided the necessary condition for capital to establish and dominate the state. To some, this formed the only way out from overcrowded agricultural work in the countryside, whereas to others, the process provided opportunities for part-time peddling and trading in between rice-planting seasons, when they would return to their villages in the countryside. Within a fifty-year span, the town saw a prolific growth of petty traders largely made up of the commoner class.[4] Thus in August 1975, the town's business sector comprised thousands of mobile and uncontrollable petty traders and peddlers, almost 3000 trishaws, about 1600 of which are unregistered, about 102 limited companies and 8 banking institutions. On the entertainment side, there are 4 cinema halls, and also about half a dozen clubs and voluntary associations.

This expansion of population and economic activity in the town thus created acute problems of accommodation. Even as early as 1931 the "old town area is . . . dirty, congested and contains many foul houses." (Reid *op. cit.,* 5).[5] This is further accentuated by the town's population natural increase at 3% per annum, and by the continuous immigration of the people from the surrounding rural areas who, when faced with the problems of housing would turn to friends and relatives who are already in the town. This is done either by adding one or two rooms to the existing structure, or by partitioning and occupying the "spaces underneath the houses which are meant to be left vacant" (Town Board 1949, 5). As a result the area of the older settlement, that is along the east bank of Sungai Kelantan, is highly congested. The temporary structure of the houses, though not quite what Shepperd meant by Kelantan houses becoming more utilitarian (Mubin Sheppard 1969), are then arranged back to back with only narrow paths and lanes in between, and are thus very prone to hazards like fire (Sa'ad Shukri *op. cit.,* 144).

Though more differentiated, the town in the 1970's is structurally similar. The emergence of the Town Board in 1948[6] as an agent for regulating housing construction, taxing and licensing of trades, turned out to be more commonly known for its function of 'scavenging, sweeping all roads and back lanes and drains, cutting grass on sides of roads, and periodically cleaning of earth drains'. This is simply due to its weakness to combat elusive traders, powerful land owners and to some extent its failure to avoid 'politicking' in the enforcement of town laws. An officer of the Town Board (*Lembaga Bandaran*) emphasises that the hawkers and peddlers may be elusive, but the main problem is in dealing with the wealthy, powerful 'ruling class' who sometimes have the backing of the top-most power, the Sultan.

Kota Bharu, then, forms the core of Kelantan social life. It is also the centre from which the forces of capitalism radiate out into the countryside. Any changes in Kelantan social life are manifested first in Kota Bharu, even if this is not where they are most observable. Consequently, Kota Bharu social life is to some extent different from the whole of Kelantan: it is the most 'modern', most capitalistic and most 'advanced'. In fact, it has become the point of reference for 'modernity' or '*hilir*' for Kelantan people as a whole.[7]

It is this aspect of Kelantan that is the subject of the present inquiry. Features emanating from dominance of capital in an indigenous precapitalist framework and generally, the impact of penetration of capital may be best observed here. Indeed the nature of social relations around which social life revolves is an expression of changes in the latter. To make the processes of such change more intelligible, the evidences from Kampung Bendahara, a residential ward of Kota Bharu town may be presented.[8] The kampung was a subject of close observation and participation over several months in 1975. To put it in proper perspective however, we must see how the kampung grew into the present town ward.

The Growth of Kampung Bendahara

The kampung originated from the 'fort' of Tengku Bendahara which gradually broke down with the expansion and growth of the town generally. On the death of Tengku Bendahara in the early 1940's, the fort land was subdivided equally according to his will among five of his children while the land on the fringe of the fort (the land between the concrete pavement and Northern road: map 5) was given to the descendants of his specialists (*bomoh* and *nujum*).[9] Though the land in the fort was subdivided, the fort as a community still existed under the rule of his eldest son, Tengku Wiria, who, together with own his five sons, maintained the traditional style of ruling, primarily on the incomes derived from inherited estates in the district of Pasir Puteh.[10] The fort community thus persisted until the death of Tengku Wiria in 1952. Since then, the fort slowly began to be penetrated by commoners from the nearby areas and from the rual areas. This is reported to have taken place in the following manner:

a) In the late 1940's, during the later part of the Tengku Wiria's rule, Che' Minah from a nearby kampung was a well known traditional masseuse (*takang urut*) who won the favour of Tengku Wiria's wife and other royal persons in the fort. As the kampung where she lived was too overcrowded, Che' Minah applied to live within the enclosures of the fort. This was with a warm welcome by Tengku Wiria and by other royal persons in the fort such that Che' Minah was allowed to set up a house free of any rent. In subsequent years, Che' Minah requested the favour of the royal persons for her relatives from her original kampung in the nearby area to live in the fort. Though this was agreed by the royal persons, Che' Minah's brother and sister were allowed (in 1952) to do so on the condition that they pay a rent of $60.00 per year on their respective house sites.

b) With the increasing problem of overcrowding in the areas in the vicinity of the kampung as a result of the natural increase in the population as well as a result of immigration of rural people who came to find work in the town, there were increasing number of applications for renting of house sites in the fort. Hj. Pa'min is a case in point. He told the writer that after coming from a rural fishing village in the district of

Tumpat, about fourteen miles away, in 1956 to work in the match factory, he had to apply to rent a house site in the fort because the accommodation provided by the factory was unsatisfactory. As he was also a pious man, the royal persons in the fort decided to build a prayer house and requested him to led the nightly prayers. Thus he became a tenant as well as the *Imam* (leader of prayers) of the kampung and in 1969 he went for the *hajj* in Mecca. His tenancy in the fort and his appointment (by the royal persons) as the leader of prayer in the fort however, attracted one of his relatives, and one of his fellow villagers, who also came to find work in the town. As they were pressed for accommodation, Hj. P'min felt obliged to recommend them to the royal persons for renting house sites in the fort. This was again followed by a relative of his fellow villager who came to work as a driver with a government department in the town.

Such a process of settlement in the fort by commoners from rural areas, which subsequently created a heterogeneous community in the fort, and at the same time transformed the traditional fort social life into that of a town ward, was further complemented by the subdivision and sales of portions of the land in the fort. For instance, a son of the late Tengku Wiria sold his share of inherited land to a commoner. This is reported to have occurred in the following manner: As he was a son of the ruler of the fort, he was spending money lavishly on women, food and gambling. When his father died, his regular source of income was immediately cut off. He resorted to borrowing cash and certain amounts of rice every month from a retail shopkeeper, Che Hasan, in the vicinity of the fort. Over the years his debts accumulated until repayment was beyond his means. Consequently he had to sell his land to Che Hasan. This at the same time gained him some extra cash.

A similar process of transfer of land also took place in the case of his three elder brothers, two of whom subsequently fled to Kuala Lumpur in poverty and shame (it is reported that one of them went to seek employment in a factory in Kuala Lumpur). Consequently he and his brother presently live on house sites belonging to other royal persons in the kampung.

The ownership of the subdivided land of the fort however was constantly changing hands. For instance, after buying a 28/1008 '*depa*' of land[11] from a royal person, Bidah believed that her land contained some hidden treasure from the old fort. So a specialist (*nujum*) was summoned to determine the nature and location of the treasure. After spending a substantial sum of money which she borrowed from Dollah, a person in a nearby kampung, it was discovered that the sacks, which were at first thought to contain the treasure, were only full of sand. Ashamed of the whole concern, especially when the residents began to ridicule the whole venture, she approached Mariam, also from a nearby kampung, for cash to go to *hajj* in Mecca. On her return from Mecca both Dollah and Mariam demanded the money owed to them. Unable to repay in cash, Bidah decided to repay them in the form of land. So the two latter persons were each given 10/1008 and 9/1008 '*depa*' of land respectively.

In this fashion, the subdivision of the fort land into small sizes suitable only for house sites, and constant change of ownership of such land, occurred.[12] Consequently, rich rural petty-bourgeiose came to town to carry out trading activities were able to buy these house sites. These rural people were later followed by their relatives who came to rent house sites from royal persons and work in the town. Notable in this case is a middleman from the rural district of Pasir Puteh about thirty miles away. When he came to buy a small portion of the land in 1968, he was subsequently followed by four of his relatives who came to settle as tenants on house sites belonging to the royal persons of the kampung.

As the process of selling land and settlement by tenants on house sites continued, the walls of the fort literally broke down in the early 1960's. Together with the area on the fringe of the fort, the town ward known as Kampung Bendahara was born (cf. Appendix I).

So in 1963, the land ownership in the Kampung was divided into twenty-two portions of varying sizes and were shared by 26 people as may be shown in the following table:

Table 2
OWNERSHIP OF LAND

		Ownership by titles:			
Sizes in *depa*	**Total No. of Holdings**	***Tengku***	***Nik***	***Wan***	**Commoners**
168/1008	3	2			1
84/1008	2	1	1	3	
48/1008	1				1
28/1008	2			1	2
24/1008	6	1	1		4
14/1008	2				2
12/1008	2				2
10/1008	1				1
9/1008	2			1	1
8/1008	1				1
Total	22	4	2	5	15

Source: Land Registration Office, Kota Bharu.

As may be seen from the table, only four out of nine original holders (royal persons) of land remained, while the rest of the land was subdivided into small portions owned by 18 others. Out of these eighteen holders however, 15 holders of land have no claims to an association with the traditional ruling (*daulat*) class, i.e. they are purely commoners.

On the examination of land ownership of the kampung in 1975 however, the picture changes dramatically: that is while the four original (royal persons) holders of the land are still maintaining control over their respective land, the *Niks* and the *Wan* (the lesser '*daulat*' sub-class), save for two *Wans* have lost control of their land. What is worth noting therefore is the fact that within a span of twelve years, the commoners were able to buy off 3 shares of the land belonging to the *Wans* and 2 shares of the land belonging to the *Niks* of the kampung, thus controlling 16 shares of the land in the kampung. Thus the old character of the fort — the dominance of, and the monopoly of land ownership by the royal persons — is now almost completely wiped out. In short, the fort has now become a residential town ward or Kampung Bendahara as it is now known in Kota Bharu.

Footnotes

1. Chan Su-Ming (1965) outlines a detailed chronology of bureaucratic development in the state.

2. Electricity was supplied to houses and streets in December 1926, the roads were tarred in May 1927, a new market was constructed in April 1928, March 1935 pipe-water was supplied to the town, October 1936 the foundation for an airport was laid down.

3. The case of Kampung Bendahara is exemplary.

4. As an illustration, we may observe the rise of small businesses in Kota Bharu in 1949 and 1970 in Appendix 3a and 3b respectively.

5. In 1975 the situation has somewhat worsened. The gross density of the population in town is estimated at 25 persons per acre. However, the net residential density stands at 63 persons per acre, while in some areas a figure of 120 persons per acre may be found. (Haji Mohamad Yussof, Chairman of Lembaga Bandaran.)

6. A concise history of the Town Board since 1896 has been summarised by Tengku Adbullah Tengku Ahmad, as '*Sekapor Sireh*' in *Chendramata Pesta Kebudaya'an dan Perdagangan Kelantan,* 1975.

7. Traditionally the term '*hilir*' means a boat journey downstream. The term persists to describe any journey to town or any urban area. Thus the town is associated with '*hilir*' i.e. urban or modern and the town's people are '*orang hilir*' as opposed to the peasants or '*orang darat*'.

8. For convenience, I would use the term 'kampung' in the following discussion to refer to this town ward.

9. Tengku Bendahara had 14 children altogether. However, on his death the fort land was willed to be divided equally among 2 of his sons and 3 of his daughters. The eldest son, Tengku Wiria was to continue to be the ruler of the fort. As such he was also given the padi estates in the rural district of Pasir Puteh. His share of the fort land was however, subsequently subdivided on his death in 1956, by 5 of his sons who, save for one, subsequently sold it to commoners. During the period of fieldwork, one of Tengku Wiria's sons was selling his inherited share of the padi estates in the district of Pasir Puteh.

10. Though details are scanty, it is observed that royal persons or the traditional ruling class own considerable proportion of land in urban as well as rural Kelantan. For instance, they own 36.4% of land in Mukim Gunung, Bachok (Mohd. Nor bin Mohamad 1974) and 12% of all land in Kota Bharu town (Syed Husin Ali 1978, 39). Two of them are in fact among the three biggest landowners in Kota Bharu, holding about 87 acres or 6% of all real estate land (Evers and Goh Ban Lee 1976, 26).

11. "'*Depa*' means in linear measurement a length of 6.6 feet, and in square measure an area of 43.56 square feet or one thousandth part of an acre", (Government of Kelantan, Enactment No. 28, 1938, 137).

12. Private individual account for 586 acres or 18% of land subdivision and transfer in Kota Bharu in 1970–75 (Evers and Goh Ban Lee *op. cit.*, 15). The average lot size however remains relatively large, i.e. 48% of all lot is still larger than 5000 square feet (*op. cit.*, 7). However, it may be noted here that house sites being discussed are not coterminous with lot size because a lot may be rented out into several house sites.

CHAPTER THREE

IMAGES OF CLASS

What we have been arguing so far is that the rapid process of capitalisation of Kota Bharu town since the incursion of capital in the early years of the present century has led to the growth of town wards or urban kampungs within a radius of one mile around the town's business centre. We noted that such growth was accompanied by, if not directly caused by, an increase in the town's population and by an influx of people from rural areas who came to find work in the town. Consequently there was pressure for accommodation which forced some to settle in areas which were traditionally the residences of royal or '*daulat*' persons, their personal followings and their servants, such as the fort of Tengku Bendahara.

However to turn to the original question of how far capital affected changes within the indigenous social formation of Kota Bharu, let us now examine Kampung Bandahara, the history of which has been dealt with in Chapter Two. In this Chapter, I shall discuss the composition of the population of the kampung briefly and then describe images of class or what people say about their respective positions in kampung social relations.

The People

When the fieldwork was conducted, the total population living in the kampung numbered 321 people. They were made up of the following categories:

adult males	57
adult females	66
youths — males	23
females	29
children in school	92
minor children	54
Total	321

These people belong to 68 households and live in 66 houses spread unevenly around the kampung.[1] These households are again made up of the following types:

a) males with wives and children which comprises 50 households.
b) males with children, 2 households.

c) husbands and wives who have no children, 5 households.
d) females with children comprise 8 households, one of which has two adopted children and one other is living with one grandchild.
e) females without children, 3 households.

The cases of single parents and single women without children are people who are either divorced or widowed.

As may be noted from the incongruent number of households and the number of houses above, one household of type (a) need not necessarily live in a house separate from another household of the same type. In fact, there are two houses which contain two such households which consist of husband and wife living with their children. One of these households further includes a married daughter, her husband and her children. Just as in the cases of single women living alone, especially beside prayer houses, such sharing of houses is widely found in Kelantan.[2]

In terms of house occupation, households in the kampung vary from the case of one single adult woman occupying a separate house to that of a nuclear family (parents and children) sharing a house with another nuclear family. To some extent such sharing of house does not inhibit the households from being separate economic units (cf. Rosemary Firth, *op. cit.)*.

Place of Origin

Being a town ward which evolved from a traditional conglomeration which centred upon a royal family, the population of the kampung now consists of people who originated from different places, that is, it is made up of some of the descendants of Tengku Bendahara who are royal, and commoners, who are either the descendants of the traditional royal specialists and servants, or settlers from the areas in the vicinity of the kampung or the rural areas.

Counting only the 68 heads of households for the present purposes, the places of origin of the people may be shown as follows:

Local born:	
royal persons	8
commoners	6
Settlers:	
from areas in vicinity	24
from rural areas	30
Total	68

As may be seen above, the population of the kampung now consists of 14 local born people, 8 of whom are royals and 6 commoners descended from the royal specialists and servants, and 54 settlers who originated either from the areas in the vicinity of the kampung or the rural areas. These differences in the kinds of birth (royal-commoner) and the place of origin among people are further complicated by the diversity of places of origin of the settlers.

Firstly, the 24 people who originated from the areas in the vicinity of the kampung came from 9 different areas. The level of concentration of migrants from particular areas may be shown as follows:

Table 3
SETTLERS FROM THE AREAS IN THE VICINITY

Town Wards or kampung	*Approximate Distance from the kampung (miles*	*No. of People from same town ward*
1. Kapor	0.5	10
2. Keladi	0.75	2
3. Penambang	0.5	2
4. China	0.5	3
5. Palekbang	2	1
6. Menuang	1	1
7. Sireh	2	1
8. Pasu	0.75	1
9. Balek Kota	1	1

Thus the settlers originated from various areas, although there is a high concentration of emigrants from one area (Kampung Kapor). Such a difference in the areas of origin is more marked in the case of settlers who originated from rural areas. Some of these came from the outer Kota Bharu district, and others came from districts in the state as far as thirty miles away. This may be shown in the following tables:

Table 4
SETTLERS FROM OUTER KOTA BHARU DISTRICT

Villages	*Approximate Distance (miles) from kampung*	*No. of People from same village*
1. Kaula	6	3
2. Tapang	5	1
3. Badang	5	1
4. Baung	5	2
5. Chepa	6	1
6. Peringat	13	1
	Total	9

Table 5
SETTLERS FROM OTHER DISTRICTS IN THE STATE

Districts	*Approximate Distance (miles) from Kota Bharu*	*No. of People*	*No. of People from Same Village**
1. Tanah Merah	30	1	—
2. Machang	16	2	—
3. Pasir Mas	12	6	2 (1)
4. Bachok	22	2	—
5. Tumpat	14	4	4 (1)
6. Pasir Puteh	26	6	5 (1)
	Total	21	11 (3)

* Number of villages in brackets

As shown in Table 4, there are 9 people who originated from 6 villages in the outer rural areas in Kota Bharu district with 5 people originating from 2 villages, and there are 21 people who originated from areas in the rural districts of the state (Table 5). The latter group of settlers are again distinguished from one another in terms of the different villages from which they came. There are 11 people who came from 3 different villages in different districts while the rest of the settlers came from different villages within a district, as well as from different districts.

We indicated earlier that some settlers settled in the kampung through the help of relatives and friends, or through marriage and some settled through purchase of small portions of land for house sites. The people may be divided, therefore, into landowners (owners of house sites) and settlers. Again, some of these people have relatives in the kampung while others do not. Let us now see how they differ from one another on the basis of land ownership and kinship.

Land Ownership

Although we have discussed the process of land division in the last chapter, a short note here is necessary. The land in the kampung consisted of two types: i) the land on the fringe of the fort which was traditionally given by the ruler of the fort to his specialists, and ii) the fort land where the ruler of the fort, Tengku Bendahara, resided with his personal following and servants. On the dissolution of the fort, both types of land were subsequently subdivided. The former type of land was subdivided among the descendants of the specialists and the latter type was subdivided among some of the descendants of Tengku Bendahara, who are royals. What is significant here, however, is the land of the royal persons. This is because some of the subdivided land was subsequently sold to commoners with the result that some of the royal persons are now landless. Some of them resorted to migration to Kuala Lumpur and some chose to remain in the kampung as free settlers on the land belonging to their relatives who were able to maintain their ownership of the land.

To reiterate what has been shown in Chapter Two, there are now 4 royal persons and 18 commoners who are owners of land in the kampung. However, it must be noted that one of the royal persons and all of the commoners own only small parcels of land. In fact, their holdings are big enough only for house sites. This is in contrast to the land owned by 3 royal persons, who own bigger holdings of land which are rented out to tenants. The 3 royal persons now have 16, 15 and 9 tenants respectively. At the same time they allow their landless relatives and those they favour like the descendants of the traditional royal servants to stay on the land free of charge.

Consequently, the people in the kampung may be divided into four categories: landowners who are rentiers (royals); owners of house sites; free settlers; and tenants. This may be shown in the following table:

Table 6
LANDOWNERSHIP IN THE KAMPUNG BY ORIGIN

People by Origin	*Rentiers*	*Owners of House Sites*	*Free Settlers*	*Tenants*	*Total*
Royal persons	3	1	4	—	8
Commoners:					
descendants of specialists	—	4	—	—	4
descendants of servants	—	—	2	—	2
settlers from vicinity	—	10	1	13	24
settlers from rural areas	—	4	1	25	30
Total	3	19	8	39	68

What is evident from the table is that settlers from various places of origin are now living in the kampung either as owners of house sites or as tenants. The landless royal persons and those who are traditionally associated with the royal family are living in the kampung free of charge on their house sites or as free settlers.

Kinship: Relatives

On the count of kinship, there are 44 people in the kampung who are related to one another either through descent or marriage, and there are 24 people who have no relatives living in the kampung. As the kinship system of Kelantan Malays is strongly bilateral similar to other Malays in the Peninsula save for those in Negri Sembilan (Djamour 1965; Swift 1965) all consanguines living in the kampung are described as relatives (*waris*). To some extent, the affines are also described as relatives because of their marriage (*waris sabit*). The affines are also described as in-laws (*ipar* or *menantu*) and they remain so as long as the relevant marriage lasts.[3]

However, the relatives who are consanguines in the kampung are classified somewhat differently from Djamour's classification (*op. cit.*, 23 ff.). They are as follows:

i) very close relatives (*waris dekat benar*) which include brothers and sisters, brother's and sister's sons and daughters, father's and mother's brothers and sisters, and one's direct descendants and ancestors.
ii) close relatives (*waris dekat*) which include cross and parallel first cousins, sons and daughters of first cousins, second cousins and the parent of one's second cousin who is the first counsin of either one of one's parents.
iii) in one particular case however, ego describes a daughter of his first cousin as a relative instead of a close relative.[4]

Generally, then we may say that the people in the kampung who are relatives are related to one another either as consanguinal relatives or affinal relatives. They then form 9 consanguinal and 6 affinal groups as may be shown in Table 7.

As may be seen from this table, at least two thirds of the people in the Kampung are related to one another. However, apart from extending help in formal occasions like feasting, help in the form of 'negotiation' for a job (shall be shown later), and help in providing a relative with a house site or recommending a relative in renting a house site, the relatives within each consaguinal and affinal group seem to be highly independent of one another. This is shown not only in the actual carrying out of their daily economic activities, but also in the different types of employment which the relatives pursue. In any case neither the consanguinal nor the affinal groups seem to form corporate groups. As cases in point, let us consider some of the kin groups shown in the table above.

We may begin with the kin group of 6 consanguines who originally came from the rural areas. This consists of one owner of a house site who

Table 7
RELATIVES IN THE KAMPUNG

Categories of people by origin	*No. of people with relatives** *Consanguines* *1*	*1*	*Affines* *1*	*1*	*No. of people without relatives*	*Total*
Royal persons	8 (1)					8
Commoners:						
descendants of specialists and servants	4 (1)				2**	6
settlers from areas in vicinity	9 (3)	2 (1)	2 (2)	6 (3)	11	24
settlers from rural areas	6 (1)	4 (2)	3 (1)		11	30
Total	27 (6)	6 (3)	5 (3)	6 (3)	24	68

* The number of the consanguinal and affinal groups are in brackets.
** These are the two commoners descended from the traditional royal servants who are living in the kampung.

is a wholesaler (dealer) of fish and fruit and who is economically well off by the kampung standard,[5] and 5 tenants on the land belonging to the royal persons of the kampung. Out of the 5 tenants, 4 are involved in petty trading at the central market and retail some of the fish and fruit of the relative who is the wholesaler, and one is involved in pedalling a trishaw which was bought with a loan from the wholesaler.[6]

Likewise is the case of 4 consanguines who belong to two kin groups from rural areas. Though both kin groups are tenants, these 4 people show variation and independence in terms of employment. For instance one kin group consists of an overseer in a sawmill and a labourer (female) in the match factory, and the other kin group consists of a vendor of bread and a driver with a Government Department.

The same is true with the case of 3 affines who originated from rural areas and settled in the kampung as tenants through marriage with the daughter of a tenant settler from an area in the vicinity. Though one of the affines (*menantu*) is employed as a night watchman just like his wife's father, he is employed in a factory different from his wife's father. The other two affines are also differently employed — one as a contract driver and the other as a construction labourer in Singapore.

Let us now take the case of the nine people who originated from areas in the vicinity and who belong to three consanguinal groups with each group having three relatives: one group consists of three owners of house sites, a retired teacher, a school teacher and a retired woman who is living with her daughter who is a clerk. Another group consists of a retired woman who is living with one of her grandchildren, her son who is a tenant and a petty trader at the central market, and her grandson who is a clerk and who is living with his wife's father; and another kin group which consists of three consanguines who are all tenants and made up of a firewood retailer and two sellers of pre-cooked foodstuffs (rice and sweetmeats) at the central market (cf. Rosemary Firth 1966, Appendix).

The case of the two consanguines who originated from an area in the vicinity is also similarly interesting. Though these two people are cognates (a brother and sister), one is a trishaw pedaller who is also a tenant on the house site belonging to a royal person, the other is a relatively rich owner of a house site who runs one of the retail shops of the kampung and whose husband is a driver (car) with a Banking Corporation in the town.

So, though some of the people in the kampung belong to several kin groups, the relatives within a group show remarkable diversity in their daily economic activities. To some extent, indeed, there is a tendency for relatives to be independent from one another. This is very marked in the case of the consanguinal group of the 8 royal persons who may be first divided into the 3 rentiers, 1 owner of a house site and 4 free settlers. Second, they are again distinguishable as 2 clerical workers, an army officer, an entrepreneur, a night guard (watchman) in the employment of a Chinese-owned firm (sawmill) and two retired persons, one of whom was formerly employed as a clerk and the other was a housewife.

Given such differences among the 44 people who are relatives and taking into account the fact that there are another 24 people who are not related to any other person in the kampung and who again differ from one another in terms of employment (as shall be shown later), we may consider the population of the kampung as a heterogeneous one. By way of summary, they may be considered as such at least on two counts: First, the population consists of people who are local born and settlers, with the former category distinguishable into royalty and the commoners, and with the latter broken into commoner immigrants from near by and those from rural areas. Second, though two-thirds of the people are related to one another forming 9 consanguinal and 6 affinal groups, these relatives tend to be independent from one another at least insofar as their daily economic activities are concerned.

Images of Class

Though the majority of the people in the kampung are related to one another as we have shown, they themselves emphasise that, apart from the kin group of the royal persons, the kinship factor is not a strong influence on their daily life. Rather, factors like wealth, types of employment and the degree of overt religiousness — measured by the frequency of attending the prayers at the kampung's prayer house and commitment to religious rituals of feasting — are considered by the people as important factors affecting their daily lives.

On the count of the royalness or '*daulat*' as we proposed in Chapter Two, the people in the kampung assign the 8 royal heads of households and their members a different position from commoners living in the kampung. The royals consequently are referred to by the people as the royal group (*puak raja*) and they carry the title of '*Tengku*' in front of their name.[7] In order to see how the royal-commoner differences are conceived by the people of the kampung, and thus what people say about an aspect of their social relations, I will take a member of the royal group, Ku Man, and a member of the commoner group, Pa'Lah, as examples.

Ku Man is a royal person who has sold all his inherited land, and is without any formal educational background. He is now employed as a night watchman at one of the sawmills near the kampung at a salary of approximately M$150.00 per month (cf. Appendices 4, 5). He lives in a house made of low quality timber with an aluminium-zinc roof on a rent-free site belonging to his father's sister. His most valued material possession seems to be a bicycle. After divorcing his wife in 1972, Ku Man now lives by himself with visits from his only daughter (13 years of age) about 3–4 times a month. His daughter spends most of her time with her mother, who lives in a different part of the town. Daily, Ku Man spends most of his leisure hours conversing at a coffee shop on the fringe of the kampung with some commoner fellow-residents.

As a royal person (*raja*) belonging to a once powerful ruling house, Ku Man romanticises his ideal past when, as a son of the then ruling house of the fort, he enjoyed complete freedom and luxury. For instance he told how he enjoyed the excitement of lifting women's dresses in public, how he enjoyed the company of prostitutes whenever he wished, and how he used to find pleasure in gambling for days on end, and the luxury of good food.

Though he is now impoverished, he seems to have pride in his royal origin. For instance, he places very high importance on his monthly royal allowance from the royal treasury,[8] and on the occasion when his ex-wife threatened to file a suit against him in the religious court for his failure to keep up his monthly maintenance payments for his daughter, he hurriedly paid the alimony (Shariah Courts 1974, 37). This, he explained, is because his royalness (*daulat*) would be severely demeaned if he had to go to court over failure to maintain his own child.

In matters of living in the kampung, Ku Man likes to perpetuate the glory and power of the royal group in the kampung by claiming monopoly over decision making affecting the kampung as a whole. Thus, according to him, every new prospective resident has to go through him to the landowner on whose land the resident proposes to build a house. He also emphasises that a resident who displeases any royal person will suffer the consequences like eviction from the kampung. For instance, Ku Man warns the writer that his father's sister, Ku Sah, supposedly one of the most influential landowners, dislikes rowdiness, noise and unfriendliness among the residents. He claimed that a few residents were told to leave the kampung on such counts.[9] Ku Man explains such action by Ku Sah as an effort to keep the kampung as a good place for the poor people who have no other place to live. He further illustrates the power of royal persons by referring to his first cousin (father's sister's son) as someone who is very hot tempered, and just like the original Tengku Bendahara, he slaps anyone in the kampung who displeases him.

Thus, Ku Man claims that the royal group has absolute control over the kampung, as if the kampung belongs to them. He explains that the fruit trees, the coconut trees and the '*chengal*' trees (a type of hardwood in the kampung) belong to the royal group rather than to individual royal persons on whose land such trees grow. Likewise he emphasises that the land in the kampung belongs to the royal group despite the fact that some portions of the land have been sold to commoners. According to him, the commoners can only be tenants on land belonging to the royal group. In fact, he says, the kampung itself belongs to the royal group. So, if the stories about the sacred cannons (discussed in chapter one) are too intangible to convince strangers that the kampung belongs to the royal group, more stories are told about the spirit (*jin*) belonging to the original Tengku Bendahara. It is said that the spirit would destroy crockery at marriage feasts unless the people holding such feasts had previously consulted it. This then shows, according to Ku Man, that the royal group still has control over the kampung and consider the people who have settled there as being under their protection. As further evidence, Ku Man claims that even the Chinese operator of the sawmill on the fringe of the kampung where he is employed 'invites' (to use his own words) him to become the night guard of the sawmill.[10] What he implies here is that there is a strong respect for and recognition of the indispensability of the role of the royal person in the kampung.

In accordance with such respect, he also emphasises that the royal persons in the kampung enjoy the luxuries of modern living. For instance he always cites the ideal case of his elder brother Ku Nor who is a chief clerk in the State's Public Service, and who lives in a 'big house' with modern facilities. Ku Nor also owns prestige goods like a television set and a motor-car with which Ku Man compares possessions of others in the kampung. Every year, Ku Nor holds a feast to celebrate the birth of the Prophet Mohamad[11] and unlike Ku Man, he occasionally attends the nightly prayers at the kampung's prayer house. Also he does not spend his leisure time conversing at coffee shops or on roadsides. He is thus regarded by the whole people of the kampung as an 'honoured' (*mulia*) person.

According to Ku Man, Ku Nor is not only very highly respected but he is also feared by the residents of the kampung. As a royal person who maintains the attributes of life-style associated with '*daulat*' class he would then be accorded deference by the commoners of the kampung. A commoner would give way to Ku Nor on meeting him on the kampung land and certainly one would not raise one's voice during the use of completely 'court language' in conversing or addressing Ku Nor. In addition, Ku Nor's wife does no other work beside looking after her house and garden, and she is described by Ku Man as refined and well mannered (*sopan santun*) typical of the traditional royal females. To complete the whole of Ku Nor's family, Ku Man regards two of Ku Nor's children very highly, not only for reasons that they are employed as clerks in two Banking Corporations in the town, but also for the reason that they belong to a family which is regarded as 'honoured'.

So though Ku Man is poor, landless and uses coarse and sometimes vulgar language especially while conversing at coffee shops, he likes to associate himself with the royal group as a whole. Thus, at times he does not seem too pleased when he is not addressed as "*Ku*", a term of address traditionally used for addressing royal (or *daulat*) persons.

* * * * * * * * * *

Pa'Lah, a commoner tenant, conceives the kampung people in somewhat diferent perspective. Originating from a rural village in the district of Tumpat, Pa'Lah has been to many places to try various forms of employment. For instance, dissatisfied with fishing in his original village, he took to selling cloth, and his travels took him as far as the State of Johore in the South and the State of Kedah in the Northwest. After he settled in the kampung in 1960 as a tenant, he lived in a house similar to Ku Man on a house site belonging to Ku Man's father's brother, and started as a labourer with a sawmill nearby the kampung. He was subsequently dismissed for poor conduct. Consequently he rented a trishaw from a Chinese owner in the town and became a trishaw pedaller. Dissatisfied with the poor income, he joined the group of itinerant vendors of bread employed by a bakery in the town.

He describes himself as 'worthless' (*ta'guna*).[12] On one occasion, he resigned himself to the fact that the leaves of '*chengal*' trees are worth more than his body (*tubuh*). Daily he spends more than half of his average daily earnings of about M$3.00 to M$4.00 on coffee, sweetmeats and cigarettes at coffee shops. When asked about this, he explains such behaviour as habitual for a town dweller. Further "if you do not sit and converse at coffee shops, your friends will call you miser (*kedekut*) and pompous (*sombong*).

Pa'Lah also places bets on cockfights during his leisure which takes him to other parts of the town, and occasionally this involves travel to other districts of the State. However, he blames his poverty for having to terminate the education of his daughter at Form Two. Besides, he explains that "she is getting older and girls should not be studying too high anyway".

Pa'Lah also rarely prays at the local prayer house in spite of the fact that the leader of the prayer, Haji Pa'min came from the same village as he did. The latter however is now comfortably employed as an overseer at the sawmill nearby the kampung and lives in a relatively 'big house' and owns a television set, an item which confers prestige. Like Ku Nor, Haji P'min also gives regular feasts. Pa'Lah, therefore, regards him highly and places him in a higher position than himself regardless of the fact that the latter is also a tenant and a commoner. Pa'Lah only classifies people like Pa'Soh as his equal. Pa'Soh, a tenant, is a vendor of ice-cream and teaches the art of self-defence (*tongkat*)[13] every night in the nearby Kampung Paya across the street. Pa'Soh also attends cockfights several times a month. He regularly converses at coffee shops, especially in the later afternoon and early evening. He never attends prayers at the local prayer house.

Alongside Haji Pa'min, Pa'Lah classifies Haji Mat as superior to him, mainly due to the fact that he has his own land, lives in a big half-brick house, draws a pension as a retired clerk and nightly prays at the central Mosque in the town. Pa'Lah classifies few others in the same category. For instance:

1. Pa'Man, a man of rural origin but who is a rich wholesaler (*towkay*) of fish and fruit who operates his business with his own truck and 3 employees, and who manages to accumulate enough wealth for a brick house on the house site he bought from a royal person.

2. Che Hassan who bought his house site from Ku Man and who is a car driver with a Banking Corporation and whose wife runs the local retail shop. In addition, Che Hassan has a daughter who is married to one of the sons of Ku Sah, the renowned royal land owner of the kampung.

In fact, Pa'Lah classifies these individuals on the same plane as Ku Nor, Ku Sah and three other royal persons as people who live in comfort and people who are religious. Just like Ku Man's classification of Ku Nor, Pa'Lah conceives these people as 'honoured people' (*orang mulia*), thus they are distinguished from others in the kampung (royals or commoners). As a group, these people are more prosperous than others in the kampung, they always feast, and some of them regularly attend the nightly prayers at the prayer house.

Being what he is, Pa'Lah is of course not invited to, nor does he offer any help at the feasts of these people. Pa'Mud, however, is always invited to help prepare the feasts alongside the relatives of the people who are holding them. La'Lah attributes this to the fact that though Pa'Mud is a poor tenant just like himself, the latter is always present at nightly prayer meetings at the prayer house. However, in cases of feasts at the house of royal persons, either Ku Man or Stopa, who comes from a family with a long record in the service of the royal persons, would replace Pa'Mud in his role of helper.

Pa'Lah also mentions the case of Che'gu Him, a school teacher who came from an area in the vicinity and who lives on his own house site which he bought from a royal person. Although Che'gu Him holds feasts, Pa'Lah notes that he is different from the people classified as 'honoured' in that his feast always excludes people in the kampung and his invitees are restricted to his fellow teachers and relatives from other parts of the town. Also Che'gu Him does not attend the prayers at the Kampung's prayer house. Thus Pa'Lah conceives Che'gu Him as being someone who is not 'honoured', even though he gives feasts.

For these reasons, Pa'Lah feels uneasy when he meets people he classifies as 'honoured'. In fact he is even moreso when he has to use the 'court language' to the highly respected royal Ku Nor. In general, Pa'Lah does not talk about the royal Ku Man as highly as he talks about Ku Nor, though Ku Man always expresses sympathy with the poverty he is in. Ku Man describes Pa'Lah as a very poor person (*orang susah*). He expresses this as "we (the royal persons) always help his family as he is in our kampung. Sometimes we give his daughter clothes to wear and sometimes we lend him some money without expecting any repayment". Pa'Lah, however, describes Ku Man as one whose royalness (*daulat*) is not worthy of consideration.

From what Ku Man says, we thus have a picture of a simple division of people in the kampung into the royal and commoner classes. One is dominant over the other, similar to the indigenous social formation that we termed the '*daulat* model' earlier. This is however different from what Pa'Lah says. The latter seems to emphasis that the '*daulat*' has been turned into the concept of 'honoured'. This, he seems to emphasise, is the principle of social relations of the kampung.

Regardless of this difference in the images of classes of the kampung, one main pattern is discernible. Whether one is royal or not, one is considered as different and superior to others in terms of respect when one is relatively rich, prays regularly at the prayer house and feasts regularly. As such, there is a conceived pattern of expected behaviour that follows from such conceived differences between people. For instance, Pa'Lah states that it would be extremely unusual and presumably unacceptable for him to behave in the same manner as Pa'Man, and it would be impossible for him to carry himself in a manner appropriate to Ku Nor or any other royal person. The case is probably the same with Pa'Soh. Likewise, it would be against the 'norms' for persons whom Pa'Lah classifies as 'honoured' to carry themselves as either Pa'Lah or Pa'Soh.

However, though Pa'Lah classifies some commoners like Haji Pa'min, Pa'Man and Haji Mat in the same category as the royal Ku Nor, these commoners would still be distinguishable from royal persons according to Ku Man's classification. Though their affluence and religiousness bring them to the position of equal, in many respects, to Ku Nor, these do not give them the rank of being royal persons. As such, their deference to the economically poor Ku Man and the royal persons generally is an expected response. This seems to be emphasised by the fact that (Ku Man says) they have to use the 'court language' in their contact with such persons. This deference, from the point of view of the honoured persons who are commoners is however, only perfunctory. Regardless, they are obliged to do so simply because failing to do so would only discredit their position of being 'honoured' as lacking in the right manners (*ta'tahu adat*).

What is discernible from what Ku Man and Pa'Lah say is that some commoners are regarded in the same way as some royals in that they are 'honoured', they are different from other commoners in the kampung and they are also different from the royal persons in the kampung. In other words, we may generalise that people in the kampung are distinguished from one another on the basis of royalness (*daulat*), wealth, and religiousness. I believe, this is the normative or the conscious model by which every resident distinguishes and classifies one another in the kampung. Classes emanating from such models may then be represented as follows:

	Classes		**Sub-Classes**
1.	Royal Persons (*daulat*)	1.	Rich, religious
		2.	Poor, irreligious
2.	Commoners	1.	Rich, religious
		2.	Poor, irreligious

Underlying such class division are both economic and non-economic (ideological) determinants. Corollarily 'a set of rules' for daily expressive social relationships evolve which supposedly reaffirm and confirm the various rights and privileges enjoyed by each class in relation to others. For instance:

1. A royal person who is religious, apparently wealthy and occupies a position in the Administration is not only respected, but he expects to be feared by the commoners in the kampung, especially the poor ones. Extreme deference is therefore expected towards such persons. Unless the occasion is a formal one, such a person is expected to associate only with members of his royal group.

2. A royal person who is irreligious and poor is expected to be respected perfunctorily as 'royal', but without the extreme deference as expected to be shown towards case (1) above. He is thus expected to join the company of the poor commoners.

3. A commoner who is religious and overtly wealthy and who is included in the group that feasts expects to be treated with deference. However, they are not expected to be feared. As such any dissatisfaction expressed by these people may be expected to be taken by others lightly, if not slightly ridiculed especially in their absence.

4. A commoner who is irreligious, poor, and without any specific skill or fixed employment, expects to be described as 'worthless'. His presence is not expected to be taken into account and he is expected to be subjected to condemnation in the case of his fault, and sympathy in the case of his weakness.

These conceived classes of people form a system of hierarchy which to a large extent is sanctioned by a system of right manners and behaviour. Whether this has any relevance or importance at the level of what actually happens is the subject of the next Chapter.

Footnotes

1. Economically independent unit consisting of parent and children or adult (couple or single) living separately or sharing a house with others is counted as one household.

2. The same is true of women living with grandchildren or women who adopt children after their own children have grown up; (cf. Rosemary Firth 1966, 13–25).

3. Though the rate of divorce in Kelantan is known to be one of the highest in the Peninsula, there was only one case of divorce in the kampung in the period of six months of fieldwork. The people, including one of the '*imam*' of Kota Bharu explain that people in the town are less inclined to divorce than those in rural areas. This seems to be true when we observe the 1973 and 1974 cases of divorce. While Kota Bharu town has only about 32% of divorce out of the total number of marriages (Appendix 7a), the district of Kota Bharu (i.e. including rural areas surrounding the town) as a whole has 49.76% and 56.65% of divorce in 1973 and 1974 respectively (Appendix 7b).

4. In this case ego is the leader of the prayer house. He describes a daughter of his first cousins (*anak sa-pupu*) whom he originally helped to settle in the kampung as a relative instead of a close relative. The relative is often accused of being involved in prostitution, though she formally works as a labourer in the match factory. Such an accusation is demeaning to his strong commitment to religion, and I believe it is possible that he would not claim the relative as close relative because it would bring him 'shame' (*malu*). In contrast, the people in the kampung seem to claim close association with a relative if the relative has high prestige as the case of Kuman below.

5. The wholesaler (dealer) in this case is described by the people of the kampung as '*towkay*', a word which is traditionally used to refer to Chinese entrepreneurs (cf. Firth 1966).

6, A trishaw is a tricycle which is pedalled by a driver (usually male) for the transportation of goods and people around the town. The fare for a ride in a trishaw is not fixed and is subjected to haggling. However it is common practice that a rider is charged from 30 to 40 cents for a one-mile journey.

7. For short however, they are commonly referred to as 'Ku' and a shortened name. For instance, Tengku Osman would be referred to as Ku Man, Tengku Esah would be referred to as Ku Sah etc. For the present purpose, I would then use these common references to denote these royal persons.

8. The actual amount of the royal allowance was never disclosed to the writer. However, some of his close commoner friends estimate it as around M$50.00 per month.

9. The truth of the case is however questionable since on further investigation, the writer could not trace the people concerned.

10. The truth of the matter is that the original owner of the sawmill secured a lease on the land for 90 years from his grandfather Tengku Bendahara in order to set up the sawmill. Though the land now belongs to one of his uncles, the operator of the sawmill retains the friendship with the royal persons of the kampung by giving employment to unemployed royal persons like Ku Man. To some extent, favourites of royal persons of the kampung like the leader of the prayer Hj. Pa'min gained the position of an overseer in more or less the same way.

11. This is locally termed as '*maulud*' which may be held on any day of the month of *Muharram,* the first month of the Muslim calendar. The celebration involves a feast where guests are invited to congregate in a manner of a religious ritual. For convenience, I would use the term 'feast' to refer to this.

12. The expression of '*ta'guna*' is a Kelantan dialect which may be equal in implication to '*bangsat*' in national Malay language (cf. Swift 1965, 151).

13. '*Tongkat*' is the art of self-defence which involves the skill of using a hard wooden rod about 5 feet long and 1½ to 2 inches in diameter.

CHAPTER FOUR

EXPRESSIVE SOCIAL RELATIONSHIPS

I now propose to show that at the level of observable behaviour, group formation in the kampung differ significantly from images which people themselves hold, as described in the last chapter. I see such observable groupings as being manifested in the expressive social relationships in which the people reciprocally engage in daily life.

Following Simmel (1950, 309) that "every relationship between persons gives rise to a picture of each in the other ..." and the further elaboration of the concept by Goffman (1967) that such relationships involve ceremonial rules of conduct or etiquette, I propose to examine the expressive social relationships between heads of households in the kampung using the assumption that heads of households influence and constrain others (if any) in the domestic unit in such as way that the social behaviour of the former makes an imprint on that of the latter. Domestic relationships between husbands and wives, parents and children, and between siblings are excluded from my analysis.

The types of expressive social relationships in which an individual, in one way or another, either voluntarily or otherwise, relates to another in the kampung are various: I see this as being manifested in different kinds of greetings, conversing and chatting. These relationships, again, seem to revolve around a wide range of social involvements which include the making and using of rafts in the river, participation in nightly prayer congregation at the kampung's prayer house, occasional assembly at feasting, visiting at homes, and participation in daily gatherings at coffee shops.

For analytical simplicity however, let us begin by considering the relationships between the individuals who use the raft[1] in the river who constitute almost half of the kampung's population (36 households); later on we will show how these people relate to the other half.

The category of people who use the raft for daily cleaning, washing, bathing and defaecating is different from others in the kampung. To use their own terms, they are "people who go to the river"; they differ from those in the kampung who have a piped-water supply from the town and from those who have their own private water pumps; both of these groups have indoor sanitation facilities. The "people who go to the river'' are forced to cooperate with one another to make, mend and use the raft, and for our purposes we can refer to them as raft-users.

Raft Groupings

Though there are two wells in the middle of the kampung introduced by the local member of the State Assembly as part of his 1974 election promise — they attract only a small number of raft-users, especially those who are further up the river bank. In the main, the wells attract women and children who use the wells for fetching 'clean' water for cooking and drinking. For other purposes, the raft is indispensable to the raft-users. A continual flow of the raft-users to the river is one of the features of daily life.

Apart from a raft that was built by a Chinese owner of a batik printing factory as part of his premises, there are two principal rafts at the disposal of the raft-users. The use of either one is restricted to members of a particular raft group, though the raft belonging to the Chinese is freely used by some of the raft-users, especially at night-time, despite the disapproval constantly expressed by the owner.

A raft group consists of members who have contributed a compulsory sum of $2.00 each when the rafts were built (approximately two and one and a half years ago, respectively). The members of a raft group, however, have to co-operate in mending the raft when the occasion arises. Such occasions are rare: according to informants, they arise only once every two or three years, or whenever a flood destroys part of the raft. During the six months period of fieldwork, neither of the rafts required mending. Exemptions from participating in the actual manual work of making and mending the rafts are only given to those who have genuine demands of other more important work, or to widows and physically incapable heads of households.[2]

The actual work of making and mending a raft entails cleaning and nailing the planks together to make a platform which is then nailed on to a float made of bamboo held together by steel ropes. Almost every member knows how to do the different part of the work. However, the work is unmanageable unless more than one person is involved. Such participation in the co-operation of making and mending gives the members of the raft-users households the right to use the raft. Anyone's breach of such 'right to use' is subjectd to extreme mockery by other members. This mockery may be slight among the adults, but the children will not hesitate to demand justification for such use by 'outsiders'. Consequently non-members describe it as 'uncomfortable' (*segan*) if they attempt to use the raft to which they do not belong. Polarisation of the raft-users into two groups in terms of who is to use which raft is then inevitable. A raft-user therefore either belongs to the raft of Haji Pa'min or the raft of Kusin,[3] thus becoming a member of one of the two raft-groups in the kampung. Let us consider the two raft-groups in turn.

i) ***The raft-group of Haji Pa'min***

As described in Chapter 3, Haji Pa'min is a tenant on a house site belonging to a royal person who is one of the original holders of land. He acts as the *Imam,* or leader of prayers at the prayer house and is an overseer at the nearby Hing Bing Sawmill (Appendix 4). As far as the raft is concerned, he acted as its informal leader who was responsible for gathering those who are interested in the co-operation of making the raft. This mainly involved taking the initiative of collecting contributions from the members and the purchase of all the necessary materials for the construction of the raft. The members of 'his' raft group consists of 22 people who are made up of the following:

Table 8
RAFT–GROUP OF HAJI PA'MIN

Place of Birth	Total	Kind of Birth: *Tengku*	*Nik*	*Wan*	Commoner	Ownership of House Site: Owners	Tenants	Free Settlers
local born	1	1						1
vicinity	9			3	6		9	
rural	12			2	10		11	1
Total	22	1	–	5	16	–	20	2

Their period of stay in the kampung varies, but save for two cases of free settlers who are relatives of a landowner, the members are all tenants on their house sites. The majority of members of the raft-group are also poor and work as manual labourers as will be shown in Chapter 5.

Apart from making and mending the raft, these members do not exhibit any co-operation with one another in their daily life. Their reasons for co-operating to make the raft, then, seems to point to only one explanation: that they all need the raft, which is difficult if not impossible to erect individually. The construction of individual rafts would not be economically viable. Their co-operation however does not entail any explicit obligation on the part of any one member towards any other, even including their 'leader' Haji Pa'min. Similarly their individual behaviour and disposition are at variance with one another, especially between Haji Pa'min and the members of his raft group. For instance Haji Pa'min who is also the leader of the nightly prayer congregation at the prayer house is at one end of the religiousness continuum in contrast to some members of his raft group who are on various points at the other.[4] There is one individual, for example, who regularly prays at the prayer house and sometimes acts as the prayer caller or '*bilal*',[5] there is another who occasionally prays at the prayer house, and there are others who do not attend prayers at the prayer house at all. In fact some of the individuals in the raft-group are extremely irreligious. To an extent they make fun of prayers and overtly express their indifference to some of the daily religious practices, and so they may be described as *jahil*, or people who show laxity towards religious practices. A trishaw pedaller who spends most of his leisure time at the coffee shop is a case in point. He openly states that he is 'at war' with the leader of nightly prayers at the prayer house, Haji Pa'min, whose efforts to rectify such behaviour into what he considers as the 'proper way' (i.e. regular attendance at the prayers at the prayer house) is ridiculed during his absence if not rejected by members of his raft group.

When going about his daily business, Haji Pa'min perfunctorily greets the members of his raft-group whom we have described as indifferent to religious practices (*jahil*) on meeting the latter on the lane or pavement in the kampung. In such a greeting, Haji Pa'min briefly inquires of a member of his raft-group as to where he or she is going or what he or she is doing without really wanting to know exactly the answers, and he addresses the member by his or her name. This greeting is replied to timidly and briefly by the member to the extent that the member (and other members who show laxity towards religion or '*jahil*') is described by Haji Pa'min as someone who is 'reluctant to talk' (*berat mulut*).[6]

In response, the religiously lax members, and others having a similar attitude to religious observances, greet Haji Pa'min deferentially: these members would not only acknowledge his presence by smiling and nodding towards him, but such greeting, though also brief and involving the same inquiries, addresses him by his social position in the kampung, i.e. as the *Imam*. The greeting is uttered in a low, soft voice, normally when one directly meets Haji Pa'min and preferably before he makes his greeting. Thus the predominant pattern of greeting between those of the raft-group who are lax in their religious practices (*jahil*) and the leader of the raft-group is that the members greet the leader with smiles, deference, and nodding, while the leader greets them perfunctorily.

However, greetings between Haji Pa'min and one member of his raft-group, Wan Husin, who occasionally prays at the prayer house and is employed as a labourer with the sawmill where Haji Pa'min is the overseer, show a different pattern: Haji Pa'min greets Wan Husin more expansively and makes polite inquiries about matters relating to his family. In return, Wan Husin seems less timid than other members described above, though the greeting is performed in the similar manner, i.e. with smiling and nodding.

Another way by which a member of the raft group relates to the leader is through conversing in the lengthy and free chatting during leisure time, which may also involve visiting each one's homes. This chatting is observed to be the relationship between Haji Pa'min and a member of his raft-group Pa'su Din, who regularly attends nightly prayers at the prayer house and sometimes acts as the prayer caller (*bilal*).

ii) ***The Raft–Group of Kusin***

Being one of the sons of the royal landowner Kusah, Kusin lives on his house site rent-free. Though he possesses a manual water pump in the house, the raft is still indispensable to him and his household for some purposes like defaecating. Economically, he is involved in a small retail business which is run by his wife and he owns and manages a small batik printing factory with four employees. He attends the prayer congregation at the prayer house daily and refrains from going to coffee shops. The members of his raft-group are as follows:

Table 9
RAFT–GROUP OF KUSIN

Place of Birth	Total	Kind of Birth: *Tengku*	*Nik*	*Wan*	Commoner	Ownership of House Site: Owners	Tenants	Free Settlers
local born	2				2			2
vicinity	3			1	2		3	
rural	7	1*			6		7	
Total	12	1	—	1	10	—	10	2

*Note — Though one member of this raft-group who originated from a rural area carries the prefix of '*Tengku* in front of his name which signifies royal heritage, he is considered in the kampung as '*raja darat*' rather than '*raja berdaulat*'. This is because his kinship link (consanguinal) to the ruling royal household, if at all, is vague. Thus the title '*Tengku*' carried by '*raja darat*' implies the insignificance of such title to the extent that it is no more than just another name for a commoner.

Similar to the members of the raft-group of Haji Pa'min, these members are either tenants or free settlers, and the same socio-economic condition. However, in contrast to the members of the other raft-group, most of them have a specific relation to their 'leader'. For instance individuals who are free settlers have, behind them, a long history of service to the royal group of the kampung in that they are descendants of royal servants; thus they are allowed to live on house sites free of rent. Another is a tenant on a portion of the house belonging to Kusin; the teenage son of another is economically dependent on Kusin in that he is employed as a labourer in Kusin's batik printing factory.

Kusin's position is an extension of the traditional paternalistic royal person's relationship with his followers. The members address him with 'court language' denoting the importance of his royal heritage. The relationship between the leader and the members of the raft-group is highly deferential, in much the same manner as the relationship between Haji Pa'min and the members of his raft group. However, there is one member with whom Kusin relates differently. This is Pa'mud, another prayer caller at the prayer house who is also a night guard with an Engineering Workshop (Appendix 5). On meeting each other, Kusin initiates a few inquiries of Pa'mud as the latter shows deference and submission.

Thus the raft represents a venture by a royal person to cater for the needs of his followers; traditionally this has been the duty of such a person. The use of the raft follows the direct, indirect, implicit or explicit whims of Kusin. His influence is enhanced by the absence of an alternative, for a member of the raft-group would not only be uncomfortable to use the raft of Haji Pa'min, but more importantly would fear the 'shame' of insulting Kusin that the act might entail. As (Swift, 1965) pointed out, the 'fear of shame' (*malu*) is central to the Malay personality and in this particular circumstance, it is reinforced by the fear of the direct sanctions which Kusin has the power to impose. This is because the words and feelings of Kusin, the son of Kusah on whose land the members are living either as renters or free settlers, are forces which threaten their use of the raft but their very existence in the kampung. Further, it is a widespread belief among these members that Kusin may provoke eviction of any member (and also any resident) whom he sees as unfit to live in the kampung. So if the words of Haji Pa'min may be ridiculed by 'his members', the words of Kusin in contrast are something to be reckoned with.[7] The relationship with the 'leader', in this case, is mediated by a complex of 'fear of shame' as well as fear of coercive sanctions.

Underlying the organisation of the raft-group in the kampung is proximity to the river and the indispensability of the use of the raft. As we have seen, the organisation of the two raft-groups do not differ significantly. While the raft-group of Haji Pa'min is largely voluntaristic, his position as *Imam* also seems important. Similarly, though the membership in Kusin's raft-group involves financial membership which is again voluntaristic, it is also imbued with the factor of respect and fear for Kusin's royal heritage. In essence the organisation of both raft-groups reveals voluntaristic, financial and functional aspects. In addition, the traditional respect and fear for the royal person and the respect for the leader of the prayer congregation (*Imam*) cannot be discounted.[8]

Differential Greetings: The Raft–Users

The groups which emanate from the raft-memberships are not clear-cut groups. I see this as being shown in two respects. Firstly, though the members of the two raft-groups are distinguished from each other on the basis of the rafts they patronise, the raft-users (including the leaders) as a group are neither divided on such grounds nor do one include all the people who use the rafts. This is because a majority of the raft-users are distinguished from the two leaders and one particular raft-user, Pa'su Din, who acts as one of the two prayer callers of the prayer house. This is shown by the nature of the expressive social relationships between a) the majority of the raft-users and their leaders, b) the relationship between one particular raft-user, Pa'su Din, with the two leaders, c) the relationship between Pa'su Din and other raft-users, and d) the relationship between the two leaders.

a) As noted earlier, the relationship between the members of the two raft-groups and their leaders is manifested in the specific manner of greeting which is highly deferential. Slight variation in the timing and content of the greeting between some raft-users and their leaders are however possible.

b) However, in one particular case, a raft-user (pa'su Din) relates to the two leaders differently; while he relates to the leader of his own raft-group through conversing, he relates to the leader of the other raft group through 'chatting' or a few moments of spontaneous exchange of information on meeting each other.[9]

c) The particular way of greeting between the members of the raft-groups and their leaders (a, above) also characterises the relationship between the former and Pa'su Din. The only difference is that the majority of the raft-users use towards him terms of address which are different from those used to greet the leaders: that is, in greeting the leader Haji Pa'min, they use the prefix '*To'Imam*' or the leader of the prayer congregation; and in greeting Pa'su Din, they use the fictive kin term 'Pa'su'.[10] However, the particular term of address used by the raft-users to address Pa'su Din does not invalidate his position as being equal to the position of the two leaders. This is because he is addressed by his social position (*pangkat*) rather than his name in the same manner as the raft-users address the two leaders. Further, Pa'su Din and the two leaders address the rest of the raft-users in a similar manner; that is, they address them either by their names or by their fictive kin term (*pa'*) in conjunction with their names — like Pa'Lah or Pa'Soh as the case may be. Also, the relationship is strongly marked by the dominant demeanour of the leaders, and the deferential response of the raft-users.

d) The relationship between the two leaders of the raft-groups is also important. It is observed that when they meet, they stop for a moment to exchange information with each other. In short, the two leaders 'chat' with each other unlike the deferential responses both evoke in their relationship with members of their respective raft-groups.

On the counts of these expressive social relationships therefore, it is possible to argue that the two leaders and Pa'su Din are distinguishable as being in different positions within the local social context thus setting them apart from the majority of the raft-users. This is because the way the two leaders relate to each other, and to Pa'su Din and vice versa, is different from the way all three relate to the majority of the raft-users. This I believe distinguishes them from the majority of people who use the raft.

Secondly, this is shown further by the implications of the relationships between the three individuals (the two leaders and Pa'su Din) and the rest of the raft-users. In particular, the relationship suggests that the majority of the raft-users adopt the manner of social inferiors in relation to the three individuals concerned. As we noted earlier, the raft-users show a distinctive style of acknowledgements like smiling and nodding their heads while greeting; they do not greet loudly or harshly; and to some extent they let out information or opinions only upon request from the three individuals. In the main, this particular greeting relationship seems to be characterised by elements like 'discomfort' (*segan*), respect, fear of shame (*malu*) and to some extent direct fear. These then order and dominate the behaviour of the raft-users in their relationship with the three individuals to the effect that it deters and inhibits direct association in their daily life. The relationship is then close to what Goodenough, (1965) terms as 'one of deference' and at best, it may be described as 'deferential greeting'.

Therefore, though the two leaders and Pa'su Din use the raft daily, they do not seem to belong to the group consisting of all the rest of the raft-users. They are in fact individuals whom Pa'Lah (a raft-user) calls earlier (Chapter 3) people who are 'honoured' (*mulia*). As the concept will be elaborated further below, I believe it is important to recognize at this stage that though the people who use the raft are on first impressions divided into two different raft groupings and with separate leadership, their expressive social relationships show that the meaningful division among them is a difference of whether one is 'honoured' or not.[11]

Given the fact that these people are living close together and are simultaneously using the raft, one may well wonder how such greeting relationship persists. Apart from reasons which characterise the relationship itself, I believe this is inherent in the nature of the raft organisation and the routine of using the raft.

As noted above, the co-operation with one another involved in maintaining the raft is minimal. When there is any, the requirement which forces co-operation is spread over a long period of time. Thus the need for one another's labour is divorced of its continuity as in the cases of co-operative work in the rural Malay villages. In addition, individual habits of using the raft differ from one another; for instance it is noted that the leader of one of the raft-groups, Haji Pa'min, uses the raft preceding the morning and afternoon prayer times and again after work in the late afternoon, while one member of his raft-group uses the raft in the late morning and again in the late afternoon. Thus direct confrontation between the members and the leaders of the raft-groups and among some of the members themselves at the raft are then less likely to occur. What this means therefore is that due to differences in individual habits of using the raft, the rafts then fail to force the raft-users as a whole into a situation of intensive daily interaction with one another. In short, the deferential greeting relationship does not necessarily have to be maintained in intensive daily social interaction, which might strain it by encouraging more egalitarian modes of inter-personal behaviour.

Calling (*Singgah*) and Unsociability (*Ta'tegor*) Relationships

Excluding the three individuals above, the rest of the raft-users' relationship to one another takes a different form. This is observed to be in the form of 'calling' (*singgah*) where one is engaged in random visiting to houses of others. This is to a large extent founded on the very nature of the structure of their houses.

The houses of these raft-users are equipped with verandahs especially constructed to receive casual visitors who stop for a while to exchange gossip on their way to some other destination. One is expected to stop for a while or call (*singgah*) at a house while passing in front of it especially if the owner is not immediately engaged in any urgent work. However such 'calling' time varies from person to person and it may last for a whole afternoon or evening. In cases where a woman is dyeing or waxing batik cloth in front of her house, standing around the batik hanger (cf. Appendix 6) replaces the verandah of the house as a meeting-place. It is very rare that a casual visitor from among the raft-users is invited into the house.

Failure to conform to the custom of 'calling' attracts accusations of being pompous or not sociable to the effect that one is subjected to restricted dealings by others among the raft-users. Excuses for not 'calling' are possible, but they seem to be accepted only from a person who is rushing along the lane to attend to some immediate and important commitment. Such a person therefore has to walk hurriedly while trying to dress up properly at the same time, and when questioned the person has to blame the children, the kitchen or the wife for being late to keep the appointment. Excuses are also accepted from a person who is riding a bicycle. The only reason for a person not to call at a house while passing it is when the two persons concerned are in conflict or involved in a personal quarrel with each other.

In one way, this 'calling' relationship expresses friendliness and sociability between the persons concerned, and in another it expresses the possibility of conflict between them. In other words, while the calling relationship expresses friendliness, sociability and co-operation, at the same time it expresses the reverse characteristic of hostility. Inasmuch as it is the norm of sociability, the relationship also emphasises the existence of hostility and conflict among the raft-users.

Interaction among some of these people is face-to-face, and its main elements are conflict and sociability. The phenomena of conflict and solidarity are part and parcel of daily social life among the raft-users. Consequently, an interest in the activities and material possessions of others among them are predominant. This interest, in turn, often arouses jealousy and quarrels. As cases in point, let us consider four of the quarrels observed:

1) This incident started when Sudin, a seventeen year old son of Dollah (member of raft-group of Kusin) bought a new pair of shoes which cost about M$20.00. Proudly Sudin then showed them to everyone who called at his house. Consequently Sabri, an eighteen year old son of Ya'akob (member of the raft-group of Haji Pa'min) decided to quieten Sudin's pride by hiding the latter's new pair of shoes. On finding the pair of shoes, Sudin hit Sabri who, with the help of a friend defeated Sudin in the fight. Subsequently Sudin's mother, thinking that the whole incident was preconceived, derogatively accused (*sumpah*) Sabri's parent who is

easily aroused and who retaliated by challenging Sudin's parent, Ya'akob to a fight. Though Ya'akob did not take up the challenge, the two households which are no more than one hundred yards away from each other not only ceased their 'calling' relationship, but also refused to greet and talk to each other.

2) Ya'akob made some renovations on his house which included a new extension and painting of the whole house. The extension was however made without prior consultation with Kuman (member of the raft-group of Haju Pa'min) who, supposedly acting on behalf of the landowner (his father's sister) should have authorised the plan. As his authority is now challenged, Kuman secretly reported the case to the Town Board which acted by inspecting the premises. Though there was no negative consequences to Ya'akob, he alleged that Kuman was behind it all, and 'degoratively accused' Kuman for showing off his 'power'. In retaliation, Kuman reminded Ya'akob of his precarious position as a renter. Though the quarrel did not develop beyond the verbal confrontation, it nonetheless severed the 'calling' ties between the two people.

3) In regard to Daud (member of the raft-group of Haji Pa'min) the case is less clear. Daud was arrested by the 'Religious Supervisers' while in 'suspicious proximity' with Yah.[12] The incident forced him to marry the latter which resulted in the divorce of his wife with whom he has three children. As Kuman has been an intermediary to such an arrest previously which earned him $10.00 in reward, Daud was convinced by others that Kuman was responsible for his arrest. This was denied by the latter. When verbal confrontations and accusations of each other occurred, Kuman maintained that no matter who was responsible for Daud's arrest, the good name of the kampung is maintained.

4) The case of Pa'Lah (member of the raft-group of Haji Pa'min) and the wife of Pa'Su Din (the member of the same raft-group who acts as prayer caller) is similarly interesting. As the actual quarrel occurred prior to the period of fieldwork, the case is based purely on the narration of Pa'Lah. Pa'Lah said that one day he was looking for some feathers to use for scooping up larvae to feed his fighting fish. Failing to find any around his house, he went under the house of his neighbour, Pa'Su Din who had a big fowl. When he left, the wife of Pa'Su Din came back from shopping at the market to find that her brooch and necklace were missing. On learning that Pa'Lah had been around, she went to Pa'Lah to demand her belongings while at the same time derogatively accusing the latter as a criminal. Pa'Lah in return denied every allegation. The incident however was interrupted by Pa'Su Din who came back from work with

the explanation that he kept the necklace and brooch in a safe place after seeing it lying around in the house. Consequently Pa'Su Din apologised to Pa'Lah for the incident. His wife however was so embarrassed (*malu*) that she would not greet or talk to Pa'Lah.

These cessations of social contact between two individuals following an eruption of confrontation in which 'derogative accusations' are exchanged in the manner of fight talk is described by the residents as a relationship of 'unsociability' (*ta'baik*) or refusal to talk to each other (*ta'tegor*). This marks the severence of an intensive interpersonal relationship where one party objectionably reacts to the actions of the other because he interprets it as meddling or malicious. As shown above, Dollah and Daud defy the actions of Kuman for interfering with their respective personal affairs. Daud (Case 3) describes Kuman as "not his work; I would not have been angry if it is his job to do what he does . . . he is only interested in the ten dollar reward". Likewise, Ya'akob accuses Kuman's action as having been born out of jealously and ill-feeling.

In essence the unsociability relationship is then underlaid by factors like jealousy, suspicion, personal ambition and interest which are widespread among the raft-users. Though living in a town quite distinct and separate from rural areas, the raft-users are in certain respects similar to peasants. According to Foster, the latter's personality is, among others, characterised by suspicion, distrust, criticism, envy and frequent physical violence (Foster 1967, 298). The cases of quarrels above therefore show that some of the qualities of the peasant personality are present among the raft-users. However, unlike Foster's typology, the phenomenon of physical violence is not common.

The calling relationship among the raft-users not only signifies sociability and friendliness, but it is also the foundation on which the hostility relationship exists as implied by the exchange of the derogative accusations and the consequent unsociability that arises. The two kinds of social relationships which in turn imply both conflict and solidarity among the raft-users are then part and parcel of their daily social life. Therefore, on the one hand we may suggest that the unsociability relationship may be understood as a controlled conflict in a small world; and on the other it may be seen as the emphatic expression of egalitarianism. Like the jealousy and suspicion among rural Malays in Jelebu as shown by Swift, the unsociability relationship among the raft-users is concerned with 'maintaining the existing distictions' of the raft-users from others inthe kampung and the preservation of their similarities with one another (cf. Swift 1965, 154).

As such, individuals who are not bound by the 'calling' relationship do not in ordinary circumstances relate to those who are bound by it through the unsociability relationship. For instance the quarrel in Case 4 does not direclty involve Pa'Su Din who, as we have shown earlier relates to the raft-users under consideration, through deferential greeting. So, though his wife derogatively accused Pa'Lah, his deferential greeting relationship with the latter is in no way severed or affected. What seems important in this case is the operation of the feeling of 'embarrassment' (*malu*) which deters direct hostility between two parties. In particular, while the wife of Pa'Su Din is embarrassed for her rash action of accusing Pa'Lah, the latter is in turn dominated by his fear of shame towards Pa'Su Din to retaliate beyond denying the accusations. Had the accuser been someone whom Pa'Lah has no respect for, a mutual exchange of derogative accusations would have been possible.

Thus the unsociability relationship, which implies conflict and hostility, seems to be a kind of relationship that takes place only between two individuals who are within the same social circle and who necessarily interact with each other face-to-face. Otherwise, the feeling of shame or embarrassment (*malu*) which underlies respect as in the quarrel Case 4 above accommodates the potential hostility and conflict that might have arisen. In short, save for the three raft-users (Haji Pa'min, Kusin and Pa'Su Din) who relate to one another through conversing and chatting, and who relate to other raft-users through deferential greeting, all other raft-users relate to one another either through 'calling' or 'unsociability' relationships.

What has been discussed thus far revolves around the people who constitute about half the total number of Malay households in the kampung. In order to show the position of these people in relation to others in the wider social context of the kampung as a whole, an analysis of how they relate to the other half of the population is necessary. For this purpose I shall focus on four new individuals and see how they relate to others in the kampung. There are the two leaders of the raft-groups, Kusin and Haji Pa'min and two raft-users, Pa'Lah and Kuman. Let us now consider the following observed cases of relationships between these individuals and some others in the kampung.

1) As I have indicated earlier, Haji Pa'min converses with Pa'Su Din, a raft-user whom we have shown to be classified as an 'honoured' person and who never fails to attend the nightly prayers at the prayer house. They are often seen talking freely with each other on the verandah of the former's house on Friday afternoon when both are free from

work.[13] Also, as we would expect, these two relate to Pa'Lah and Kuman through deferential greeting, and they relate to Kusin through chatting.

2) Haji Pa'min and Pa'Su Din also seem to chat with Kunor, a royal person who is a senior clerk in the State's Public Service. The latter neither visits the former's homes nor receives them at his house. However he receives royal persons like Kusin with whom he converses and summons Awang,[14] through his son, whenever he likes.

3) In addition to conversing at homes as in 'calling' noted earlier, Pa'Lah and Kuman are also always conversing at the coffee shop at the fringe of the kampung with some other regular patrons from the raft-users of the kampung. When people like Che'gu Him[15] stops at the coffee shop to buy cigarettes (which he normally does) they always greet him and inquire about things such as where he is going and sometimes his purpose in going there, and further, they seem to expect answers from such inquiries. However, Pa'Lah and Kuman react differently when they meet Kunor; Pa'Lah is observed to use the prefix '*ku*' to greet Kunor in a deferential way, and Kuman stops to chat only briefly unless Kunor detains him.

4) Different from the one discussed so far, Che'gu Him is greeted by people like Kusin, Kunor and Haji Pa'min, and such greetings are performed in the same manner as he is greeted by Pa'Lah and Kuman (3 above). In return, he greets these people in the same way. In addition, he only visits people who live outside the kampung and likewise receives visitors from such places. In most cases these people are his fellow teachers with whom he also 'converses'. In fact Che'gu Him seems to associate mostly with people who are living in other areas of the town.

The obvious pattern discernible from these examples is that an individual may be involved in any one of the three kinds of social relationship: they are i) a chatting relationship as between Haji Pa'min and Kusin or Kunor (examples 1 and 2); ii) a conversing relationship as between Haji Pa'min and Pa'su Din (example 1), or as between Kusin and Kunor (example 2) or as between Pa'Lah and Kuman and other patrons of the coffee shops of the kampung (example 3); and iii) a mutual greeting relationship as between all these people and Che'gu Him (example 4).[16] The point should be emphasised, which will be examined more intensively later, that these three kinds of social relationships do not overlap. They are in fact highly independent of one another to the extent that 'conversing' makes 'chatting' insignificant and likewise 'mutual greeting' inhibits any other forms of social relationships. Nonetheless a point of caution seems necessary. Rather than considering extraoridinary circumstances under which an individual is forced to 'chat' with another with whom he usually 'converses', as when he meets the partner on his way to work for which he is late, we are concerned here with that part of social life in the kampung devoid of any unexpected or formal circumstances. However, to clearly distinguish these three types of social relationships, and also for reasons of simplicity, I shall analyse each of them separately.

Chatting: The Feasting Circle

Of the three kinds of social relationships, chatting appears least pervasive and incorporates a smaller circle of actors. As indicated earlier, the people explain it as a relationship between "people who know each other, but are not close friends"; thus, they exchange information for a few moments in the manner of spontaneous chatting. The subject of the conversation may centre around the immediate activity of each other and may extend to matters concerning each other's family, work and involvements in the recent past or the near future and seems to be restricted to those involvements that one deems the other party is free to know. Gossip about activities of others in the kampung may also crop up in such conversation.

As the occurrence of such a relationship is to a large extent random in that the conversants neither avoid nor seek one another out, the arenas for the relationships are many. They may include the sides of roads, retail shops, on the lane in the kampug and even at bus stops. All these arenas however point to one common principle: that at all times, the relationship occurs outside of homes, and in all cases observed a period of 'chatting' never exceeded five minutes.

However, the question why the 'chatting' relationship persists in the form it does, and does not develop into something more akin to a conversing relationship demands closer scrutiny.

This seems to be shown by the fact that people who chat with one another are observed to meet on certain occasions which to a large extent exclude the majority of other people in the kampung. These occasions are the nightly prayer congregation at the prayer house and the occasional congregation at feasting. Let us then consider each of these occasions separately.

i) ***The Prayer House:***

In order to show this clearly I believe a note on the prayer house congregation is in order. Though it was erected in the mid-1950's, the present prayer house is attributable to the efforts of Kunor, who in the guise of representing the people of the kampung, requested the local member of the State Assembly to renovate the ageing prayer house as part of his 1974 election promises. The latter obligingly agreed by donating M$500.00 which resulted in the present premises that are big enough to accommodate twenty to thirty people at a time, and include a curtained section for women *jemaah* (prayers).[17]

Being the original leader of the prayer congregation of the prayer house, Haji Pa'min continues to lead nightly prayers with the assistance of Pa'Su Din and sometimes Pa'mud[18] who substitute as the prayer caller (*bilal*). However, the prayer house does not attract all the people of the kampung. Rather it seems to attract only a handful of people who may be categorised into i) the regular *jemaah,* that is those who attend the prayers on most nights of the week, and ii) the irregular *jemaah* or those who attend the prayers at the prayer house once or twice a week. Also there are cases of individuals who go to pray either at the central mosque (*Masjid Besar*) in the town centre or at the prayer houses in the nearby kampung. The regular and the irregular *jemaah* at the kamppung's prayer house are as follows:

Table 10
REGULAR AND IRREGULAR *JEMAAH*

Jemaah	Total	People who chat (12) Royal	People who chat (12) Commoners	Raft-Users (33) Royal	Raft-Users (33) Commoners
Regular	10	3	6	—	1
Irregular	9	2	1	—	6

It may be observed that there is only one raft-user who regularly attends the nightly prayers as opposed to 9 others. Their number among the irregular *jemaah* is however the reverse, i.e. 6 out of 9 irregular *jemaah.* If the attendance at the prayer house shows anything, it is that those who attend the prayers are people who do not show total laxity towards religion. Thus they are distinguished from the majority of the raft-users (26 out of the total of 33) who do not attend prayers at all, some others who attend prayers at the prayer house outside the kampung and those who do not pray at all. However, as those who attend the prayers are again distiguished into the regular and the irregular *jamaah,* a note on the concept religiousness in this particular case seems necessary.

Attendance at prayers to some extent qualifies one to be described as a religious person in the sense that one does not object to religious formalism. Otherwise one is described as irreligious in the sense of showing laxity towards religion (*jahil*) though one may believe in the religion of Islam. However, the religiousness of those who attend the prayers seems to differ in degree. This is because the qualification of being religious demands extensive knowledge of the verses from the Holy Kor'an and to some extent its translation into Malay, as well as being able to recite the various 'prayers' (*doa*)[19] besides the most important criterion of daily practice of an adherence to the principles of the religion. As such it seems only the leader of the prayer congregation (*Imam*) who fully qualifies: he is described as being pious in that he shows sincere and strong commitment to religious practices on top of the fact that he knows how to recite the various prayers (*doa*). In varying extent, the prayer callers and the other regular *jamaah* are also described as such. On the same count the attendance at the prayers by the irregular *jemaah* seems to merit description of 'showing' religiousness in the populist sense, especially when their observance of religious practices like the prayers seems no more than a case of mere formality.

However, to take the attendance at the prayer house as the cardinal qualification for a chatting relationship between people seems to be somewhat limited. This is because such a relationship does not seem to be the uniform rule of relating among those who attend the prayer house. For instance, let us take the individuals from the social relationships above as our examples.

Regular *Jemaah*	**Irregular *Jemaah***	***Jemaah* at Prayer Houses Outside the kampung**
Haji Pa'min, Kusin, Pa'su Din, Pa'mud	Kunor, Pa'Lah	Che'gu Him

It is noted that while a consistency of social relationship exists between those who attend the prayers at the kampung's prayer house and those who attend prayers at a prayer house outside the kampung, i.e. the relationship of mutual greeting, the regular and the irregular *jemaah* at the kampung's prayer house seem to be cross-cut by different kinds of social relationships. For instance among the regular *jemaah,* we noted that Haji Pa'min and Pa'su Din relate to each other through 'conversing' relationships, they both relate to Kusin through chatting relationship in the same way as they relate to the irregular *jemaah* Kunor. Further the regular *jemaah* Kusin relates to the irregular *jemaah* Kunor through 'conversing' relationship. However, all these people relate to another irregular *jemaah* Pa'Lah through 'deferential greeting' relationship. In addition, one of the prayer callers, Pa'mud who is a raft-user and obviously a regular *jemaah,* relates to all these people (except Pa'Lah) in a deferential manner though this may involve inquiries or request for opinions by the latter. Paradoxically though, Pa'mud related to Pa'Lah (who is another raft-user but an irregular *jemaah*) through the 'chatting' relationship.

Thus, to some extent attendance at prayer at the kampung prayer house does not seem to explain the phenomenon of the 'chatting' relationship. In any case it is not the only reason underlying such a relationship. Therefore some further explanation seems warranted.

ii) ***The Feasting***

This seems to be provided by the second kind of occasion where people who chat with one another occasionally meet; that is the religious ritual of feasting which in this case is the celebration of the birth of the Prophet Mohammad. In Malay this is termed as '*maulud*' which may be carried out on any day of the month of *Muharram,* the first month of the Muslim year. This celebration involves the giving of a feast where guests are invited to feast free of any charge or presents.[20] For the purpose of the present study, this celebration shall then be referred to in short as 'feasting'. During the period of observation, the following people held such 'feasting':

1) Kunor, an irregular *jemaah* at the prayer house. His principal invitees include 7 regular *jemaah* who are commoners, 3 regular *jemaah* who are royal persons and 1 irregular *jemaah* who is a commoner. His principal helpers are 1 regular *jemaah* who is a raft-user commoner, 1 royal person who is a raft-user and 3 raft-users who are free settlers and who are descended from royal servants.

2) Pa'su Din, one of the prayer callers. His main invitees are also people who are invited by Kunor, including the latter. However, his helpers include 1 regular *jemaah* who is a raft-user commoner who also helps at Kunor's feasting (he is also the other prayer caller), and his relatives.

Although the feasting at the house of Kunor was more elaborate, extensive and varied, both feasts are typical of the *maulud.* The invitees at both feasts centred around the same group of individuals, none of whom belongs to the raft-user group of people. The raft-users are only involved in such feasting, if at all, as helpers in the preparation of the feast. In the main, feasting involves all the regular *jemaah* at the prayer house and a few irregular *jemaah.* In any event, according to Haji Pa'min, they are individuals who in previous years had celebrated the feasting and thus they are reciprocally invited to the feasting of others in the kampung. In fact they are the individuals whom the raft-users call "people who are religious, people who have wealth, and if there is any feasting or celebration in the kampung, they are the ones who are involved". The people concerned however, prefer to categorise themselves as "people who are religious" in the sense of claiming that they are the only individuals in the kampung who seem to show keen interest and respect for the religion, that is to say they have a high commitment to religious practices. However, because feasting also involves people who are irregular *jemaah,* such claims seem a little weak. Nevertheless they are people whom we may call the 'feasting circle' of the kampung, and for the purpose of this study I use the term feasting circle to refer to this particular group of individuals.

What seems obvious here is that regardless of whether one is a regular or irregular *jemaah,* participation in the feasting seems to explain the 'chatting' relationship. For instance, although Kunor is an irregular *jemaah* at the prayer house, the fact that he overtly cherishes the religious ritual of feasting and is likewise invited to such occasions means that he is different from some regular and irregular *jemaah* who do not feast, like the cases of Pa'Lah and one raft-user commoner who helps at feasting and who are irregular and regular *jemaah* respectively. As shown earlier, Kunor relates to these two raft-users through deferential greeting; the two men have respect for Kunor and in fact classify him as an 'honoured person' together with some others who belong to the feasting circle. Some of these people would be regular *jemaah* at the prayer house who chat with Kunor, like the leader of the prayer Haji Pa'min.

So the fact that Kunor and Haji Pa'min 'chat' with each other shows that 'chatting' is not only a kind of social relationship between the members of the feasting circle, but it is also a relationship between the 'honoured' persons of the kampung. In any event we may argue that while attendance at the prayers at the prayer house is necessary, participation in the feasting is an important if not the sufficient condition for the 'chatting' relationship. On this basis, there are 12 people in the kampung — 6 royal persons and 6 commoners who variously relate to one another through a 'chatting' relationship. In terms of ownership of land, the royal people include one free settler, while the commoners have 2 tenants and one free settler.

Table 11
THE FEASTING CIRCLE

Place of Birth	Total	Kind of Birth: *Tengku*	*Nik*	*Wan*	Commoner	Ownership of House Site: Owners	Tenants	Free Settlers
local born	7	6			1	7		2
vicinity	2				2	2		
rural	3				3	1	2	
Total	12	6	—	—	6	8	2	2

At this stage, however, to regard the attendance at prayers and participation in the feasting or, in short, commitment to religious practices as the direct qualifications for a person to be honoured seems in need of further justification. I see this as folows:

a) Firstly, feasting is religious in nature, that is, it is a good deed (*kebajikan*) done in accordance with the principles of religion. The periodic revitalisation of good deeds by the participants seems to give continuing legitimacy to the status of the participants as 'honoured' persons. The fact of adhering to the norms of attending the prayers at the prayer house and, more importantly, feasting therefore seems to function as a claim to such respectability by the respective participants. This is especially obvious in the case of an individual like Kunor, whose participation in feasting seems to override his irregularity in attending the prayers at the prayer house.

b) Secondly, following Swift (1967) any kind of feasting among the Malays in Malaysia involves a certain level of extraordinary expenditure which in essence is a claim for prestige through showing high wealth. The kind of feasting being discussed is an example. This is because the feasting is done purely as a good deed, the holder of such a feast does not expect any contributions from others and has no expectation of any returns or profit. The feast, then, is a pure exhibition of possession of surplus wealth which may be expended freely. Therefore participation in the feasting not only shows a high commitment to religion but it also shows possession of economic surplus, i.e. wealth beyond immediate need for daily consumption.

c) Thirdly, though such respect is traditionally the prerogative of royal birth, it seems that it is now in need of being supported by attendance at prayers and participation in feasting. Otherwise, royal birth falls in importance. For instance Kuman has been variously mentioned as being denied his inherited respect, as is implied by his deferential greeting relationship with the leader of the prayer congregation, Haji Pa'min. This seems to be directly due to the fact that he fails to attend prayers at the prayer house as well as his non-participation in the feasting. On the other hand the royal people like Kusin and Kunor who are regular and irregular *jemaah* respectively and who are both participants in the feasting are able to maintain if not enhance their inherited respectability. Therefore commitment to religion seems necessary to maintain the respectability of the royal persons in the kampung.

Thus the feasting circle or the honoured persons who chat with one another belong to an exclusive social category within the kampung. For instance, it may be noted from the cases of some social relationships that individuals who relate to Haji Pa'min through the chatting relationship neither belong to the raft-users, nor are they bound by 'calling' or 'unsociability' relationships. Instead the members of this 'chatting' network relate to the raft-users through the deferential greeting relationship. This is especially shown by case 3 in the examples we have given.

From this we may argue that individuals who chat with one another and collectively relate to the raft-users through the deferential greeting relationship are thus socially distinct from the latter. The fact that they are able to amass sufficient surplus to hold a feast is also a significant economic consideration in the kampung. They are thus not only respected by raft-users but their subordination of the latter as implied by deferential greeting is also instrumental in delineating their social boundary.

This group of individuals who chat with one another are therefore sharing what Weber has called the 'equality of social esteem' (Gerth and Mills 1948, 187) to the effect that it becomes the qualification for the 'chatting' relationship, and as such it separates them as a group from the raft-users or any group in the kampung (as will be shown later).

Though we may speak of a feasting circle, these people are not as socially close to one another, as the raft-users discussed earlier. To show how this is so, let us take the cases of two individuals within the group, Kunor and Haji Pa'min.

Kunor is a royal person who is a senior clerk in the State's Public Service, and he is also one of the landowners of the kampung. In contrast Haji Pa'min is a tenant on a house site belonging to one of the royal persons in the kampung (Kunor's father's sister) and employed as an overseer by one of the Chinese owned sawmills nearby. His pre-eminence in religious knowledge and practices however makes the latter an indispensable member of the kampung both at feasting congregations as well as at the nightly prayer congregation at the prayer house. Consequently he is well respected and held in high esteem by the people of the kampung, comparable to if not equal to the position of Kunor. Kunor irregularly attends the prayers under the leadership of Haji Pa'min, and both participate in the feasting and are thus members of the feasting circle of the kampung. They respect each other though Haji Pa'min is obliged to use the 'court language' to talk to Kunor just as any other commoner in the kampung would do towards a royal person.

However, the two do not associate with each other beyond 'chatting'. The main reason for this seems to be that the basis of their claims for respect in the kampung are somewhat different. While Kunor is a royal person, a burearucrat and an owner of his own house site, Haji Pa'min is a commoner, an overseer with a sawmill, a tenant on his house site and the leader of the prayer congregation (*Imam*) of the kampung. Thus, though they are equally respected by the people in the kampung and they respect each other, the fact remains that the respect they gain is based on different factors as obviously implied by these personal charcteristics. To some extent, this is also the result of their different ways of life, especially economic and natal status; they are not familiar with each other and they do not share common activities in daily living apart from daily prayers at which again Kunor's attendance is irregular. In short, though the two individuals share the common attribute of being respected in the kampung, they are forced to relate to each other in the manner of 'chatting' at places other than at feasting simply because their claim for respect springs from different if not competing factors and they belong to different class positions in the town's productive system and are thus unfamiliar with each other's way of life.

'Chatting' is thus a relationship between individuals who share the quality of the 'honoured person' which gained them respect from the raft-users of the kampung. The relationship implies mutual respect, and underlying the relationship is the fact that they are not socially close to one another mainly because they claim respect through different factors and they are not familiar with one another's way of life. However, the net effect is that they are distinguished from others in the kampung as people who belong to an exclusive group of people which we may call feasting circle.

Mutual Greetings: The Individualists

Another kind of expressive social relationship is mutual greeting. This is a relationship where an individual greets another without any inhibitions. Such greeting is a relationship between two people who, to use their own words, "know each other but are not friends". If we may recall the examples of the various social relationships above, it is noted that Che'gu Him relates to all the people discussed so far through mutual greetings. Likewise he is also greeted by these people in the same manner.

It is also worth noting that Che'gu Him neither attends the prayers at the prayer house in the kampung (though he is not described as irreligious in the present sense — *jahil*), nor does he attend the kampung's coffee shops. Further, since the kampung is a town ward which is hardly isolated from the rest of the town, he goes to visit people outside the kampung freely, he frequently receives visitors from such places and at times he also attends coffee shops outside the kampung especially in the town centre which is only about 0.7 of a mile away. In fact Che'gu Him does not seem to participate in the social life of the kampung at all. In addition, his house is located beside the main road and this seems to facilitate his movement out of the kampung and without arousing any unnecessary inquiries from other people. In other words, unlike the members of the feasting circle and the raft-users, the social activities of Che'gu Him are oriented towards the outside of the kampung. As a case in point, this is shown by his feasting which in this particular case is the ceremony of 'shaving' (*cukor*) of his newborn grandson.[21]

The ceremony was carried out one Friday morning and it involved a light breakfast meal. His invitees however did not include any individual from the kampung, rather they were mainly his fellow teachers and relatives from outside. Even the leader of the prayer congregation (*Imam*) of the kampung, Haji Pa'min, whose role and service in such an event is usually indispensable, was left out of the ceremony.

Both the feasting circle and the raft-users describe the people in the kampung who share the social characteristics of Che'gu Him as "people who take no notice of other people" and who for the present purposes we may call the "individualists". This is because of the following reasons: if such people hold feasts, their feasting involves helpers and invitees who are living in areas other than the kampung; if at all, they attend prayers at prayer houses situated outside the kampung; and if they spend their leisure time at coffee shops, they would choose ones which are located outside the kampung, especially those in the centre of the town. They do not associate with other people in the kampung to the extent that they do not seem to show any desire to significantly involve themselves in its social life. Consequently, whenever and wherever they meet other people in the kampung, they greet them in a perfunctory way.

Included in this category are 23 people who are made up of commoner owners of house site (13) who are largely settlers of the kampung as may be shown in the following:

Table 12
THE INDIVIDUALISTS

Place of Birth	Total	Kind of Birth: *Tengku*	*Nik*	*Wan*	Commoner	Ownership of House Site: Owners	Tenants	Free Settlers
local born	4	1			3	3		1
vicinity	11		1	3	7	7	4	
rural	8		1		7	3	5	
Total	23	1	2	3	17	13	9	1

The probable reasons underlying the social relationship adopted by the individualists seem several. First, the individualists are not bounded by face to face relationships with others in the kampung. They are relatively independent from others in the kampung, and their social world is less parochial. In any case their social life centres around Kota Bharu town rather than being restricted within the enclosure of the small town ward. Given such a situation, the individualist may then afford to be individualistic as far as the kampung's social life is concerned.

Second, being in the town, the individuals in the kampung as a whole may also choose not to spend their time in the kampung. This is especially so when one works in the town centre and associates mostly with fellow workers who may come from other areas. One's active social life may be spent in the town centre itself or in the areas of the town where fellow workers live. For some people, the kampung is no more than a dormitory area. Given the fact that it is a town ward within a bigger town environment, the kampung's social life is thus less significant to some people who choose to remain out of it. This is especially so when, as indicated earlier, the main town centre which houses the core of business and entertainment in the state of Kelantan is less than a mile away.

Third, it is noteworthy that the houses of the individualists are situated along the major roads and payment of the kampung. This seems important at least in one respect: that the situation of the houses favours a quick and easy access to the outside of the kampung, sometimes without even being noticed by other kampung inhabitants.

In short therefore, the mutual greeting relationship in the kampung seems to be founded on two main factors: i) the individuality of one particular category of people, and ii) more importantly, the physical and the social environment of the kampoung is part of the wider town (urban) environment of Kota Bharu.

'Conversing'

To turn to another kind of social relationship prevalent in the kampung, let us now consider the conversing relationship. As briefly indicated above, this relationship implies a long period of conversation between two people when both are not engaged in any form of work. Such a relationship seems to occur on the basis of mutual fricndliness where both parties freely talk on a wide range of subjects including important discussions on private and personal matters. However, such a relationship may also extend to 'empty talk'.

The time taken up by such a relationship may last until tiredness and the lateness of the hour at night force the participants to come to a stop, or until a matter that needs urgent attention crops up. As distinct from the chatting relationship, the conversing relationship takes place either at home or in coffee shops. Also different from the chatting relationship, this kind of relating to one another to some extent involves the action of choosing the houses or the coffee shops as the arena for conversing. An individual therefore knows and is familiar with the other party with whom he is conversing. His assumption that he is acceptable to the other is reciprocated, and he is welcome by the other.

For the present discussion however, it seems necessary that we reiterate the cases illustrated earlier: it is noted that Haji Pa'min converses with Pa'su Din; Kunor converses with his royal kin and sometimes receives a visitor who is a clerk, and the son of the traditional royal entertainer (*bidari*). Further Kuman and Pa'Lah converse with some others either at home during their 'calling' at one another's houses or at coffee shops.

What is implied by the nature of the relationship is that familiarity and common interests seem to underlie the personal choice of partners in such a relationship. The basic common interest in matters regarding religious practices, for instance, seems to determine the choice of Haji Pa'min to converse with Pa'su Din and vice versa. Further, both are tenants on house sites belonging to a royal person and both have gone through the process of settling in the kampung from the same rural village. Similarly, familiarity and sharing of common, mainly economic experience with one another among the raft-users underlies their conversing relationship, first at homes as shown in their 'calling' relationship and second, at the coffee shops.

So similarity of interest and/or familiarity with one another eases the social distance between partners so that a free relationship takes place. In addition, conversing may also occur in the manner of a traditional entertainer as in the conversing between Kunor and the son of his father's entertainer.

However, it is worth mentioning that different groups of people seem to converse at different places, that while the feasting circle seem to prefer to converse with one another at home, the raft-users seem to be less discriminate; that is they converse both at home and in coffee shops with perhaps a slight preference for the latter. There is also a difference in the manner in which the conversing is carried out; while the conversing at home seems to be strongly characterised by politeness, conversing at coffee shops is dominated by rowdiness, the use of vulgar language and with conversation tending to centre around the themes of women and "empty talk". This however does not discount the fact that problems of employment, wages and even local politics are also discussed at the coffee shops. At night time the conversing relationship at coffee shops is followed by games like draughts or cards.

Conversing at coffee shops is generally regarded as degrading especially by people who converse only at home and people whom we have called the feasting circle or the 'honoured' persons of the kampung. In effect, these people choose to be excluded from conversing at coffee shops. On the other hand, it seems to be a matter of common practice if not compulsion for the majority of the raft-users to congregate and converse at the coffee shops. This seems to be related to the ideology of 'what is proper';[22] it appears that while it is 'proper' for the raft-users to 'converse' at the coffee shops, it would be 'improper' for the feasting circle to do so. To some extent conversing between the two groups of individuals, if any, is not only regarded as 'improper', but more importantly both the feasting circle and the raft-users seem mutually 'uncomfortable' (*segan*) in each other's presence; that is, the feasting circle seems unable to adjust to the presence of the raft-users and likewise the raft-users do not seem to 'feel at home' in the presence of the feasting circle. So in as much as it is an improper place for the feasting circle to 'converse', the general social awkwardness that they would create significantly deters them from attending coffee shops. The resultant separation of places for 'conversing' between the feasting circle and the raft-users then is accepted as one of the main aspects of the norms of the kampung; i.e. while the raft-users 'converse' in coffee shops and at home during their 'calling' relationship, the feasting circle 'converse' only at home.

Though the 'conversing' relationship appears as a free and an uninhibited relationship between individuals, it is in fact severely restrictive. While the parties involved are determined by personal choice, such choice is constrained by the ideology of 'what is proper'. In addition, the place for 'conversing' is specifically segregated for certain groups of people, otherwise one would not only feel 'uncomfortable' but one would also be socially degraded. In short, the conversing relationship is a relationship which has a strong moral emphasis.

Recapitulation

To recapitulate these various kinds of expressive social relationships in the kampung here is to emphasise a general character of social relationships as a whole: that is, respectability or the quality of being 'honoured' is shared unequally by individuals in the kampung. This then determines the kind of social relationship in terms of which a person opts to relate to another to the extent that these relationships appear to be the 'given' way of relating.

The various relationships discussed above may be seen as the sets of rules of relating in the kampung. Thus if an individual is endowed with respectability or is 'honoured', his relationship with another individual in the kampung may take any of the following forms:

1) 'Deferential' greetings seem to dominate his relationship with an individual who has no such respectability. Thus he is also excluded from 'calling' and 'unsociability' relationships in which the latter would be involved.

2) 'Mutual greetings' seem to govern his relationship with people who neither seem to have respect for him nor for whom he has any respect. In any case such people relate to others in the kampung through mutual greeting regardless of their respectability.

3) 'Chatting' seems to order his relationship with an individual who shares similar respectability but whose attainment of such is through factors different from his. In any case he is not familiar with the way of life of the other, though he respects the other and is likewise respected by him.

4) He seems to choose the 'conversing' relationship to relate to individuals who share the same quality of respectability and whose respectability is founded on factors similar to, if not the same as his. He is thus familiar with the other and this eases his sense of social distance, making his relationship freer and more open.

5) To some extent he seems to recognise the traditional monopoly of respect by the royal persons. This is expressed by his usage of court language in addressing or chatting with such persons. However, such a monopoly is becoming less of a reality, i.e. it can also be achieved by commoners like him. Thus when he uses the 'court language' towards some royal person in deferential greeting, such use is only token. If it means anything at all, it is that his respectability is enhanced as someone who knows the custom (*adat*).

We may then look at the expressive social relationships in the kampung in terms of horizontal relationships as well as the vertical ones. This may be summarised broadly by the following diagram:

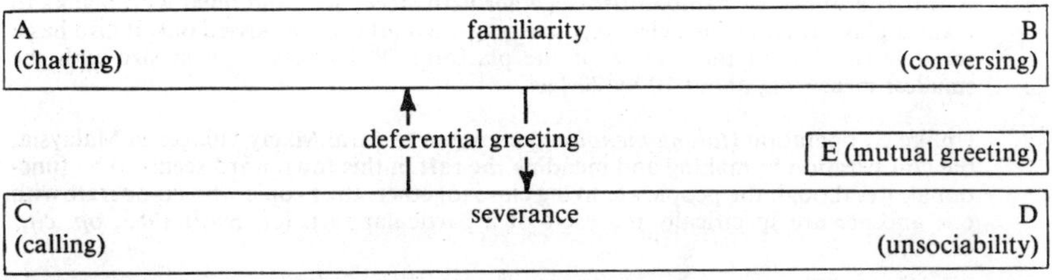

Each point on the diagram represents a kind of expressive social relationship: A is the 'chatting' relationship which implies similarity of respectability; the familiarity of one another may induce two or more individuals into a conversing relationship at point B; point C represents the 'calling' relationship which implies closeness and egalitarianism which, when severed changes into the unsociability relationship at point D; point E represents the mutual greeting relationship which essentially implies individuality and outside orientation. In any case it is outside the kampung's social life.

In addition, individuals who relate to one another through A and B form a divided entity endowed with respectability which is denied to individuals who relate to one another through C and D. This is signified by the deferential greeting relationship between A and B, and C and D. When individuals in E relate to individuals in both A & B and C & D through one and the same manner of relating, i.e. mutual greeting, it is obvious that they do not have any definite place in the respectability scheme of the kampung.

As these kinds of social relationships are the norms of relating, nonconformity to such rules of relating would then bring the ideological sanction of being labelled improper behaviour. Each kind of social relationship is highly independent of one another (cf. Simmel 1950, 321).

Thus the people of the kampung express distance to some and closeness to some others through these social relationships. The net effect is that they may be seen as falling into three main divisions — the feasting circle, the raft-users and the individualists. As these divisions are subjective, it is perhaps possible, for purposes of analysis, to speak of them as social categories. Whether they constitute status groups, or they coincide with objective class situations of people within it is the subject of the following discussion.

Footnotes

1. A raft is a bunch of bamboo tied together with steel ropes and lined with planks to make a platform on which cleaning, washing and bathing are carried out. It also has a small latrine-hut in the middle of the platform. Rafts may vary in size with the smallest measuring about 10 by 20 feet.

2. Unlike co-operation (*tolong menolong*) common to rural Malay villages in Malaysia, the co-operation in making and mending the raft in this town ward seems to be functional, i.e. though the people are living close together, the people who co-operate with one another are specifically the users of a particular raft: (cf. Swift 1965, *op. cit.,* 48–50).

3. Though the raft is communally owned, the association of these individuals with the two rafts in the kampung is founded on the fact that they initiate and organise the making and mending of the two rafts such that the rafts are known after their names. This involves collection of funds and buying of necessary material for such work, besides mobilising those who are interested in joining their respective 'raft-group'.

4. This is taken to represent the differences in the degrees of reverence for religion in the kampung. At one end of the continuum an individual is extremely religious to the point of total dissociation from other people or what the residents term as '*alim*'; at the other, an individual is characterised by manifested indifference to religious principle to the point of its neglect as described by the term '*jahil*'; and at the middle of the continuum, an individual is characterised by his close adherence to the principles of the religion and leading a life accordingly but not at the cost of social life, i.e. meeting and mixing with others who have more or less similar degree of respect and reverence for the religion. This category of individuals is described by the indigenous term of '*lebai*'.
5. A '*bilal*' or prayer caller is officially a position appointed by the State Council of Religion which is technically lower than that of *Imam* or the leader of the prayer congregation. His main task is to call the members of the prayer congregation to prayers when such times come. This is done by beating the drum in a particular rhythm which is then followed by the Muslim call for prayer (*bang*). He also recites a short verse loudly to mark the beginning of prayer when the congregation is ready. The *imam* and the '*bilal*' in the present case are however unofficial positions since the present prayer congregation is only local and centres around a prayer house (*madrasah*) rather than a mosque to which an official *imam* would be appointed. In the case of Kota Bharu town for instance, there are two official *Imams* (cf. Nash *op. cit.*).

6. '*Berat mulut*' is a term used by a person in the kampung to describe another person who would not talk openly and freely. Another way in which the people in the kampung describe the phenomenon is 'one reply to one greeting' (*tegor sa-patah, jawab sa-patah*).

7. This is an outcome of a quarrel in the vicinity of Kusin's house. The incident arose when a fight between two children extended to involve their parents. After an intense exchange of fight talk between the two, Kusin interfered to find a peaceful compromise. However this was neglected; the fight developed into a physical contest. So working on the report by Kusin, Kusah ordered Kuman to terminate the tenancy on the house site of one of the fighting parties who was regarded in the wrong. In addition, mention of the noise created by youngsters in the house rented by the present writer (about 50 yards from Kusin's) is also in order. On leaving the kampung for a week to attend to some other demands, the writer gave the key to the house to an Upper Sixth Form male student to use the house for study purposes. However being friends of the kampung youngsters and unable to check their attendance to the house, the youngster turned the house into premises for a nightly meeting place to play cards and get together that went on until the early hours of the morning. On the writer's return, the owner of the house complained of the dissatisfaction showed by the landowner concerning the matter. The writer was then told that the house may be used only conditionally; that no youngsters were to be allowed to remain on the premises after dark. This was obediently observed.

8. Traditional respect and to some extent power of *Imam* in Kelantan affects social life significantly (cf. Roff, *op. cit.,* 102–152).

9. Further elaboration on the kind of social relationship shall be taken up later in the chapter.

10. Fictive kin terms of address which are predominant in the kampung are mostly *Pa'* for males and *Mak* for females. It is only in this particular case that the term *Pa'su* is used, though such terms are not uncommon in Kelantan.

11. As the three individuals among those who use the raft are distinguished here as different from others in that they are 'honoured', I would use the term 'raft-users' from now on to refer to the group of people who use the raft and who relate to the three individuals concerned through 'deferential greetings'. In addition, I shall show shortly that the term 'raft-users' only refers to the group of people who relate to one another either through 'calling' (*singgah*) or 'unsociability' (*ta'tegor*) relationships.

12. Being "in retirement with and in suspicious proximity to any woman", who is by religious law marriageable to the man is an offence under the religious law of the State of Kelantan. The offence is termed '*Khalwat*' and fines for such offence is the minimum of $100.00 or one month imprisonment (Shariah Court 1974, 39). However, it is common practice for the arrested couple to get married to escape the fines. Though the law is part and parcel of the Muslim law of the State, the implementation of the law is recent and much of the operation is unofficial; it started in 1969 with 2 officers and 7 assistants who are locally known as 'Religious supervisers' (*Pegawai Pencegah Maksiat*) and they operate by giving unofficial rewards of $10.00 for any information which leads to an arrest.

13. Friday is the official holiday of the week for the State of Kelantan.

14. Awang is the son of the favourite entertainer (*bidari*) to the Tengku Bendahara. He is forty-two years of age and runs a business as a washerman who is locally known as '*dhobi*' or '*tukang dhobi*'.

15. Che'gu Him is a Malay school teacher who purchased a house site in the kampung in 1956.

16. I have here translated the Kelantan concepts of (1) '*kechek*' as 'chatting' which means that two individuals are involved in short conversation at random meetings. The individuals concerned know and are familiar with each other. So one describes his chatting partner as "if I meet him, we talk for a while". This then distinguishes the (2) conversing which is translated from the Kelantan concept of '*bual*'. This signifies a state of high familiarity and closeness with each other where conversation consequent-

ly extends to a much longer period similar to 'calling' (*singgah*) relationship discussed earlier. These two concepts are then again different from (3) 'mutual greeting' which is translated from the Kelantan concept of '*sama-sama tegor*'. This essentially implies that the two are 'not uncomfortable' (*ta'segan*) to greet each other. However this does not extend to 'chatting' conversation; they say "we know each other but we are not friends". So for the purpose of the present study, I would use the English equivalents of these concepts in the hope that the original connotations of the concepts are maintained.

17. Due to lack of an appropriate English equivalent, I am using the concept *jemaah* here to refer to people who go to pray at the prayer house. It is a common feature in the design of the prayer houses in Kelantan to provide a section for women *jamaah.* In this case the section is separated by a curtain which separates the men from women *jemaah.*

18. Pa'mud is a member of the raft-group of Kusin. He is employed as a night guard with a Chinese-owned firm (Engineering Workshop: Appendix 5) and is a tenant of Kusin's mother.

19. Literally '*doe*' would be the English equivalent of 'prayer' or that verbal request or gratitude for some gifts from the God. These are invariably set prayers of different kinds and lengths and which are uttered in Arabic language to suit the particular occasion.

20. This is in contrast to the wedding feasts in Kelantan where guests are expected to contribute presents either in monetary or material forms (cf. Rosemary Firth 1966).

21. '*Cukur*' may be translated as cutting hair from one's body. The ritual of '*cukur*' involves cutting at least a few strands of hair from a new-born baby. This is preceded by a few prayers (*doa*). Normally the ceremoney itself lasts for no more than half an hour after which food is served to guests. In certain respects the '*cukor*' is similar to the feasting discussed above (*maulud*) in that the guests are invited without being expected to contribute any presents, monetary or otherwise.

22. 'What is proper' refers to a cojuncture of ideal behaviour, actions, use of language, items of consumption and to some extent employment and marriage. At the level of perfection, it expresses the ideals of custom and tradition, and more important, the religious (*Islam*) values as it is understood (through the local clergy) locally. The notion of 'honoured' (*mulia*) discussed earlier is a form in which it is manifested.

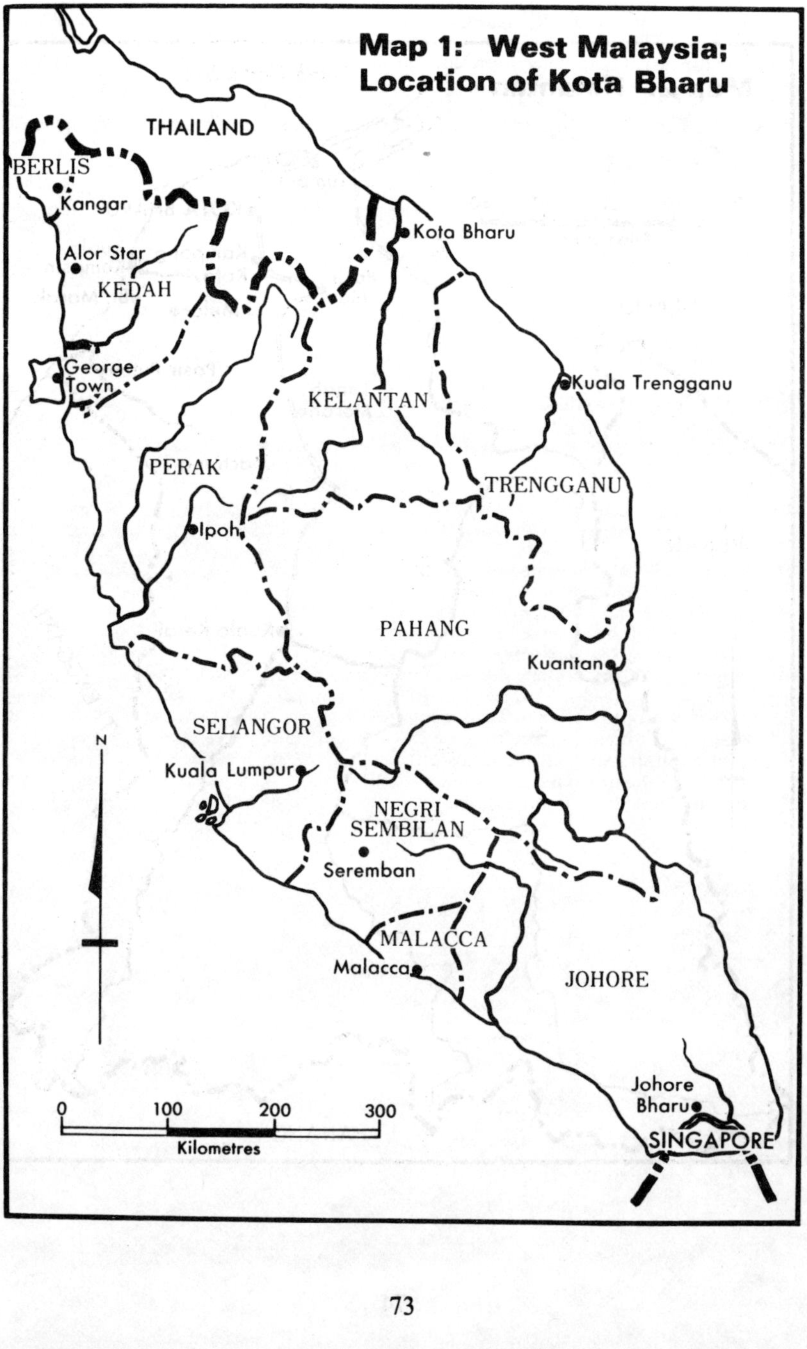

Map 1: West Malaysia; Location of Kota Bharu
THAILAND
BERLIS
Kangar
Alor Star
KEDAH
George Town
Kota Bharu
KELANTAN
Kuala Trengganu
PERAK
TRENGGANU
Ipoh
PAHANG
Kuantan
SELANGOR
N
Kuala Lumpur
NEGRI SEMBILAN
Seremban
MALACCA
Malacca
JOHORE
Johore Bharu
SINGAPORE
0
100
200
300
Kilometres

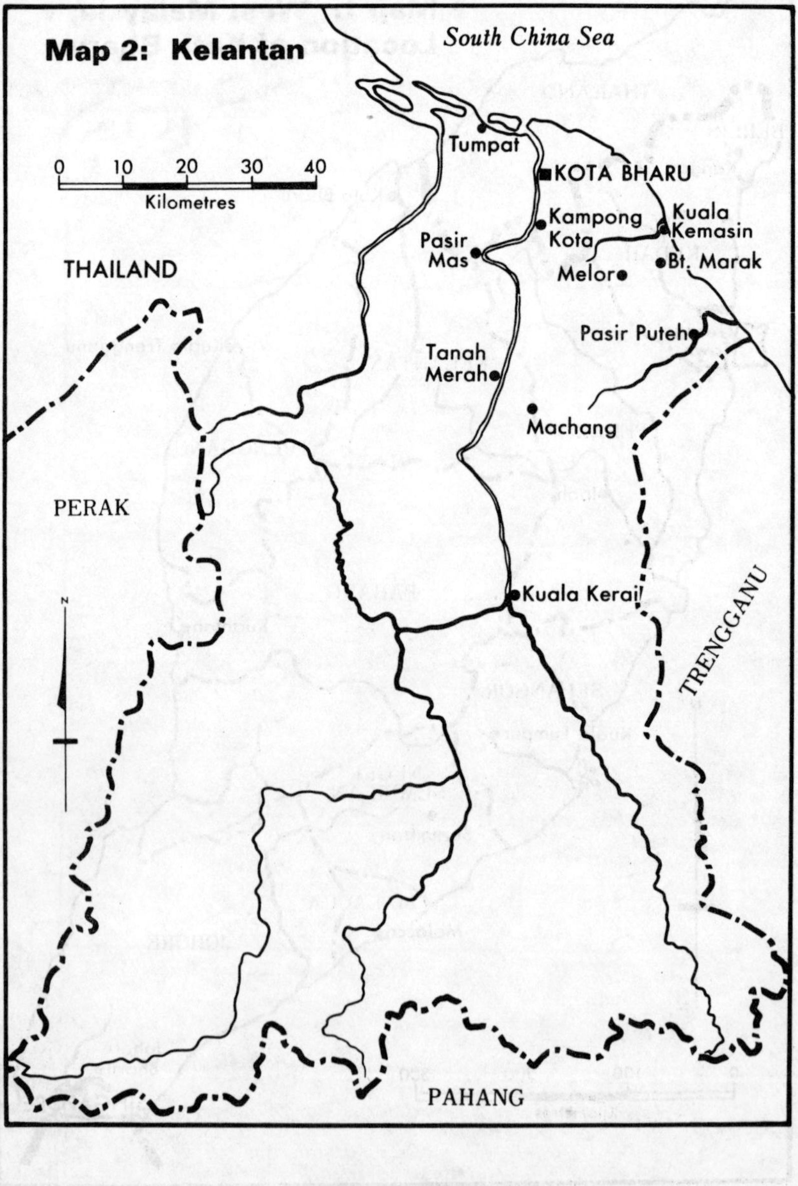

Map 2: Kelantan
South China Sea
Tumpat
0 10 20 30 40
Kilometres
KOTA BHARU
Kampong
Kota
Kuala
Kemasin
Pasir
Mas
Bt. Marak
Melor
THAILAND
Pasir Puteh
Tanah
Merah
Machang
PERAK
Kuala Kerai
N
TRENGGANU
PAHANG

Map 3: Kota Bharu Town in Early 1900's

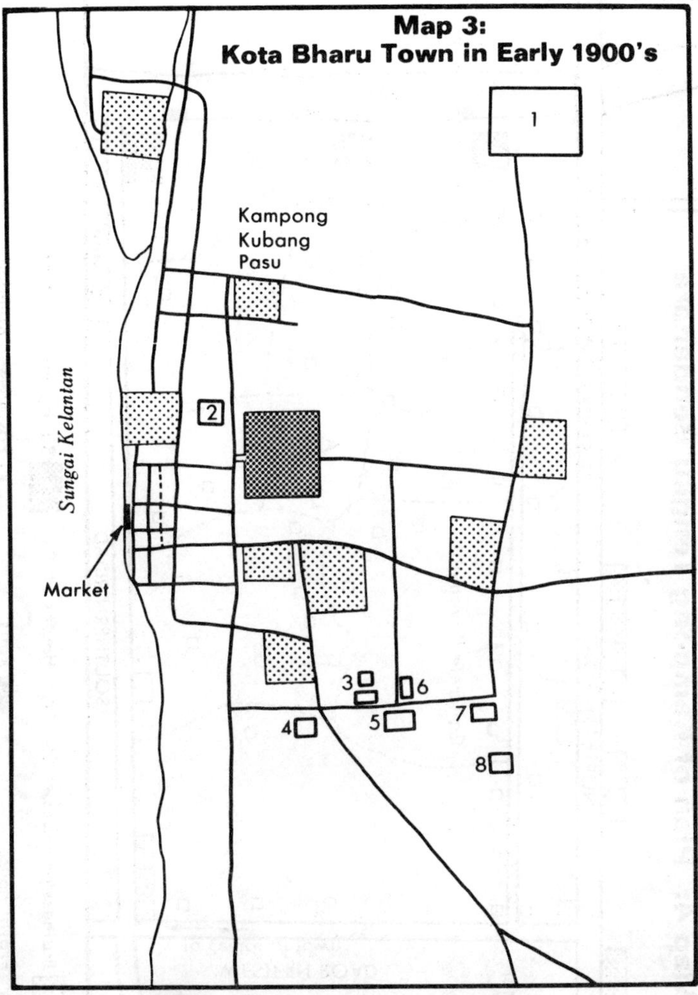

'Dalam Kubu' (fort of the Sultan)

Forts of Royal Families

1 'Kebun Sultan' (Garden of the Sultan)
2 Central Mosque
3 General Hospital
4 Rest Home
5 Residence of Captain Anderson
6 Hospital for Europeans
7 Malay School
8 Jail House

Map 4: Plan of Kampong Tengku Bendahara

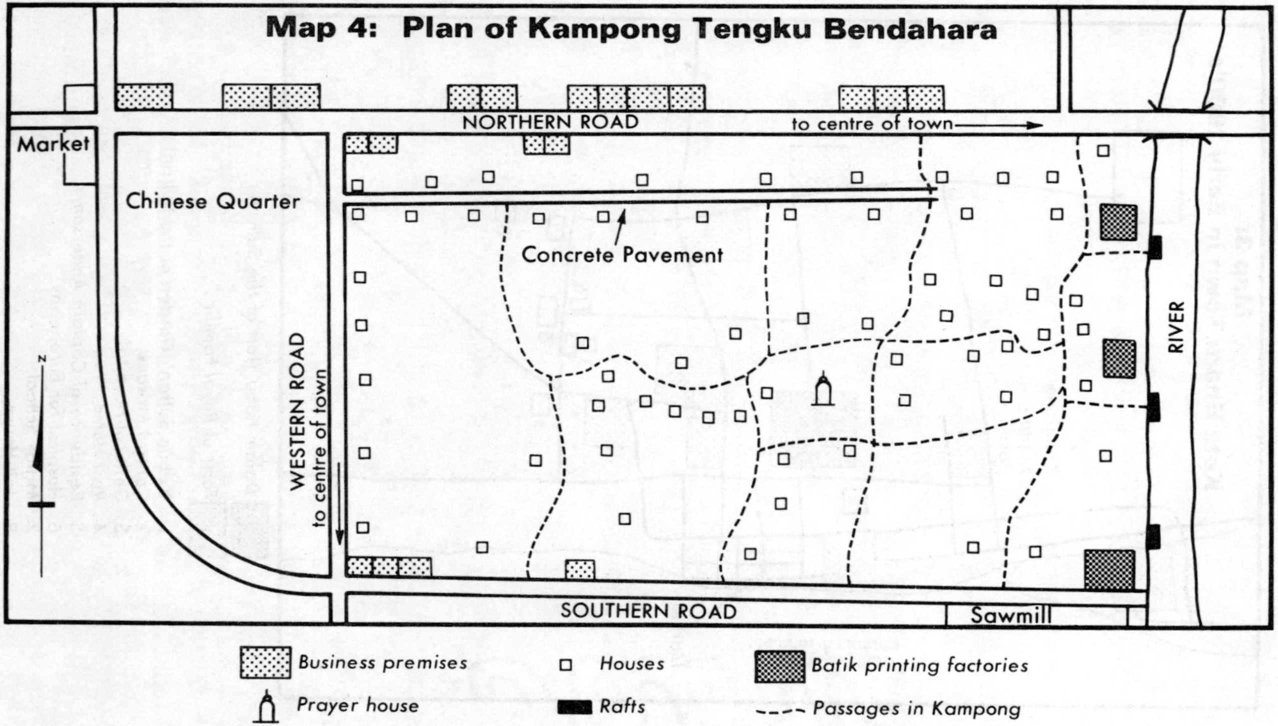

CHAPTER FIVE

ECONOMIC DIFFERENTIATION AND CLASS FORMATION

The observations about expressive social relationships in the last chapter establish three distinct categories of people living in the kampung. Paradoxically these categories do not show similar groupings on economic grounds. In this chapter I shall discuss the areas of economic life which I believe show significant similarities between the three groups of people. These are their patterns of consumption, employment and the employment of women and children in the households. This should indicate the position in which people from various categories are located in the productive system of the town.

Patterns of Consumption

Patterns of consumption are significant because differences in these strongly reflect differences in the class position of individuals, though their position within the productive system of the town is by far the stronger determinant (cf. Giddens 1973, 109).

The consumption goods which I see as significant for these purpose in the kampung are i) houses, ii) prestige goods like motor-cars, television sets, motor-cycles and to a lesser extent bicycles and transistor radios. These goods may be seen as the storage or the constant identifier of differences between people and groups of people in the kampung. Let us now consider the distribution of such goods in the kampung separately.

i) ***Houses***

The 66 houses in the kampung differ from one another in several ways — including their architecture, their size, the materials from which they are constructed, their exterior decoration and the size of their sites. In general the houses may be categorised into four main types.

a) Low quality timber houses with aluminium-zinc or atap roofs which are normally called 'huts' (*bangsal* or *pondok*). They are raised on stilts and the area underneath is used for storage of such items as firewood for cooking, and bicycles. There are 30 houses of this type.

b) Medium quality timber houses with tiled roofs, usually called 'tiled houses' (*rumah bata*). These are also raised on stilts and the area underneath some of them is also used for storage purposes. There are

20 houses of this type.

c) High quality timber houses with asbestos roofs constructed on brick foundations. There are 13 houses of this type.

d) Brick houses of which there are three.

Though this classification of houses is based on a number of physical characteristics as mentioned above, it significantly emphasises the difference between the ideal or the desirable mode of living and the functional shelter. The latter seems to be assigned to the huts and the former to the last two categories of houses which are known locally as 'big houses' (*rumah besar*). The main reason is that the last two categories show aspects of quality. For instance they are bigger in size, their architecture is 'up to date' and they have some desirable aesthetic qualities. The houses contain two rooms or more, they are painted on the inside as well as on the outside, they have a fenced compound or, failing that, the compounds are kept clean and are decorated with flowers and fruit trees. The fence and the gates, if any, are also well decorated. On these counts they are then described as the 'big houses'. They are different from the rest of the houses in the kampung, especially if they are compared to the 'huts' and some 'tiled houses' which are generally small in size and aesthetically pleasing.

Two other reasons may be adduced for describing the last two categories as 'big houses'; the first is that the conception of 'big houses' as an expression pertaining to urban houses, while 'tiled houses' and the huts are likened to rural houses. The implication of such conceived equivalences are then significant. As I have indicated earlier, the prevailing conception of urban and rural differences in Kelantan implies a difference between people who are 'modern' (civilized and refined) and 'traditional' people who are vulgar and backward respectively. For the same reason I believe the big houses' are evaluated as higher in prestige than the 'huts' or the 'tiled houses'. Another reason, and I think a more important one, lies in the relative costs incurred in building the houses. A 'big house' in most cases cost more than M$7000.00 while the cost of a 'hut' on average is about M$500.00. The cost of a 'tiled house' is usually about three times that of a 'hut'.

The different conceptions of houses and the differences between them lie, therefore, in physical as well as in aesthetic aspects, and more importantly in the relative costs of the houses which signify the wealth of their owners.

Given the fact that these are only the general differences between the houses in the kampung, a note of caution is necessary: that is there are some minor similarities between the houses concerned. This may be shown as follows:

Table 13
DIFFERENCES AND SIMILARITIES BETWEEN HOUSES

Category of Houses	*Number*	*Two or More Rooms*	*Painted*	*Fenced/ Compound*
'big houses'	16	16	16	11
'tiled houses'	20	13	12	3
'huts'	30	2	1	—
Total	66	49	38	14

Let us then consider how these different types of houses are distributed among the three categories of people in the kampung.

i.i) ***The Houses of the Feasting Circle:***[1]
Standing out from the mass of houses in the kampung are the houses of some people of the feasting circle. These are the 'big houses' of the kampung, the mere sight of which is sufficient to produce a deferential feeling among the poor people who own the 'huts'. As one of the poor puts it, "if I were ever to be invited into such a house, I would not know how to sit down". As an example let us describe one such house belonging to Kupar, an individual of the feasting circle category.

Kupar's house is considered as the biggest house in the kampung. It is made of high quality timber with an asbestos roof, and it is constructed on concrete foundations on a site of about 200 square yards. The compound of the house is littered with flower pots and plants, and it is surrounded by a steel fence which has a decorated front gate. It has three bedrooms, a spacious lounge and a concrete floor kitchen area. Both the inside and the outside of the house are painted white.

The houses of the people in feasting circle category, however, do not share identical characteristics. Apart from the fact that all of them have two rooms or more, there are significant differences between them which may be stated as follows:

a) In terms of types of houses, the people of the feasting circle own both 'tiled houses' and 'big houses'. Their composition may be shown as in the following:

Table 14
HOUSES OF THE FEASTING CIRCLE

No. of People		*Types of Houses:* Huts	*Tiled Houses*	*Big Houses:* Timber	*Brick*
Royal persons	(2)	—	1	4	1
Commoner tenants	(2)	—	1	1	—
Commoner owners of house sites	(4)	—	1	1	2
Total	12	—	3	6	3

b) The houses in the group are further differentiated from one another on the grounds of exterior decoration like painting, fencing and decoration of compounds with flower and fruit trees, and on the grounds of differences in the materials from which the steps of the houses are constructed and the nature of the kitchen floor Again these differences may be shown in the form of the following table:

Table 15
DIFFERENCES IN EXTERIOR DECORATION, STEPS AND KITCHEN OF HOUSES OF THE FEASTING CIRCLE

No.of Houses		*Fenced Compound with flowers & fruit trees*	*Painted*	*Steps:* Wooden	*Concrete*	*Kitchen Floor:* Wooden	*Concrete*
Royal Persons	(6)	3	5	1	5	—	6
Commoner Tenants	(2)	—	2	1	1	2	—
Commoner Owners of House Sites	(4)	1	4	2	2	2	2
Total	(12)	4	11	4	8	4	8

We see, then, that people in the feasting circle own three 'tiled houses' and nine 'big houses'. The latter type of house is again differentiated into the high quality timber houses and the brick houses. In addition the main features of the houses also show some differences: namely, there is one house which is not painted and there are four houses which have steps and kitchen floor made of wood. This rather downgrades such houses relative to other houses belonging to the group, especially if they are compared to the house of Kupar described above.

At this point, the ownership of house sites seems worthy of mention. This is simply because unless one owns a house site or one is willing to rent a wider area of land, the availability of the land to be fenced away for a compound is limited. Nonetheless there are only four cases of the three rentiers and five owners of house sites in the category who have fences around their houses. These four cases consist of two rentiers who are royal persons and two owners of house sites one of whom is also a royal person. The fences among the rentiers again do not circumscribe the area of the land owned. What this tends to show is that fencing of compounds in these cases is not so much determined by the desire to mark the boundaries of the land as it is instigated by a concern that the compound be kept clean and adorned with flower and fruit trees for aesthetic reasons.

The differences among the houses make some of them more aesthetically pleasing than others; some of the houses are closer to the ideal of the 'big house', even if they do not achieve it as fully as the house of Kupar described earlier.

i.ii) *The Houses of the Raft-Users:*

Just as there are variations among the houses of the feasting circle, there are also some differences among the houses of the raft-users. While some of the raft-users have atap roofed and aluminium-zinc roofed houses or 'huts', others have 'tiled houses'. These two types of houses are distributed among the raft-users in the following manner:

Table 16
HOUSES OF THE RAFT-USERS

Number of Houses		*Type of House:* 'Huts'	'Tiled Houses'	*Size and Decoration:* Two rooms or more	Painted
Free settlers	(4)				
royal person	(1)	1	—	—	—
commoners	(3)	2	1	—	—
Tenants					
Commoners	(28)	22	6	2	2
Total	(32)*	25	7	2	2

*One 'tiled house' is shared by two households.

From the table above, it may be seen that out of the total 32 houses of the raft-users, there are only two houses which are painted and contain two sleeping rooms.[2] These are the two houses among the eight tiled houses of the category. To some extent, the differences among the houses of the raft-users seem to be outweighed by their similarities. On the one hand none of the raft-users owns a 'big house', and on the other, most of the houses contain one sleeping room, have verandahs at the front; and are all served by wooden steps.

Also, save for the four houses belonging to free settlers, all the houses of the raft-users are built on sites rented from royal persons who are some of the original holders of land in the kampung. As tenants, these raft-users have no choice on the location of their houses, which is determined by the landlords. In addition, their house sites are small in size. This is because the raft-users are poor (as will be shown later) and thus renting a wider area of land for a compound would entail unnecessary costs. Consequently the houses of the raft-users form a mass of huts closely packed together on one side of the kampung with the few 'tiled houses' scattered among them

i.iii) *The Houses of the Individualists:*

Unlike the two categories discussed so far, the category of people whom we have called the individualists own all types of houses ranging from 'huts' to 'big houses'. In particular, more than half of the houses are 'big houses', while the other half are 'tiled houses' and 'huts'. This variation is shown in the following table.

Table 17
THE HOUSES OF THE INDIVIDUALISTS

Number of Houses		*Types of Houses:* *Huts*	*Tiled Houses*	*Big houses (Timber)*	*Size and Decoration:* *Two or More Rooms*	*Fenced Compound*	*Painted*
Landowning individualists	(12)	2	3	7	18	8	12
Tenant individualists	(9)	3	6	—	6	3	6
Free settler royal person	(1)	—	1	—	1	11	18
Total	(22)*	5	10	7	18	11	18

* One 'big house' is shared by two households.

One fact that emerges from the table is that the houses of individualists differ from one another depending on whether the owner is an owner of a house site or a tenant. All the 'big houses' of the individualists belong to the landowning individualists. Let us test this generalisation by examining the houses of these two sub-categories of individualists separately.

First the landowning individualists: As may be seen from the table above, there are seven 'big houses' owned by some of the landowning individuals. These have fenced compounds which occupy the whole area of the house site, somewhat similar to the houses owned by some people of the feasting circle discussed above. By this very fact these houses are different from the three 'tiled houses' and two 'huts' owned by the rest of the landowning individualists. In fact these latter types of houses are similar to houses of some raft-users discussed earlier, and form a direct contrast to the 'big houses' owned by the landowning individualists and others in the kampung.

Moreover, the houses of the landowning individualists also differ from one another in terms of size and exterior decoration. As shown in the table, there are two houses which are so small as to contain one sleeping room in contrast to other houses which contain two or more, unlike all the others, there is one house which is not painted.

Second, the tenant individualists: The differences among the houses owned by the individualists are again shown in the types of houses owned by the tenant individualists. As shown in the table, there are seven 'tiled houses' (including the house of the free settler who is a royal person) and three 'huts' owned by this sub-category of individualists. Further, there are three among the seven 'tiled houses' which are somewhat different from others: though they are classified as 'tiled houses', they show some characteristics of 'big houses' in that they are painted on both the inside and the outside, they are within compounds (rented) and they contain at least two rooms each. However, since they are built from medium quality timber and are raised on stilts instead of lying on concrete foundations, they are thus pure 'tiled houses' nor 'big houses' as they have been defined so far. Instead, they show some characteristics of both types, are considered by the people of the kampung as a little 'better' than other 'tiled houses'.

At this stage, we may generalise that there are substantial differences in the types and size of the houses owned by each category in the kampung, but that there are also significant similarities in the houses owned by people from different categories. By way of summary, this may be shown in the following table:

Table 18
DISTRIBUTION OF HOUSES AMONG GROUPS[3]

Types of Houses		*Feasting Circle*	*Landowning*	*Individualists: Tenant*	*Free Settler*	*Raft-Users*
big houses	(16)	9	7	—	—	—
tiled houses	(20)	3	3	6	1	7
huts	(30)	—	2	3	1	25
Total	(66)	12	12	9	1	32

In other words, while people of the feasting circle own the 'tiled houses' as well as the 'big houses', the individualists own all types of houses. The raft-users however, own only the 'tiled houses' and 'huts' with the majority being the owners of 'huts'.

What this implies is that the type of house within each category in the kampung is not homogeneous. On the basis of ownership of houses, their pattern of consumption cross-cut the division of people into the feasting circle, the individualists and the raft-users. This is shown further by another aspect of consumption, — the possession of prestige goods.

ii) ***Possession of Prestige Goods:***
The prestige goods which indicate class differences between people in the kampung are motor-cars, motor-cycles, television sets and to some extent bicycles and transistor radios. Such goods are all visible and they are the point of reference to differentiate and evaluate the economic status categories of people.

Let us consider the distribution of the prestige goods among the people in the kampung, which appears in the following table:

Table 19
DISTRIBUTION OF PRESTIGE GOODS[4]

Categories of People	*Total No. of People*	*Prestige goods possessed: Motor-Cars*	*Motor-Cycles*	*Television Sets*	*Bicycles*	*Transistor Radios*
feasting circle	12	3	1	11	4	12
landowning individualists	13	3	3	9	9	13
tenant & free settler individualists	10	—	2	2	4	10
raft-users	33	—	—	—	7	3
Total	68	6	6	22	24	38

As shown in the table, the general pattern of ownership of prestige goods is that motor-cars, television sets and to some extent motor-cycles are heavily concentrated in the hands of people in the feasting circle and among landowning individualists. Possession of such goods drops sharply in the category of tenant individualists where there are only two people who own motor-cycles and television sets, and ownership is completely lacking among the raft-users. The last two categories of people show possession of bicycles and transistor radios, although these are few in number. One reason for such a distribution of prestige goods among people in the kampung is the differences in their level of income. I have left further elaboration of income differences below.

It is also worth mentioning that even though bicycles and transistor radios are relatively cheap and are regarded as less prestigious than other prestige goods, they are highly valued by the poor in the kampung. I observed that the bicycles are kept clean and are well guarded by some raft-users. In contrast, they are regarded by some people in the feasting circle category mainly as a means of transport for their children to commute to school. This is further shown by the fact that some people of the feasting circle regard transistor radios as 'toys' for children while they, on the contrary, are regarded by the raft-users as highly prestigious goods.

iii) ***Clothing:***
To some extent, clothing is also considered as a prestige item, but this is more pronounced among the youth than any other age group in the kampung. For instance, expensive materials of clothing, especially imported ready-made clothing and footwear from Europe or the United States seem to be highly regarded by these youth regardless of their parents' economic or social status. As the youth are considered here mainly to show the recruitment process into different economic groups, such consideration of clothing as prestige goods is beyond the present discussion.[5]

As far as the head of households are concerned, they seem less concerned about the prestige of their clothing. Instead they seem more concerned about its tidiness. It is observed that though their clothes are made of the same material, for instance batik clothes, some are better kept than others. At various times it is said by a person in the feasting circle category that dressing shabbily is embarrassing (*malu*). On the other hand, the raft-users seem to be less embarrassed about the way they dress regardless of how shabby they may look. In some cases even the cleanliness of the clothing itself may be questioned.

Nevertheless there are visible differences in the clothing of the people in each group. While the raft-users and some tenant individualists wear the same, mostly batik, shirts over a span of a few days, the feasting circle and some of the land-owning individualists seem to own a wider range of clothing. This is especially so among the people of the feasting circle when their day-time clothes are not appropriate to be worn for prayers at night. However this does not discount the fact that some raft-users and tenant individualists sometimes wear clean clothes, especially when they are attending a wedding feast; in one particular case, a raft-user was observed to change into a clean set of clothing when he was about to visit a dentist.

These differences in clothing betwen people seem to be largely determined by the differences in the nature of the work or employment and incomes.[6] As I shall show shortly, some raft-users and some tenant individualists are unskilled manual workers. Consequently the clothing they wear daily is made of low quality, cheap materials. In contrast, some people of the feasting circle and some landowning individualists are employed in relatively higher income employment with some employed as white collar workers. With their higher incomes and cleaner work, they are able to wear better quality, clean clothes.

Though the quality and cleanliness of clothing differ between people, such differences are not coterminous with the three categories. Instead they seem to follow the differences in terms of ownership of different types of houses and ownership of different prestige goods, i.e. wealth.

In other words, the categories of people do not show significant differences from one another in their patterns of consumption. Instead, differences cut across and divide people into high, intermediate and the low consumption groups. The first group consists of some people of the feasting circle and some landowning individualists; the second group consists of some people of the feasting circle, some landowning and tenant individualists as well as some raft-users; and the third group consists of some individualists who are both landowners and tenants, and the majority of the raft-users. If the differences in the patterns of consumption may be taken as a reflection of class position in the kampung, the classes formed obviously do not coincide with the categories which emerge from their pattern of expressive social relationships.

Employment

It should be clear at this point that while an inquiry into the amount of the distribution of income among the individuals in the kampung is necessary, the nature of the employment through which they reproduce their respective economic position also demands attention. The first step is to describe the nature of employment in the kampung and later we will show how the incomes from these employments differ and how they are distributed among various categories.

In 1975, the people in the kampung were involved in various types of employment as Table 20 reveals:

Table 20
TYPE OF EMPLOYMENT IN THE KAMPUNG

Types of Employment	*Male Heads of Households*	*Female Heads of Households*
Employees of Government Departments (including the State Council of Religion):		
Officers	2	—
School Teachers	2	—
Clerks (including Chief Clerk)	3	—
Drivers (cars and trucks)	1	—
Labourers	1	—
Employers of Private Capitalist Organisations: (including domestic servants)		
—	Clerks	2
Overseers	1	—
Drivers (cars and trucks)	10	—
Nightguards (watchmen)	3	—
Labourers (including 2 in Singapore)	7	1
Domestic Servants	—	1
Self-Employment		
Entrepreneurs (*towkay*)	3	—
Firewood retailers	2	—
Middleman (*peraih*)	1	—
Sellers/petty traders at Market	1	5
Tailors and Carpenters	3	—
Food/Drink stall operators	2	—
Trishaw pedallers	4	—
Self-employed on commission (vendors)	3	—
Itinerant batik sellers	1	—
Taxi drivers (unlicenced taxi)	1	—
Retired Government Servants	4	—
Retired and dependent	—	4
Total	57	11

One formal classification (Statistics Department 1970) breaks employment into the following categories:

1) professional workers which include teachers of the kampung,
2) clerical workers,
3) sales workers which include sellers at the market and vendors,
4) service workers,
5) production and related workers, and
6) transport equipment operators and labourers.

According to this classification, most kampung dwellers would fall into the last four categories. Such classification is obviously inadequate to describe the actual utilization of labour among the kampung residents. This is because people place so little importance on the nature of their work preferring to emphasise the regular receipt of income. In a raft-user's words,

> Money is needed for everything; we have to buy everything, rice, vegetable, fish and all; people in villages (rural areas) are different, they do not have to buy everything (rice, vegetable and fish).

Accordingly, employment may be classified according to whether it brings a regular and fixed supply of money in wage earning employment (*kerja makan gaji*), or the irregular and variable income generated by self-employment (*kerja sendiri*). The contrast may be shown as follows:

1) ***Wage earning employment,*** (*kerja makan gaji*) includes: officers, teachers, clerks, overseers, drivers, watchmen, and labourers in government and private business organisation.	2) ***Self-employment*** (*kerja sendiri*) includes: entrepreneurs, tailors, middlemen, carpenters, food/drink stall operators, trishaw pedallers, itinerant sellers, vendors and sellers at market.

The category of wage earning employment (*kerja makan gaji*) signifies a fixed and a regular wage accrued from the sale of labour to government organisations and capitalists in the town. It changes only when a worker receives a wage increase and/or a promotion. In contrast self-employment emphasises independence and control over one's labour. The income derived from self-employment is therefore believed to vary according to the skill of a worker and the intensity of his labour. For instance, entrepreneurs are expected to succeed when they are shrewd and enterprising, the sellers at the market (petty traders) will be successful when they are dedicated to their employment and trishaw pedallers and vendors will receive higher income if they are physically strong and industrious.

The income from self-employment also depends on other factors beyond the control of the workers. For instance, apart from the variable demand for their products as with sellers and entrepreneurs, incomes are also affected by weather conditions: wet weather hampers the drying of batik cloth, for example, and also hampers the operations of sellers at the market who conduct their business on an unsheltered pavement. Trishaw pedallers and vendors, similarly, cannot operate effectively during wet weather. Further, the entrepreneurs who deal in wholesaling fish are affected by the worst of the wet weather when fishing comes to a halt, i.e. during the monsoon months of October to January. Generally the incomes of the self-employed are lower during the wet weather which runs from September to February.

There are also important distinctions to be made within these two categories. In particular, there are substantial differences in the amount of income each form of employment brings, and there are also differences of personalities involved in each form of employment. Some of those in wage earning employment are teachers and bureaucrats (officers and clerks) who have a minimum of grade six Malay school education (1950's) and who also earn higher incomes. In contrast, some are pure proletariat who are free to sell their labour as drivers, nightguards and labourers and are somewhat lower in the literacy scale if not totally illiterate and who also receive lower incomes. In fact the incomes of these workers are among the lowest in the kampung. As shown in Table 21, these labourers earn no more than $150.00 a month, an income officially classified as the poorest in the State (Kelantan, 1979).

Table 21
EMPLOYMENT AND INCOMES

	Income Range:	*Forms of Employment:*
I.	$300.00 and above $250,00 to $300.00	Entrepreneurs, senior clerks, officers and teachers. Clerks.
II.	$150.00 to $250.00	Overseer, drivers, operator of food and drink stalls, middleman, firewood retailer, night guard and labourers in Singapore.*
III.	$150.00 and below	Labourers, vendors, trishaw pedallers, itinerant batik sellers, tailor, carpenter and sellers at the market.

*Though the labourers in Singapore receive an income of $10.00 per day, the extra expense incurred in travelling and accommodation makes the take home wage less than $300.00 per month. As such I have included them in the category of income which is less than their actual income.

The situation is similar among those who are self-employed. For instance, there are petty bourgeois who operate business ventures, like the three entrepreneurs, one of whom operates a batik printing factory, with the other two being wholesalers of fish, fruit and copra. The first owns his factory premises; the others each own a truck which is used to transport goods. Their incomes are somewhat higher when compared to such self-employed people as the firewood retailers, middleman, and operators of food and drink stalls as shown in the Table 21 above. In fact their incomes are as high as if not higher than bureaucrats, i.e. above $300.00 per month. The incomes of the latter self-employeds are again higher than those who are self-employed as petty traders, vendors and trishaw pedailers whose incomes are seldom higher than $5.00 per day.

Following the differences within each category of employment, there are differences in the nature of work involved. Within the wage earning employment for instance, there are white-collar workers (teachers and bureaucrats), manual workers (drivers, overseers and nightguards) and heavy manual workers or labourers. Similarly the nature of self-employment differs from one case to another. For instance, while entrepreneurs employ their labour in the least manual way because the actual manual work is carried out by their labourers,[7] all other forms of self-employment involve manual work if not heavy manual labour: the trishaw pedallers, for example, work long hours, from early morning till night time.

If the forms of employment in the kampung may be classified at all, a classification which incorporates the personalities of the worker, the income derived from such employment and the nature of employment itself would probably be meaningful. To use their own terminology, the people in the kampung seem to regard the use of their labour as being dichotomised into 'comfortable' (*kerja senang*) and the 'toilsome' (*kerja susah*) employment. The former classification primarily signifies i) a high amount of income, ii) 'easy' and less physical exertions where leisure and pleasure rather than 'work' appear to be associated with such employment,[8] and iii) the fact that a certain level of literacy and shrewdness is required by such type of employment, the personalities involved are also described as 'intelligent persons'. Included within this type are the officers, teachers, clerks, entrepreneurs and to a lesser extent the overseers, drivers and retailers of firewood.

The latter type of 'toilsome' employment however, emphasises the reverse: i) it does not only imply that the income from such type of employment is low, but also expresses an insecurity in the flow of the income; ii) different from the 'comfortable' types of exployment which are associated with leisure, the 'toilsome' types of employment are regarded as 'real work' which are invariably dirtying and tiring; and iii) as this type of employment requires mere physical strength and endurance, the individuals involved are usually described as 'unintelligent'.[9] The forms of employment which this type includes are labouring, vending, trishaw pedalling and to some extent selling at the market.

This clear-cut classification however, again has its difficulties in describing the various forms of employment in the kampung. This is because some forms do not fall into either of the two types. For instance, operating the food and drink stalls is strenuous work, but the income derived from it is better than other manual forms of employment. The same is true with the middleman, sellers at the market, carpenters and tailors where economic calculation, skill and shrewdness are important. Further the cases of the drivers and nightguards are also not clear. These jobs are semi-manual in nature and the income derived from them seems to be neither too high nor too low by the kampung standard. I believe these forms of employment may be regarded as in a middle rung, between 'comfortable' and 'toilsome' employment.

Employment in Town

The nature of employment of people in the kampung is then different from that in rural areas. Save for one case of a small scale market gardener (in an area about 1/10 of an acre) who is in fact a retired clerk with the State's Public Service and who is currently drawing a monthly pension of about M$100.00, the types of employment in the kampung may be called town employment. This term is used for at least two main reasons. Firstly, these types of employments are described by the people concerned as 'town employment' (*kerja bandar*). This is because the income derived from such types of employment is in the form of salary, wages, profit and payment for the services rendered. It is different from 'rural employment' (*kerja kampung*) which emphasises working the land, and often becomes a point of comparison by people who migrated from rural areas.

To some extent the income derived from town employment is also different from that of rural employment. The income from the latter consists of goods from subsistence production and cash from cash crops, while the income from the former is solely in the form of cash. This is shown in the case of the poor people in the town and the rual areas. While both are described as 'having enough to eat' which is commonly interpreted as 'subsistence', the income for the two kinds of people are different. Subsistence in the rural areas means cash as well as production, whereas subsistence in the town means a low monetary income, though they are both tied and dominated by capital.

Secondly, town employment, in contrast to employment available in the rural village, is more diverse. As shown in Table 20 above, the 68 heads of households observed are involved in 18 different forms of employment. Further, even when some of these people are involved in the same form of employment, (for instance clerical, semi-manual workers and labourers), they again differ in that they have different employers. Some are employed in government service, while others are employed in private capitalist organisations. In addition, people thus employed are fairly independent and alienated from one another save for one entrepreneur who deals in the wholesaling of fish and fruit, and distributes some of his trading goods to his relatives who are retailers at the market. This case of dependence however, still is characterized by the usual contract arrangement between a wholesaler (*toway*) and a retailer.[10] In general therefore, the employment of people in the kampung is highly specialised and separated from one another, and thus they are different from the somewhat homogeneous employment in the countryside, which to some extent favours co-operation between people.

It is important at this stage to consider how these various types and forms of employment are distributed among the three categories of people in the kampung. The distribution determines the level of income of the people in the three categories and this in turn, determines the patterns of consumption discussed above.

The distribution of people by employers and incomes may be shown in the following table:

Table 22
EMPLOYERS OF CATEGORIES OF PEOPLE IN THE KAMPUNG

		Groups of People:				
				Individualists:		
Types of Employers	*Monthly Income Est. in in M$*	*Feasting Circle*	*Land-owning*	*Free Settler*	*Tenant*	*Raft-Users*
Government:						
senior clerks	500	2	—	—	—	—
officers	400	2	—	—	—	—
teachers	400	—	2	—	—	—
clerks	250–300	—	—	—	1	—
drivers	150–250	—	—	—	—	1
labourers	150 below	—	—	—	—	1
Sub-Total		4	2	—	1	2

Private Capitalist Organisations:						
labourers in Singapore	300	—	—	—	—	2
clerks	250–300	—	—	—	2	—
overseers	250	1	—	—	—	—
drivers	150–250	1	5	—	2	2
night guards	150–200	—	—	—	—	3
labourers	100–150	—	—	—	2	4
domestic servants	90	—	—	—	—	1
Sub-Total		2	5	—	6	12
Self-Employment:						
entrepreneurs	above 300	2	1	—	—	—
stall operators	200	—	—	—	—	2
middlemen	150–200	—	—	—	1	—
taxi drivers	150–200	—	—	1	—	—
firewood retailers	150	1	—	—	1	—
vendors	below 150	—	—	—	—	3
trishaw pedallers	,,	—	—	—	—	4
itinerant sellers	,,	—	—	—	—	1
tailors/ carpenters	,,	—	1	—	—	2
sellers at market	,,	—	—	—	—	6
retired on pension	150–200	2	2	—	—	—
retired, dependent on children		1	2	—	—	1
Sub-Total		6	6	1	2	19
Grand Total		12	13	1	9	33

It may be noted that 9 people in the kampung are employed in government services, 25 in capitalist organisations and 34 are self-employed. Capitalist organisations and self-employment make up the majority of the available labour in the kampung (86.8%) with the latter employing almost 50% of the labour. In terms of distribution among categories of people, it is noted that while people from every category are employed in all branches of employment a greater number of the raft-users are employed in capitalist organisations and self-employment. This is significant especially when the raft-users' incomes are taken into consideration. None of the raft-users ever receives an income of more than $250.00 per month regardless of their employers or form of employment. Even if the labourers in Singapore receive an income of about $300.00 per month, it is highly doubtful that all of the money may be brought back to Kota Bharu.

To compare their income fully, the following table is necessary:

Table 23
DISTRIBUTION OF SOCIAL CATEGORIES

Income Range	*Employment*	*Feasting Circle*	*Land-owning*	*Groups of People: Individualists: Free Settler*	*Tenant*	*Raft-Users*
I	*'comfortable'*					
M$300.00 and above	entrepreneurs	2	1	—	—	—
	senior clerks	2	—	—	—	—
	teachers	—	2	—	—	—
	officers	2	—	—	—	—
M$250.00 to M$300.00	clerks	—	—	—	3	—
Sub-Total		6	3	—	3	—
II	*'middle range'*					
M$150.00 to M250.00	overseers	1	—	—	—	—
	stall operators	—	—	—	—	2
	drivers	1	5	1	2	3
	middlemen	—	—	—	1	—
	firewood retailers	1	—	—	1	—
	night guards	—	—	—	—	3
	labourers in Singapore	—	—	—	—	2
Sub-Total		3	5	1	4	10
III	*'toilsome'*					
M$150.00 and below	labourers	—	—	—	2	5
	vendors	—	—	—	—	3
	trishaw pedallers	—	—	—	—	4
	itinerant sellers	—	—	—	—	1
	tailor/ carpenter	—	—	—	—	2
	sellers at market	—	—	—	—	6
	domestic servants	—	—	—	—	1
Sub-Total		—	1	—	2	22
Retired persons		3	4	—	—	1
Grand-Total		12	13	1	9	33

On the examination of employment and incomes in the kampung as illustrated above (Table 23), one generalisation is in order: that is, regardless of their employer (government, private capitalist organisation or self-employment), some people of the feasting circle are employed in forms of employment we have classified as the 'comfortable employment', some are employed in what we have called the 'middle range', while the majority of the raft-users work in 'toilsome employment'. The individualists, however, are distributed throughout all forms and types of employment ranging from 'toilsome' to 'comfortable'. There is therefore a marked difference in income between people of the feasting circle and the raft-users. The former enjoy an income above $150.00 per month with 6 out of 12 people receiving above $300.00. Two-thirds of the raft-users on the other hand receive a maximum monthly income of $150.00 with only 10 people receiving a monthly income between $150.00 to $250.00. The individualists are fairly distributed in all the income categories.

What this means is that on the basis of employment and income or their objective economic positions in the productive system of the town, 12 people in the kampung may simply be classed into the relatively wealthy and comfortable bureaucrats (including school teachers) and petty bourgeois who receive more than $300.00 per month, 23 people are subsistent townsmen who are able to use or sell their labour power efficiently, and there are 33 people (48.5%) who are extremely poor either because they are exploited by capitalist organisations as in the case of labourers or because they are dominated and controlled by bigger and stronger capital operating in the town as in cases of self-employed persons.

What I am suggesting is that the objective positions of people in production relations of the town show a strong similarity in types and forms of employment between people of different categories, and people in the same category are also employed at different income levels. Let us now note such similarities between people of different categories and then examine how people within each category differ from one another.

One form of employment which people from all categories pursue is that of a driver in the service of government, private capitalist organisation or a driver of a private taxi. As may be seen in Table 23 above, there are 12 individuals thus employed, consisting of 3 raft-users, 8 individualists and 1 individual in feasting circle category. Though the employment varies a little in the sense that one may drive a car instead of a truck, or one is employed by the government rather than by a capitalist or the income derived does not vary significantly. For instance a truck driver employed by a capitalist earns about $180.00 as compared to a car driver in a government department, who earns about $200.00 per month.

Although forms of employment other than driving are not shared by people from all three categories, they are still variously pursued by people from different categories. For instance the type of employment we have classified as 'comfortable' in which the income derived therefrom is among the highest by kampung standards and the nature of employment is the least manual if not totally white-collar, are shared by people from both the feasting circle and the individualist categories. Direct sale of one's labour is another example. As may be seen from Table 23, there are 2 tenant individualists and 7 raft-users who are employed as labourers (including labourers in Singapore).

It is worth emphasising at this stage that apart from the poor forms of self-employment like vending, trishaw pedalling and selling at the market which are monopolised by the raft-users, all other forms of employment in the kampung are shared by people from different categories. There is thus no clear-cut division of people into the three categories when the types and particular forms of their employment and incomes are considered. Instead, the employment differences between people in each category is significant.

i) ***The Feasting Circle***

First, let us consider the feasting circle category. As is obvious from Table 23 above, the main difference in the types of employment among people in this category is that they are differentiated into people whom we may call bureaucrats and petty bourgeois employed in 'comfortable' employment and those who are employed in the 'middle range' subsistence employment.

Those who are employed in the former type of employment consist of senior clerks, officers and entrepreneurs who receive high income and whose nature of employment is the least manual and the least dirty. Their nature of employment involves wearing clean clothes and relaxing in the evening. Some such as the officers and the senior clerks enjoy the benefits of financial loans and bonuses (Shariah Court 1974, 58). Employment among these people provide security in every sense especially in their old age as exemplified by those who are on pensions after retiring from the government service.[11]

In contrast, the nature of employment among those who are employed in the middle range subsistence employment are somewhat manual and they receive a lower income. This is exemplified by the cases of the driver, overseer and especially by the case of the firewood retailer: while the work of the driver and the overseer are not so physically demanding and are less dirtying, the work of the firewood retailer involves cutting, storing and delivering the wood by hand cart to customers in which case it is dirtying as well as physically demanding. His income is not only low but it is also highly variable because it depends largely on the demand for the fire wood.

If there is a general pattern in the forms of employment and income among people in the feasting circle category, it is that they are employed variously in forms of employment ranging from the most 'comfortable' to the lowest in the middle range subsistence type of employment.

ii) ***The Individualists***

As indicated above, the individualists are employed indiscriminately in all types of employment. In particular, 3 of the landowning individualists are employed in 'comfortable' employment, 5 are employed in 'middle range' subsistent employment, and one is employed in 'toilsome' employment. Apart from one carpenter, the landowning individualists are employed in forms of employment which are more or less similar to people of the feasting circle discussed above. In fact three (2 teachers and 1 entrepreneur) people of this sub-category are equally comfortable as six people of the feasting circle, while five others are more or less within the same income range as the rest of the feasting circle. There are also two individuals in the sub-category who are on a pension just like two pensioners of the feasting circle.

The tenant individualists are similarly distributed in various types of employment: 3 are employed in the comfortable employment, but their incomes are slightly lower than others in such employment, 5 people (including one free settler) are employed in 'middle range' and 2 are employed in 'toilsome' employment. One of these tenant individualists, the firewood retailer, differs from those employed in 'middle range' employment in this sub-category in that his employment involves much more manual labour. Further, there are two labourers among the tenant individualists whose incomes are \$3.50 and \$5.00 per day respectively. These incomes are markedly lower than any other forms of employment followed by the people in the sub-category and are typical of the income derived from a 'toilsome' employment.

iii) ***The Raft-Users:***

If the people in the feasting circle category are employed mainly in the 'middle range' and 'comfortable' types of employment, the employment among the raft-users is the reverse of this pattern. They are largely employed in forms of employment within the 'middle range' and the 'toilsome' types of employment, with a heavy concentration in the latter.

From Table 23 above, it may be noted that there are 10 out of the 33 raft-users who are employed in the 'middle range' type of employment. There are operators of food and drink stalls, drivers, night guards and labourers in Singapore. The incomes from these forms of employment are also higher than any other type and forms of employment pursued by raft-users. As may be seen from Table 23, the incomes are above the average of $150.00 per month.

However, most of the raft-users are employed either as wage labourers or in various forms of self-employment which are classified as 'toilsome' employment. The labourers are mainly concentrated in sawmills on a daily wage of less than $5.00,[12] in batik factories on a daily wage which does not exceed $5.00,[13] and in the match factory where their daily wage is about $3.00 per day.[14]

Due to this low and fixed income from wage labour, some of the raft-users turn to self-employment like selling at the market, vending and trishaw pedalling. Some of them explain that they choose forms of self-employment because they see themselves as capable of earning more income than those offered to a labourer by private capitalist organisations. This is mainly due to the fact that the income from such forms of employment depends largely on personal strength and enterprise. They seem to believe that they can manipulate their daily income according to their needs, i.e. they can work harder and for longer hours if it is necessary for the particular day or week. This is shown especially in the case of trishaw pedalling and vending where the people involved estimate their incomes differ considerably from each other: the three vendors for instance estimate their incomes as being between $4.00 and $6.00 daily, and the four trishaw pedallers also estimate their income differently from one another ranging from the lowest of $3.00 to the highest of $7.00 per day. Such variability in the incomes of people involved in the same form of employment is also shown by the case of 6 sellers at the market who estimate their incomes differently from one another ranging from $2.00 to $5.00 per day. On the average, the incomes of the raft-users who are employed in 'toilsome' employment do not seem to be higher than $150.00 per month.

There are obviously many reasons which force the raft-users into such forms of employment and into poverty. Their level of literacy is very low and they lack particular and specialised skills which are required by production in the town. Their education seldom exceeds two years in a vernacular school. If they possess skills like tailoring and carpentery, the serious competition from capitalist enterprises in the town reduces their production to the level of subsistence. In any event, the value of their labour is hardly sufficient for their existence, and it supports only a bare subsistence level of existence in the town.

The raft-users who are employed in 'toilsome' employment are therefore the poorest people of the kampung, along with the two labourers who are tenant individualists. On the same count, they are also different from other raft-users who are employed in the 'middle range' employment discussed above.

From our examination of employment and incomes in the kampung, we may suggest that there are significant differences between people in all the three categories, and we may also suggest that there are similarities between people from different categories. To put it simply, there are bureaucrats and petty bourgeois who are employed in 'comfortable' employment from both the feasting circle and the individualist categories, there are subsistent townsmen from all the three categories who are employed in 'middle range' employment and there are extremely poor tenant individualists as well as the majority of the raft-users who are employed in 'toilsome' employment.

From our observation on the patterns of consumption, types and forms of employment and the amount of incomes among the three categories of people in the kampuing, it is obvious that the economic differentiations between people do not coincide with their different social positions manifested by the patterns of their expressive social relationships. This may be summarised in diagrammatic form:

Consumption/Employment/Income	*Categories of People*
High consumption/'comfortable' employment	Feasting circle, landowning individualists
Medium consumption/'middle range' employment	Feasting circle, landowning and tenant individualists and raft-users
Low consumption/'toilsome' employment	Tenant individualists and majority of raft-users

It seems clear that a low level of consumption is directly related to poor income which again is related to the 'toilsome' employment regardless of whether an individual is employed by the govenment, private capitalist organisation or himself. The reverse is also true. The least manual or comfortable forms of employment are directly related to high income and high consumption. Between these extremes, fall the middle range employment and incomes.

On the basis of their employment or their objective position in the productive system of the town, the people in the kampung may be seen as divided into three classes which do not coincide with the categories which emerge from their expressive social relationships discussed in the last chapter. In order to see the reality of their class difference further, let us briefly discuss the employment patterns among their women and children.

Employment Among Women

Let us first consider the employment of women in the kampung generally. This will show the objective economic status of each household within the three categories because people who are economically well off seldom allow their women to be employed in jobs which are dirtying and which also bring poor income — for instance the dyeing and waxing of batik cloth.[15] Also they seem to regard such employment as socially degrading and economically unrewarding.

Consequently women from the wealthy class are employed, if at all, in such employment as teaching and shop keeping. This is also attributable to the fact that they either possess the appropriate educational qualification for teaching school, or their household economy provides sufficient resources to run a retail shop. Otherwise the women resort to 'not working'[16] which is again possible when members of their household, usually their husbands, have sufficient income to maintain their household economy. In fact it has been shown in Chapter 2 that the wives and women of the rich and powerful royal persons and aristocrats have traditionally been non-working. Today the non-working wives are typically those of the bureaucrats, including teachers (*orang makan gaji*), notably the bureaucrats in high positions like District Officers and those on whom is conferred the honorary title of 'Dato' (cf. Kah Bador 1973).

In any case the employment of women in the kampung should show the differences and similarities of the objective economic conditions of the household concerned.[17] This is especially so when it is observed that the form of employment among the wives in the kampung are more or less as widely spread in income and status as the employment of heads of households discussed in the last chapter, though the variety is somewhat less. This may be shown in the following table:

Table 24
EMPLOYMENT OF WIVES

Types of Employment	*Monthly Income Est. in M$*	*Feasting Circle*	*Land-owning*	*Groups of People: Individualists: Free Settler*	*Tenant*	*Raft-Users*
dyeing & waxing batik cloth	30	3	4	1	5	15
labouring in a factory	90	—	—	—	—	3
traditional masseuse	0	—	—	—	—	1
selling at the market	90–100	—	3	—	1	1
house wife	—	5	4	—	3	3
shopkeeping	above 100	2	—	—	—	—
school teacher (religious teacher)	300	1	—	—	—	—
	Total	11	11	1	9	23

Generally, the forms of employment among wives in the kampung are observed to fall into five main categories: i) housewife, ii) light work as shopkeepers and teacher, iii) labouring in the match factory, iv) dyeing and waxing of batik cloth, and v) petty trading or selling at the market.

These are, however, not absolute forms of employment since in all cases observed, the wives are never completely detached from their household duties. All the wives look after their houses and the members of their households like housewives in the western world. What is significant is that while all the wives are performing their basic duties as housewives, a substantial number of them are gainfully employed in economically important employment apart from and on top of household duties. The question now becomes why some of these wives are employed in extra work whereas some others remain as housewives or 'not working'.

It may be argued that the employment pattern among wives is largely determined by the amount of income of their husbands. This means that where possible, wives would employ their labour to increase the incomes of their well-off husbands, and wherever necessary, the wives would employ their labour to supplement the poor incomes of their husbands. Whenever it is neither possible nor necessary to supplement the incomes of their husbands, the wives would choose to remain as housewives or 'not working'. This pattern is observable when we consider the non-working wives in each category. It also explains how and why other women are employed in their respective forms of employment.

i.i) ***The Wives of the Feasting Circle:***
First, let us consider the women of the feasting circle, for I believe it is important that we consider the employment of wives in relation to the types of employment which their husbands pursue. In the case of the feasting circle, this may be shown as follows:

Table 25
EMPLOYMENT OF WIVES AND HUSBANDS OF THE FEASTING CIRCLE

Husband's type of Employment	*Total No.*	*Employment of Wives:* Housewife	Shopkeeping	Teaching	Dyeing & Waxing Batik Cloth
'Comfortable' Employment					
Senior clerks	2	1	—	1	—
Officers	2	2	—	—	—
Entrepreneurs	2	1	1	—	—
'Middle Range' Employment					
Drivers	1	—	1	—	—
Overseer	1	—	—	—	1
Firewood retailer	1	—	—	—	1
Retired persons on pension	2	1	—	—	1
Total	11	5	2	1	3

There is a high correlation between non-working wives and the types of employment of their husbands: that is the wives of people who are employed in 'comfortable' employment are the majority of those who are not working in the group. In contrast, those wives whose husbands are employed in the 'middle range' employment are found to be employed even in poor income and dirtying forms of employment like the dyeing and waxing of batik cloth.

It is necessary to note that there are two wives who are actively employed among those whose husbands are employed in 'comfortable' employment. These are the wives of an entrepreneur and a senior clerk. They are both royal persons. The probable reason for their employment, I believe, is that one has the appropriate educational qualification to be teaching religious studies (*ustazah*) and the other's husband has sufficient capital resources to set up a retail shop for the wife to look after. In any event, they are both non-dirtying and much more economically viable than the forms of employment of other wives in the kampung. In fact the wives are economically better off than the majority of the heads of households among the raft-users.

It is significant to mention here that one of the wives of the two retired persons is working in dyeing batik cloth whereas the other is not working. The reason seems to be that the incomes of their husbands are different. Even though both husbands are on the government pension scheme, the husband of the wife who is not working (a royal person) has an extra income from rent on his house sites, while the other relies solely on the pension. The latter's wife seems compelled to work to supplement the income of her husband even though the income from her employment is little.

In other words the wives of heads of households who are employed in 'comfortable' employment are only employed in non-dirtying, employment which may bring substantial increase in the total income of their households. Otherwise the fact that their husbands already have a high income makes it unnecessary to be employed, especially in the poor and dirtying forms of employment. In this case they adopt the alternative course of not working.

i.ii) ***The Wives of the Individualists:***

This economic argument seems even more valid if we consider the economic activities of wives in the other two categories of people in the kampung: the individualists and the raft-users. None of the wives of the individualists who are employed in 'comfortable' employment are gainfully employed. This is shown by the cases of wives of two teachers and the wife of an entrepreneur in the category. As point of comparison with other wives in the group, they may be shown in Table 26.

The table show that there are four wives in the category who are not working. These are the wives of people who are employed in the middle range employment (drivers) and one of the retired persons. This does not discount the relationship between the employment of the husband and that of the wives, for on closer examination, two of these wives are childless, and the other two are young mothers who have one and two small children respectively, for whom their children prevent them from working in other than their house work. Though this may be true to some extent, it seems that such an explanation is not sufficient in view of the fact that other wives in the group, who also have small children, are

Table 26:
EMPLOYMENT OF WIVES AND HUSBANDS AMONG THE INDIVIDUALISTS

Husband's Occupation	*Total No.*	*Occupations of Wives:* *Housewife*	*Selling at Market*	*Dyeing & Waxing Batik Cloth*
'Comfortable' Employment				
Entrepreneurs	1	1	—	—
Teachers	2	2	—	—
Clerks	3	—	—	3
'Middle Range' Employment				
Drivers	8	3	1	4
Middleman	1	—	—	1
Firewood retailers	1	—	1	—
'Toilsome' Employment				
Labourers	2	—	—	2
Carpenters	1	—	1	—
Retired persons on pension	2	1	1	—
Total	21	7	4	10

working (cf. Appendix 2).

What seems important is the question of the varying level of economic pressure at different stages of the family cycle. The wives who are not working in the group are wives of people who have less economic pressure. In particular they have only one or two small children who are below the school age. Thus they are less compelled to work to supplement the income of their husbands. This is especially shown by the case of the retired person in the category who has no children and whose wife does not find it necessary to work.

From these, it seems reasonable to believe that while the employment and income of husbands determine the forms of employment of their wives, it is also necessary to note that the intensity of economic pressure on the household in a particular period of time may also determine the types and forms of employment that the wives pursue. To some extent this explains why some of the wives are working while some other do not.

i.iii) ***The Wives of the Raft-Users***

The relationship between employment and income of the husbands and the employment of the wives in the kampung may be seen from cases of wives in the category of raft-users. For the present purposes, this may be shown as follows:

Table 27
EMPLOYMENT OF WIVES AND HUSBANDS AMONG THE RAFT-USERS

Husbands' Type of Employment	*Total No.*	*House-Wife*	*Dyeing & Waxing Batik Cloth*	*Labouring in Factory*	*Selling at Market*	*Traditional Masseuse*
'Middle Range Employment						
Stall operators	2	—	1	1	—	—
Drivers	3	1	2	—	—	—
Night guards	2	1	1	—	—	—
Labourers in Singapore	2	—	2	—	—	—
'Toilsome' Employment						
Labourers	4	1	2	—	1	—
Vendors	3	—	1	1	—	1
Trishaw pedallers	4	—	4	—	—	—
Itinerant sellers	1	—	1	—	—	—
Tailors	1	—	1	—	—	—
Carpenters	1	—	—	1	—	—
Total	23	3	15	3	1	1

As shown in the table, the majority of wives of the raft-users are employed in poor income and dirtying forms of employment. Beside those who are employed in dying and waxing batik cloth, there are also those who are employed in the match factory as labourers, and those who are selling at the market. Only three are not working. They are the wives of two raft-users who are employed as a night guard and driver respectively and whom we have classified as being employed in the 'middle range' employment. The other is the wife of a labourer.

While we may argue that the wives of the night guard and the labourer are not working due to little economic pressure, that is, they both have one small child each, the wife of the driver is different. She has four children, one of whom is a seventeen year old boy who is unemployed with two attending primary school and one a child of less than school age. The reason for her not working is difficult to ascertain. This is because generally 'not working' wives in the kampung are confined to those whose husbands are employed in 'comfortable' employment or those from households which have less economic pressure. If this case of 'not working' wife shows anything, it is that she has the choice either to remain non-working or to be employed in order to supplement the income of her husband. In other words, employment for wives whose husbands are employed in the 'middle range' employment may be voluntary.

In contrast, the wives of the raft-users who are employed in toilsome employment are compelled to work in order to acquire a reasonable amount of income to meet their daily needs. As may be seen from Table 27, they are all employed in poor income forms of employment which are invariably dirtying.

Non-working wives in the kampung, therefore, consist of i) wives of people who are employed in 'comfortable' employment, ii) wives of those people who are not immediately compelled by economic necessity to be employed, and iii) wives of those people who are employed in 'middle range' employment who choose to remain 'not working'. At this point we may generalise the patterns of employment among wives in the kampung as follows:

i) The wives whose husbands are employed in 'comfortable' employment are either employed in the forms of employment which are non-dirtying and which also bring substantial income, or remain as housewives.

ii) Though the wives of people who are employed in 'middle range' employment are gainfully employed, they seem to do so voluntarily to supplement the income of their husbands.

iii) Unless the immediate economic pressure is extremely low, the wives of those people who are employed in 'toilsome' employment are compelled by economic necessity to seek employment in any form available in order to supplement the poor income of their husbands.

However, it is important to emphasise that the employment patterns among the wives do not only indicate significant differences in economic status of households within each category, but also the similarities of economic status of households between the three different categories of people. In particular, the above discussion shows that:

i) Wives who are not working because their husbands are employed in 'comfortable' employment are found among the feasting circle and the individualists, especially the landowning individualists.

ii) Wives who choose to be employed among those whose husbands are employed in the 'middle range' employment are found in all the three categories.

iii) Wives who are compelled to seek employment due to the poor income of their husbands are found among the individualists notably the tenant individualists, and the majority of the raft-users, who are mainly employed in 'toilsome' employment.

In other words, the discussion suggests that on the basis of employment among the wives as an indicator of economic status of households, the division of people in the kampung into the three categories (feasting circle, individualista and raft-users) cannot really be justified. This is further shown by the employment and education of their children.

Employment and Education of Children

The employment and education of children in the kampung is an equally important indicator of economic status of households. Following Parkin (1971), I will examine the hypothesis that the economic status of each household determines the education and consequently the employment of children. Indeed, I see this as one of the main aspects in which we may observe the process of reproduction of the household economy, class, and its relations in the local social formation. To begin with the observed cases, the employment of children in the kampung may be shown in Table 28.

Table 28 shows that the children of the kampung are employed in the following manner: ten are employed in white collar employment, which includes school teachers, clerks, typist and an office boy; three are employed as light manual labourers which include two shop assistants and a driver; and fifteen are employed as labourers in the match and batik factories in the town and in factories in Kuala Lumpur. The majority of the children, however, remain unemployed.

The distribution of children in the various forms of employment takes the following pattern: that is, while white collar employment is almost confined to the children of the feasting circle who are also royal and the children of the landowning individualists, the majority of the unemployed children are found to be children of tenant individualists and of the raft-users. While jobs in factories (including those outside the state) are pursued by children from all groups, light manual labour seem to be confined only to the children of the feasting circle and tenant individualists. Let us then consider each form of employment closely.

i) *White Collar Employment*

One explanation for the distribution of white collar employment among the children in the kampung seems to be their level of education. For instance, those children who are working as clerks all possess the minimum of Grade Three Malaysian Certificate of Education, and both the typist and the office boy possess the Lower Certificate of Education. Consequently those children who are without education, which in the present case is synonymous with standard six vernacular education, either seek

Table 28
EMPLOYMENT AND EDUCTION OF CHILDREN

Children/ Categories of People	*Highest Qualifications:** Std.6*	*L.C.E.*	*M.C.E.*	*Total*	*Forms of Employment:*** Unemployed*	*Labourer*	*Labourer in Kuala Lumpur*	*Light Manual Labourer*	*Business*	*White Collar*	*Total*
Feasting Circle:											
Royal persons	—	1	3		—	—	—	—	1	3	
Commoners:											
landowners	1	3	1		—	—	1	2	1	1	
tenants	3	—	—		—	2	1	—	—	—	
Sub-Total	4	4	4	12	—	2	2	2	2	4	12
Individualists:											
Landowners	—	1	4		—	—	—	—	—	5	
Tenants	—	5	2		6	—	—	1	—	—	
Free settlers (royal)	—	2	—		—	—	2	—	—	—	
Sub-Total	—	8	6	14	6	—	2	1	—	5	14
Raft-Users:											
Free settlers	2	—	—		2	—	—	—	—	—	
Tenants	22	6	1		18	8	1	—	—	2	
Sub-Total	24	6	1	31	20	8	1	—	—	2	31
Grand Total	28	18	11	57	26	10	5	3	2	11	57

Key: * 1. Std. 6 denoted a primary 6 vernacular school education.
2. L.C.E. denotes Lower Certificate of Education or Form Three level education.
3. M.C.E. denotes Malaysian Certificate of Education or Form Five level education.

** 1. Light manual labour refers to drivers and shop assistants.
2. White collar employees in these cases include school teachers, clerks, typists and office boys.

employment as labourers or remain unemployed. But while it is true that employment in white collar jobs is determined by the level of education, it is again possible to argue that education is in turn determined by the availability of finance for it.

As we have shown, some people of the feasting circle and some of the landowning individualists are people who are employed in 'comfortable' employment, some people from all three categories are employed in the 'middle range' employment, and some of the tenant individualists and the majority of the raft-users are employed in 'toilsome' employment. As these various types of employment are coterminous with the differences in terms of high, medium and poor income, it may be suggested that the achieved level of education, which sets the chances for employment of children in white collar jobs, is largely determined by the availability of finance. For instance, 8 out of the 11 children who are educated to Form Five level and are employed as teachers and clerks are the children of the feasting circle and landowning individualists who are employed in 'comfortable' employment; 18 children who are educated up to Form Three level are the children from all groups whose parents are employed in the 'middle range' employment; and 24 out of 28 children who are educated up to Standard Six vernacular school are children whose parents are employed in the 'toilsome' employment who are all raft-users.

The relationship between the low level of education and lack of available finance for education is shown further by the fact that children from the poor income group do not continue their education after failing the Form Three examination. Instead they remain unemployed. In contrast, the children from the high income group who fail the examination continue their education in private schools.[18] The case of a child of a royal person from the feasting circle illustrates this. After failing his Form Three examination, he was sent to study to be a motor mechanic, and during the time of fieldwork, he was engaged in teaching 12 students who were paying a monthly fee of $25.00 each. Obviously such a pattern of education after failing to continue schooling in government schools is related to the availability of finance. Thus the children whose parents are employed in 'toilsome' employment and to some extent those children whose parents are employed in 'middle range' employment are hindered from continuing their education in the privately run schools or in trade schools.

The situation is shown again by the differences in the types of school in which children are currently enrolled. This may be shown in the following table:

Table 29
ENROLMENT OF CHILDREN IN MALAY AND ENGLISH MEDIUM SCHOOLS

Children/ Categories of People	*Types of Schools:** *Primary*	*Secondary E.M.*	*M.M.*	*Rel./School*	*Tertiary*	*Total*
Feasting Circle:						
Royal persons	—	4	—	—	—	
Commoners:						
landowners	2	6	—	—	—	
tenants	2	—	3			
Sub-Total	4	10	3	—	—	17
Individualists:						
Landowners	5	11	3	—	2	
Tenants	9	1	10	—	—	
Free settlers (royal)	—	2	—	—	—	
Sub-Total	14	14	13	—	2	43
Raft-Users:						
Free settlers	2	—	—	—	—	
Tenants	16	1	11	2	—	
Sub-Total	18	1	11	2	—	32
Total	36	25	27	2	2	92

**Keys:*
1. E.N. denotes English Medium Schools and M.M. denotes Malay Medium Schools.
2. Tertiary education in this case includes one child who is attending a Technical College in Kuala Lumpur and one studying in England.

Table 29 shows that all children from all categories of people who have reached the age of seven years old are enrolled in schools (primary). However, the number of children from the tenant individualists and the raft-users categories drops significantly at the secondary level, especially in the English Medium secondary schools. The main reason is that English Medium secondary schools are more expensive than the Malay Medium schools (Murad Bin Mohd. Nor, 1973). In fact if the children from the poor income groups are enrolled in secondary schools at all, they are heavily concentrated in the Malay Medium schools. This is shown by the cases of children from the feasting circle (tenants) and the individualists who are employed in the 'middle range' employment, the children of the tenant individualists and the raft-users who are all employed in 'toilsome' employment.

In addition, the differences in parental attitudes towards education is also worthy of consideration. As we have seen, a raft-user attaches perfunctory importance to the education of his children. Consequently, only among the children of tenant individualists and raft-users are cases found of children leaving school at an early age, or only intermittently attending school — girls because they are helping their mothers in dyeing batik cloth, boys because they prefer to join with the adult men in gambling. This inevitably leads to failure at school examinations, especially at the Form Three level. This is shown by the fact that there is only one case of a child from the two categories who has passed the Form Five examination and who is now working as a clerk, and at present there is only one case of a child who is currently in Form Five class.

Such attitudes towards the education of their children is perhaps another dimension of poverty. Firstly, the children are needed to look after the young ones in the family in order for the mothers to go out to work to supplement the income of their households, and secondly, the poor groups take it for granted that failure at school examinations is part and parcel of the nature of education of their children. In addition they seem to believe that even if their children acquire the necessary educational qualification, they would not be able to find employment in the white collar employment simply because they do not have the necessary contacts to 'negotiate' for such an employment, as will be shown shortly.

So while the employment pattern in white collar employment among the children depends on the level of education, it is also important to note that the level of education is in turn determined largely by the income of the parents. In effect, the employment of parents and the economic status of each household in the kampung determines the employment of their children.

ii) ***Unemployment:***

Though such an argument has a good deal of explanatory value, there are exceptions which must be taken into account. There are children from all the three categories who possess the Lower Certificate of Education and the Malaysian Certificate of Education qualifications who are unemployed. As may be seen from Table 28, there are two unemployed children who possess Malaysian Certificate of Education and Lower Certificate of Education respectively among the children of the feasting circle; there are six unemployed children of whom five hold Lower Certificate of Education and one holds Malaysian Certificate of Education among the children of tenant individualists; and there are five holders of the Lower Certificate of Education among children of the raft-users who are unemployed. From these cases one may conclude that consideration of additional factors is necessary to account for the unemployment pattern among the children of the kampung. These are two: the prevailing procedures of getting employed, especially in white collar employment; and the lack of the available opportunities.

The procedure for getting employed in the private capitalist organisation and in government departments in Kelantan today is known as 'negotiation' (*kira*). This means that a person who has the necessary qualification (or even a lesser qualification than that which is required, e.g. a Lower Certificate of Education instead of the required Malaysian Certificate of Education) has to have an intermediary to negotiate for a position. The intermediary may be a kinsman or a close friend, who is also a friend of the employer or who is a prominent person in the government department, who has the authority to choose the candidate for the particular position. The intermediary however, may or may not do so for a certain sum of cash. It is however usual for a friend to prescribe a certain sum of cash for the 'negotiation'.

Consequently, those children who have the necessary qualification but whose parents are not friendly with any of the prominent persons in the state, whose parents do not associate with people who know such persons and more importantly whose parents lack the financial resources to negotiate, would inevitably lose in the competition for a particular employment opportunity. As an example, the son of Che Mat (a tenant individualist who is working as a firewood retailer) has been unemployed for the last three years after completing his Malaysian Certificate of Education with Grade Three. During the period of fieldwork, the position of a 'store keeper' with the State's Public Service was advertised. An intermediary was found who demanded an initial fee of M$200.00. As the job was not positively guaranteed by the intermediary, the deal was called off because of the parents' fear of shame if the money was paid without securing the position. This is also because the case was always compared by the residents of the kampung with that of another parent who was able to 'negotiate' the position of an office boy for his son free of any charge.[19] In addition, the latter only possessed a Lower Certificate of Education which at present is generally recognised as being useless for employment in any white collar employment.

To some extent, this is also the explanation given for white collar employment among childen of the feasting circle and the children of the landowning individualists as shown in Table 28. As we have seen the parents of these children are either employed in the bureaucracy or they are people who have friends through the nature of their work as in the case of drivers. In short they are people who have access to the 'right' persons who can successfully 'negotiate' for employment. As it is expressed locally, they have the 'proper contacts' (*ada orang kenal*). This is especially true for children from the royal group of persons whose parents have friends and more importantly kinsmen in the prominent bureaucratic positions in the state. Their educational qualification, however minimal, would be reinforced by such 'power contacts' to secure employment.

Negotiation also affects the employment of children in light manual labour. In fact it underlies all kinds of employment in the town of Kota Bharu, even when formal educational qualificatins for a position is not required. This is most observable in the practice of private capitalist organisations, such as the Match Factory. In its forty years of operation, the factory has never advertised a single post whether clerical or manual. Every vacancy in the factory is spread by word of mouth and consequently, the clerical positions are staffed by friends and relatives and similarly the manual workers are either friends or relatives of one another.[20] The same is also true with those who seek employment as a trishaw pedaller: unless a man is able to purchase a trishaw which costs about M$300.00, he has to have a guarantor before he is able to hire a trishaw from an owner who charges M$1.30 per day. The guarantor is therefore inevitably a person whom he knows and who is also trusted by the owner of the trishaw.

Given such a situation, the son of Che Mat and others like him, rightly attribute their failure to be employed in a desirable white collar job to the fact that their parents do not know prominent persons who can 'negotiate' for a position. At the same time they lack the financial resources to pay such intermediaries. This applies especially to the children of the raft-users and children of the tenant individualists simply because they seem to associate only with people of their category or their fellow workers who are in the similar situation. In addition, the parents cannot afford to spend money which may be wasted in the process of 'negotiation'. They are unwilling to enter into 'negotiation' unless they are positive of securing the position. As a result they seem to subscribe to a common belief that education for their children at the Forms Three and Five levels is useless because they do not have the 'proper contact' to make such qualifications meaningful.

The discussion so far, however, does not take into account the important structural factor of lack of opportunities for employment among children with qualifications such as the Malaysian Certificate of Education and the Lower Certificate of Education. Given the fact that secular education produces in the minds of people who have received it, however briefly, the aspiration of entering 'occupations associated with an urban milieu and a division of labour based on industry and commerce' (Nash *op. cit.,* 139–40) and to a large extent the good image of white collar employment, there is therefore an extreme lack of opportunities for the children who are educated only up to Forms Three and Five levels. In fact the procedure of 'negotiation' for a position is largely related to, if not directly the outcome of the lack of opportunities to utilise such qualifications. Consequently, boys who possess such qualifications migrate to cities like Kuala Lumpur where there are greater opportunities of employment, at least as labourers in the factories. As shown in Table 28, five of such children are now employed as labourers in factories in Singapore and Kula Lumpur.[21] The majority of the children however remain unemployed in the kampung.

Girls who have had similar education are less mobile. They tend to stay at home to extend help in the daily chores. At the same time they may also be employed in dyeing batik cloth in the vicinity of their homes. They are collectively described as 'maidens who are awaiting proposals for marriage'. Their main concern is to familiarise themselves with the female routines of handling household chores, minding the younger ones in the family and learning the techniques of dyeing batik cloth. At the same time they attend to family shopping which gives them the opportunity to 'advertise' their presence and availability, if not beauty, in the marriage market. The cases of two children (female) who are both attending a religious school (Table 29) are also considered to be within this category of the unemployed children.

iii) ***Wage Labourers***

The children who are rural born and who followed their parents to settle in the kampung from rural areas are different from their siblings in many ways. They demand a separate analysis. They are hardly literate and their education, if any, does not exceed that of standard six in vernacular schools. Also, they do not aspire to white collar employment like the children who are locally born and who have had some education. Subsequent to their settlement in the kampung, therefore these children follow the footsteps of their parents and seek any form of employment in the town which was available to them.

These children, then, are involved in employment which does not require any formal education, this invariably means labouring in batik factories for the males and labouring in the match factory for the females. These are the ten children who are shown in Table 28 as being employed as labourers. It seems to be a general rule that with their little education these children have lower aspirations than the others and consequently they do not seem to mind working in dirtying and poor income employment as labourers.

Such a pattern of employment for rural born children cuts across the categories in the kampung. As shown in Table 28, there are two such children from the commoner tenant feasting circle and there are eight from the category of the tenant raft-users.

We may suggest here that on the basis of employment, the children in the kampung may be seen as divided into two main divisions: one of rural born children who are employed as wage labourers and the other of local children who have some education and who aspire to white collar employment. When the latter group of children are hindered from fulfilling their expectations due to a lack of education or of resources to 'negotiate', they migrate to cities to work as labourers in factories or they remain unemployed in the kampung.

Recapitulation

Insofar as patterns of consumption, employment and the employment of women and children may be regarded as manifestations of economic status of households in the kampung, we may conclude by emphasising that these households are in fact distinguishable into the well-to-do bureaucrats and petty bourgeois on the one hand, and the subsistent and extremely poor townsmen and proletariat on the other. Whether or not they are wage workers, all the people of the kampung are dominated by the capital in the town either directly as bureaucrats and proletariat or indirectly as petty bourgeois, subsistence petty traders, poor vendors, hawkers and servicemen. The economic status cuts across the social categories of expressive social relationships.

Footnotes

1. The category of people whom I call the feasting circle has been distinguished in the last chapter from the other two categories of the kampung, i.e. the raft-users and the individualists. I am using these categories here as analytical categories.

2. One of the houses which has two sleeping rooms among the houses of the raft-users is shared by two households.

3. As indicated earlier, the 68 households in the kampung are living in 66 houses. There are then 4 households who are sharing 2 houses. These are the 2 households among the

landowning individualists who are sharing 1 big house, and there are 2 households among the raft-users who are sharing 1 tiled house.

4. There is however one motor-car owned by a free settler among the individualists which is used primarily as an unlicensed taxi. Since it is operated mainly for profit and income, I have classified it here as a capital good, like other motor-cars in the kampung. It is thus excluded from the Table 19 as well as from the present analysis. On the same count, I have excluded 2 trucks and 3 trishaws (the trucks belong to an individual of the feasting circle and a landowning individualist respectively, while the trishaws belong to raft-users).

5. In addition, the youth are also different from their parents. While parents are divided into the three categories discussed, the youth and children generally come together as a group on many occasions. For instance the male youth of the kampung belong to a soccer team which plays against teams from other kampungs; most of them join the coffee shop congregation whether or not their parents are patrons of coffee shops, and most of them congregate at the sides of roads at night or roam around the night stalls in the town's main business centre. I believe the youth of the kampung should be studied separately and in their own right.

6. The relationship between low income and low quality clothing is also shown in the case of footwear. This is best illustrated by citing a case of a raft-user who always wore a pair of sandals (rubber) for the whole period of the fieldwork, regardless of time and place. Presumably he does not own any other kind of footwear. However, he periodically says that whenever he has sufficient savings, he would purchase a pair of high quality leather shoes which at the time cost about $30.00.

7. The two wholesalers (dealers) have 3 and 2 employees respectively while the operator of the batik factory has 4 employees.

8. To put it generally the concept of 'work' (*kerja*) in the kampung seems to refer to any employment of labour which has economic ends. Consequently employment which demand less physical labour are regarded as leisure rather than real work.

9. One trishaw pedaller describes his 'unintelligence' as being 'stupid as a cow'.

10. The usual arrangement is that the wholesaler (*towkay*) sells his goods to the retailers (sellers) at wholesale price (*borong*). In the case of the relatives however, the cash transfer of the sale takes place after the day's work rather than immediately the transaction takes place, especially when the relative-seller has no immediate cash.

11. This pension continues for a lifetime, and the amount drawn monthly is a small proportion of the monthly income of the last day while in the service or as the Sultan may determine; (Kelantan Enactment, No. 6, 1972).

12. The wages in the sawmills vary from one sawmill to another; for instance, one sawmill has a starting daily wage at $3.40 with an increment of 30¢ per year to a maximum of $4.30 per day, and one other sawmill has a starting daily wage of $2.80 with an increment of 20¢ per year to a maximum of $3.40 per day.

13. There are however minor differences among the labourers employed in batik factories as they are found in the kampung: the printer (*pemukul*) who sets the pattern at the beginning of the process of production is considered as a skilled batik worker and is thus paid $5.00 or more per day, while the labourers are paid $3.00 per day.

14. In the match factory however, the labourers are paid slightly less: non-skilled labourers are paid $2.20 per day to the maximum of $2.80 per day after one year's experience. The women labourers are paid 10¢ less than men labourers. As part of the condition of service however, every labourer is entitled to i) advances for purchase of bicycles, ii) two *gantangs* of rice per month, iii) a yearly bonus which does not exceed

a total of one month's pay, iv) a present which is worth $12.00 on every *Hari Raya,* v) book allowances for school-going children, vi) a sum of $280.00 per birth of a child for a woman labourer, and vii) every labourer stands a chance of being chosen for a free pilgrimage trip to Mecca; the selection is however largely based on seniority of service and this is restricted to only two labourers per year.

15. This is carried out on a piece-rate basis and on contract with owners of batik printing factories. The owner pays 20¢ for each piece of batik cloth dyed and 5¢ for each of the cloth waxed. The former process takes no less than one hour and the latter process takes no more than ten minutes.

16. The local term used to describe wives who are not engaged in work apart from housework is wives who are 'not working' (*dudok saja*). Obviously the conception is an outcome of comparison with the working wives. However, it may be recalled from a previous chapter (Chapter 2) that this had been the preoccupation of ladies of high birth and wives of the nobilities. Their main duty was to serve and look after their husbands while leaving the household chores to their servants. This also entailed extreme consciousness and care about their personal appearance, proper manners and behaviour. The conception of 'not working' wives is then the present expression of the traditional ideal employment of wives of royal persons and nobilities, though its traditional elaborateness may not be as obvious.

17. We are considering here the employment among women in order to determine the economic status of their household. Households whose male head are either divorced or widowed and female heads of households are excluded in the present discussion. The latter has been treated as heads of households discussed earlier.

18. At the time of fieldwork, there are six privately run schools in the town which are charging a monthly fee of $15.00 for Form Three class, $20.00 for Form Five classes, and $36.00 for Form Six classes.

19. This is the case of a raft-user who works as a vendor of ice-cream. However, as he was formerly a driver with a government department from which he retired due to a long period of illness, it was claimed that he has friends in the government service who were responsible for the 'negotiation' of the job for his son.

20. In a separate interview with a leader of a workers' gang who is responsible for employment of Malay manual workers in a Chinese owned biscuit factory in another part of the town, he emphasised that he would first choose his relatives who are in need of work to work in the factory, and his second choice would be his friends or friends of his friends. The important factor for the choice is that he has to know the character of the workers so that he can vouch for their reliability.

21. It seems important to note here that from my correspondence, the son of Che Mat has now left for Singapore to work as a labourer with a construction company.

CHAPTER SIX

LOCAL BORN AND SETTLERS: BACKGROUND TO AN URBAN ECONOMIC STRUCTURE

The economic differentiation between people discussed above shows that it is largely related to the employment structure of the town. In this chapter, I shall discuss the socio-economic backgrounds of the people to explain how economic differentiation came about. By socio-economic backgrounds, I am concerned with one's place of origin, whether one is a commoner or royal by birth, the level of education achieved and previous employment. This analysis should also take account of the kampung as an urban ward of Kota Bharu town.

First, it is necessary to recall that the kampung developed into the present town ward as part of the growth of Kota Bharu town into an urban centre, following the intrusion of western capitalism into the state in the early 1900s. As I have shown in Chapter Two, the town soon became the centre of western capitalism in the state and came to depend on the colonial bureaucratic and educational systems and large scale private commercial organisations. This process went hand in hand with a steady growth in population, some of whom became servants of the colonial government, or servants of the private capitalist organisations, while a significantly large proportion became wage labourers and self-employed at the level of 'subsistence' and in poverty. Though the country became independent in 1957, the growth of the town was affected only in the sense that a gradual process began of replacing colonial bureaucrats with indigenous ones. The town continued to develop on the colonial model, which is to say that the town is primarily the centre of political control over the state, with commerce in a complementary role.

At the town ward or kampung level, such urban growth was first seen in the form of a change from the traditional 'fort' settlement to the present conglomeration of the town ward. This took the form of subdivision and sale of some of the land in the fort which consequently led to settlement by the commoners and the rise of a heterogeneous population in the kampung. After the dissolution of the fort's social formation therefore, the people in the kampung consisted of those who were locally born and settlers from elsewhere. The former group may be divided into those who are descended from royal persons or rulers of the traditional 'fort', and commoners who are descendants of royal specialists and royal servants.

Economically these people are employed in various non-agricultural types of employment around the town which we have classified as 'comfortable', 'middle range' and 'toilsome' employment. Let us now discuss how their origins and other factors of socio-economic background determine their employment and thus the employment structure of the town. For the purpose of analysis, I propose to consider the socio-economic backgrounds of the people according to their birth and their place of origin in the following order: i) royal persons, ii) local born commoners, iii) settlers from the areas in the vicinity, and iv) settlers from the rural areas.

The Royal Persons

The rise of the colonial government in Kelantan implied a diminution in the status of royal persons in Kota Bharu. As we have seen in Chapter Two, the increasing control over the state by the colonial government in the first half of this century meant the gradual loss of the power of the royal persons in the town. The ultimate take-over of control of the state by the colonialists came when the administration of the state was fully bureaucratised under the British in the 1930's, and when the Sultan became a mere figurehead. By this time the symbols of power and prestige had shifted from royal persons (the '*daulat*' class) to British Officers.

Instead of enjoying traditional power and the freedom to tax their subjects, royal persons now became dependant on the British either as salaried officers in the administration (bureaucrats) or as beneficiaries of royal allowance. The significant change brought about by the colonial administration is therefore that wealth accrued from taxation and other government exactions was now collected in the state's treasury instead of being shared out among the royal families.

However, this is not to deny that the royal persons were given priority to hold lower positions in the administration. In fact, a school was established for the purpose in 1904. But the royal persons now had to be qualified or literate in the secular sense in order to be dependants of the British. Otherwise, their traditionally celebrated royal birth had little significance. It is true that they were given the privilege of royal allowances; however, as I have indicated earlier, the amount of these allowances was insufficent to meet their daily needs, let alone to form a substitute for taxes which had maintained their traditional affluence. The net effect was that royal persons were forced to adapt to the new economic structure in somewhat the same manner as the majority of commoners in the town. Such pattern of the downfall of royal persons in the town of Kota Bharu is shown clearly by examples of royal persons living in the kampung today.

Leaving aside the case of one retired woman head of a royal household, let us examine the seven heads of royal households in the kampung. Their present employment, their previous employment and their level of secular education is as follows:

Table 30
EMPLOYMENT AND EDUCATION OF ROYAL PERSONS

Present Employment		*Education:* *Std. 6+*	*Below Std. 6*	*None*	*Past Employment*
Comfortable:					
Chief clerk	(2)	1	1	—	—
Officer	(1)	1	—	—	—
Entrepreneur	(1)	—	1	—	contractor (tobacco)
Middle Range:					
Taxi driver	(1)	—	—	1	
Night guard	(1)	—	—	1	Night guard
Retired:					
Retired on pension	(1)		1	—	Clerk
Total	(7)	2	3	2	

As may be seen from the table, there is a close relationship between the level of secular education and the forms of employment which people take up. For instance, with a little primary education of either standard five or six in the 1940's, one was able to secure a position such as a clerk in the colonial administration. Otherwise a royal person was forced to look for self-employment in business or for poorer employment like driving or working as a night guard.

It is also important to reiterate that the procedure of getting employment in the town is governed by 'negotiation' as well as on the level of secular education. With little education and the fact that the colonial administration favoured the appointment of royal persons, it is not surprising that even those who achieved lower educational qualifications were employed as clerks in the government service, as the cases of a clerk and the retired clerk who both achieved only a standard four primary education (Table 30).

This pattern suggests that royal birth plays a significant role as far as employment in the government service is concerned. However, it has to be supplemented by the criterion of a minimum level of secular education. Although royal birth is advantageous, it is not the sole determinant of forms of employment open to this group of people in the kampung.

Royal birth is also important another way: that is the glory of their royalness or '*daulat*' which was traditionally associated with power, prestige and affluence seems to be very much alive. This is shown in the fact that there is a tendency for the royal persons to be conscious of their heritage to the extent of trying to actualise, if not maintain their traditional way of life.

This tendency is expressed by royal persons who are employed in 'comfortable' employment in terms of fineness of living and affluence appropriately carrying the tradition of the '*daulat*' class. By virtue of the fact that they are employed in 'comfortable' employment (presently or in the past) they therefore did not have to resort to selling inherited land to maintain their affluence like other royal persons who are now employed in 'middle range' employment. Consequently, these three royal persons became rentiers to forty settlers to whom they relate through social distance and with the minimum of social contact. Though the relationship between the rentiers and the tenants is largely contractual (as implied by the M$60.00 rental fee per annum), the rentiers explain their action somewhat altruistically as 'helping the landless people', and imply that this constitutes a revival of traditional patronage relations. Coupled with their high pattern of consumption, their restricted social contact and their maintenance of social distance from the rest of the population in the kampung, it seems likely that they are trying to preserve their '*daulat*'.

These royal persons are included within the feasting circle of the kampung, as we have seen, and this implies their 'deferential relationship' with the non-honoured people of the kampung. However, their relationship with the commoners of this category is somewhat special: that is, though belonging to the same group, the commoners relate to royal persons through the use of 'court language' (*bahasa raja*) which signifies at least the special heritage if not the superiority of the latter. This custom also leads to a restricted social intercourse. While royal persons accept the commoners as part of the exclusive category of the kampung, at the same time they project the image that they themselves are a group set apart within this exclusivity, and there is a strong tendency for royal persons to try to preserve and maintain their traditionally superior position.

One such person is Kusin. He is at present self-employed as the owner operator of a batik printing factory. The obvious reason he is not a bureaucrat is that he was educated only up to Standard Three which at the time would not qualify him for a position in the Administration. Consequently, with the help of his mother, he started a retail shop in the kampung, went into trading tobacco leaves as a middleman and finally settled down as an operator of a batik factory employing four workers.

While his economic activity as an entrepreneur or 'towkay' is the main source of his income, it is important to note that his business entails control over four workers in the manner of a traditional royal person. His workers do not demand payment of wages until the time he chooses: they work at irregular hours when he so desires and more importantly, they all felt obliged to visit his wife in hospital when she was admitted for treatment.

What is obvious is that in this case the relationship between workers and their employer is not contractual as the case with other batik operators, especially the Chinese operators. Instead, the relationship is personalised, and the employer is referred to by the workers as '*Ku*'* denoting the clientage of the latter. This is different from other employers who are referred to by their workers as 'towkay'. In addition, the entrepreneur in this case is also the leader of a raft-users where his relationship with the members of the group succinctly expresses his royalness. In short, this case illustrates a conscious maintenance of a royal heritage.

The pattern is shown again by the case of Kuman. Unable to be employed in a prestigious position in the administration due to his lack of education, he has compensated for this by idealising the power and respect given to royal persons. (See Chapter Three, above) This behaviour is compatible with his economic activities: after selling his share of the inherited land in the kampung to settle his debts, he first started working as night guard with a company which was constructing a bridge near the kampung. When the work was completed, he was employed as a night guard with a sawmill near the kampung. The main reason for his choice of such forms of employment and the changes of employment within the same type were that labouring, which is the main alternative, is still regarded by the royal persons as demeaning. In any case, through the help of influential members of royal families, displaced royal persons like Kuman may still find employment which does not demand heavy physical labour, like being a night guard.

From these cases we may suggest that without the appropriate secular education, royal persons in the kampung now face an employment problem in the new economic structure. However, the fact that they are royal by birth gives them a little extra advantage in the sense of being

**Ku* = prince, short form of *tengku*.

able to avoid heavy and demeaning physical work. As such the royal persons of the kampung are distributed in both 'comfortable' and 'middle range' employment but not yet into the category of 'toilsome' employment.

In other words, the rise and subsequent dominance of western capitalism in the state which led to the growth of Kota Bharu into the administrative, and to a lesser extent the commercial centre of the state directly caused the impoverishment of some of the royal persons. The traditional royal prerogatives are now threatened and the employment of royal persons in the kampung may also be seen as the final effort by these people to retrieve their traditional positions. In this situation, some of the royal persons who are less qualified to meet the challenge of the new economic situation are increasingly losing ground.

The Local Born Commoners

As I have indicated earlier, this category of people are descended from royal specialists and royal servants. While people in the former sub-category own house sites inherited from their ancestors, the latter are allowed to remain on land in the kampung as free settlers.

With the growth of the town and the simultaneous breakdown of the 'fort' social formation, these people are now to some extent free from direct bondage to the royal families, especially in the daily running of their economic activities, and face the challenge of the new economic structure as independent townsmen, though their traditional ties with the royal families prove, in some cases, advantageous as we shall see. Their present and past employment may be shown in the following table:

Table 31
EMPLOYMENT AND EDUCATION OF THE LOCAL BORN COMMONERS*

Present Employment		*Education:* Std. 6+	*Below Std. 6*	*None*	*Past Employment*
Middle range:					
Drivers	(3)	1	2	—	Private in the Army, labourer, petty trader
Labourer in Singapore	(1)	—	—	1	labourer
Retired persons:					
On pension	(1)	1	—	—	clerk
Dependant on children	(1)	—	—	1	housewife
Total	(6)	2	2	2	

*Note: Save for one driver and labourer in Singapore, all are owners of house sites.

What the table suggests is that the pattern of employment of the local born commoners bears certain similarities to that of the royal persons; that is those who are educated up to Standard Six in the pre-war period were able to join the services of the government as shown by the case of the retired clerk and the case of the driver who was formerly in the armed forces. Otherwise they either resort to petty trading or freely selling their labour around the town as shown by their previous forms of employment.

However, it must be noted that their close contact with the royal families of the kampung has enabled some of them to change their employment from petty trading and wage labouring to that of drivers. The career of one driver, Ghani, illustrates this persistence of patronage. Starting to work as a labourer with one of the batik printing factories around the kampung, Ghani was facing serious economic difficulties in maintaining his household especially when his third child was born in early 1970 when the other two were attending primary school. With the help of a royal person in the kampung who occasionally summoned him for domestic help, especially on occasions like feasting, Ghani was able to obtain a job as a truck driver with a sawmill which has a long history of goodwill toward royal persons of the kampung.

Thus, we may suggest that while secular education is important in determining the types of employment and the economic positions of the local born commoners, it is also a fact that a traditional tie with the royal persons is advantageous.

The Settlers from the Vicinity

What determines economic differentiation between the households in the kampung discernible from these two categories of people are therefore secular educational qualifications and contacts with people who are in the position to 'negotiate' for employment. I believe this pattern to be pervasive to the town as a whole, and certainly it is the result of the growth of the town after the breakdown of the 'fort' settlement.

The pattern is also shown by the cases of people who have settled in the kampung from nearby areas. Their present and previous employment may be shown as follows:

Table 32
EMPLOYMENT AND EDUCATION OF SETTLERS FROM THE AREAS IN THE VICINITY

Present Employment		*Education:* *Std. 6+*	*Below Std. 6*	*None*	*Past Employment*
Owners of House Sites:					
Comfortable:					
Officers	(1)	1	—	—	—
Teachers	(2)	2	—	—	—
Clerks	(1)	1	—	—	—
Middle range:					
Drivers	(3)	—	3	—	—
Toilsome:					
Carpenters	(1)	—	—	1	—
Retired:					
On pension	(1)	1	—	—	School teacher
Dependant on children	(2)	—	—	2	Housewives
Total	(11)	5	3	3	
Tenants:					
Comfortable:					
Clerks	(1)	1	—	—	—
Middle range:					
Middleman	(1)	—	—	1	Trishaw pedaller
Firewood retailers	(1)	—	—	1	Trishaw pedaller
Night guards	(1)	—	—	1	Driver
Toilsome:					
Itinerant sellers	(1)	—	1	—	Driver
Trishaw pedallers	(2)	—	—	2	Fish monger, participant in land development scheme
Vendors	(1)	—	—	1	Labourer/trishaw pedaller
Labourer	(3)	—	—	3	—
Sellers	(1)	—	—	1	—
Domestic servants	(1)	—	—	1	—
Total	(13)	1	1	11	

As shown in the table, there is a marked difference between people who had the Standard Six education and those who do not have any secular education. Those who are educated up to Standard Six are employed in the forms of employment which we have classified as 'comfortable', and those who are educated below that level are employed in 'middle range' employment as drivers. Those without education are invariably employed in 'toilsome' employment.

I have argued that the amount of income derived from 'toilsome' employment is lower than the income from the other two types. Consequently, those who are employed in 'toilsome' employment have in the past changed their employment in the hope of securing a higher income. As may be seen from Table 32, all but one case[1] of those who are employed in 'toilsome' employment have previously been engaged in different forms of employment, while none of those people employed in the 'comfortable' employment have in the past been employed in different forms of employment. One worker in a 'toilsome' employment has even changed into a participant in the rural land development scheme (rubber) after previously working as a fishmonger. However, he experienced disappointment and dissatisfaction due to lack of immediate cash while waiting for the rubber to become productive; moreover, he seemed to prefer working in the town and town life. Thus he resorted to working as a trishaw pedaller.

In spite of frequent changes in the forms of employment by those people who are employed in 'toilsome' employment, there are only two people who subsequently improved their economic situation. These are the tenants employed as a middleman and a firewood retailer respectively. Both of these forms of employment are regarded as lower 'middle range' employment — a slight improvement from their previous employment as trishaw pedallers.

This therefore confirms the present contention that in the main, education or lack of it largely determines the type and the form of the employment one receives and consequently it underlies the economic differentiation between people in the kampung. As the cases of settlers from nearby reveal, education determines their employment in 'comfortable', 'middle range' or 'toilsome' employment, as the case may be. Whenever there are changes in the forms of employment due to an individual's hard work and personal dedication, they represent only small economic improvement — for instance the change from pedalling a trishaw to selling firewood.

Apart from creating such differentiated forms of employment and the resulting discrepancies in the economic situation between households of the kampung, the growth of the town has also meant a rapid natural increase in the population. A consequence is that there is a shortage of land for house sites; the town area is now congested. A significant number of people have been forced out of their original birthplaces as shown by the cases of these 24 settlers; some moved out due to family quarrels over inherited land,[2] while others opted to move simply due to either overcrowding on the family land, or overcrowding on the land where their parents were living free of any change as personal followers of the traditional landholders who were invariably royal persons or the favourites of the traditional royal households.

However, their methods of settling in the kampung differ from one another. These I believe are determined by the types of employment in which they are employed. As shown in Table 32, there is again a close relationship between those people who have always been employed in 'comfortable' and 'middle range' employment and the ownership of house sites in the kampung. In contrast, those who are employed at some stage in 'toilsome' employment seem to be exclusively settlers who are tenants.

In effect, we may suggest that the economic differences among the settlers from the areas in the vicinity are largely coterminous with their differences in terms of owners and tenants of house sites. Such an equation, however, demands a cautionary note, because there are slight possibilities of economic mobility among the tenants, one of them, in fact, is employed in a relatively high income employment as a clerk.

In general, the economic differentiation among the settlers from areas near the kampung is explicable in terms of their types of employment. This is to a large extent determined by the level of secular education which they have received, favours them in 'negotiation' for a particular form of employment. This however, does not discount the important factor of 'personal contact' in such 'negotiation'. In addition, personal dedication, shrewdness and calculation are also significant factors in determining types of employment, though they form no substitute for education. Such factors account for some people who are able to improve their economic situation a little. However, as mobility is rare, and at any rate it represents only little economic improvement, it seems plausible to argue that the economic positions of these people, and the present economic differences among them are determined by their economic positions prior to their settlement in the kampung.

Settlers from the Rural Areas

These patterns also apply to settlers who originated from rural areas.

This may be shown as follows:

Table 33
EMPLOYMENT AND EDUCATION OF SETTLERS FROM RURAL AREAS

Present Employment		*Education:* Std. 6	Below Std.6	Arabic School	None	*Past Employment*
Comfortable:						
Entrepreneurs	(2)*	—	2	—	—	—
Middle range:						
Drivers	(5)*	1	3	—	1	Labourer (1) Rural (1)
Stall operators	(2)	—	—	—	2	Waiter (1), fishing and trishaw pedalling
Overseers	(1)	—	—	—	1	Labourer/fishing
Middlemen	(1)	—	—	—	1	Rural
Night guard	(1)	—	1	—	—	Labourer/rural
Firewood retailers	(1)	—	—	—	1	Trishaw pedalling/fishing
Labourers in Singapore	(1)	—	—	—	1	Labourer/rural
Toilsome:						
Tailor/carpenters	(2)	—	—	1	1	Rural (2)
Labourers	(6)	—	—	—	6	Rural (6)
Vendors	(2)	—	1	—	1	Fishing/labourer trishaw pedalling /itinerant seller (1), driver Forestry Dept. (1)
Sellers	(3)	—	—	—	3	Rural (3)
Trishaw pedallers	(2)	—	—	—	2	Fishing (1), fishmonger (1)
Retired	(1)	1	—	—	—	Clerk
Total	(30)	2	7	1	20	(25)

*Note: The two entrepreneurs, one of the drivers and the retired clerk are owners of house sites.

The table shows that the factor of secular education again determines the forms of employment which the settlers from the rural areas pursue. For instance, individuals who are employed as entrepreneurs, clerks and drivers (which, according to our classification, would be classified as comfortable and middle range employment, have had some secular education. This, therefore, forms a significant contrast to the 15 people who are employed in 'toilsome' employment and who, save for one case of the vendor who was formerly employed as a driver with the Forestry Department, are all uneducated and illiterate. From this, we may suggest that differences in types of employment among these settlers are therefore attributable to the differences in their achievement of secular education.

This however does not discount the personal efforts of the entrepreneurs: that is, though both are educated up to no more than Standard Three, their education is supplemented by their personal dedication and shrewdness in business. This energy forms the foundation on which they achieve a economic status comparable to others who are employed in similar or other forms of 'comfortable' employment.

While such an explanation has some force, I believe an additional and perhaps more important explanation for the economic differentiation among the settlers from rural areas lies in their original economic position while they were in the rural areas. I believe this also explains the nature of their settlement in the kampung.

An individual's economic position and the differences among them prior to their migration to town are variables which must be examined in explaining the migration itself, the nature of their settlement in the kampung, and most importantly, the resultant differences in the forms and types of employment they are pursuing at present.

As may be seen from the table, the entrepreneurs, the retired clerk and the drivers have never changed their employment. In fact they migrated to town mainly to be close to the place of work in the case of the clerk, or to extend their business operations in the cases of entrepreneurs. They have always been better off than other rural migrants, and this has enabled them to purchase house sites in the kampung. In any case their migration to town was mainly for reasons of further improving their economic position, which had already been relatively high in the rural areas.

In contrast, all the other rural migrants were previously engaged in rural employment prior to their settlement in the kampung. They were sharecroppers or share tappers, and some were fishermen. They were either landless or their parents' land was not big enough to accommodate their group. It is a widely accepted view that land concentration and proletarianisation of rural population in Malaysia today is widespread (Syed Husin Ali, 1972), and this has thrown a large proportion of the rural poor into economic insecurity. This insecurity has pushed them into town because they believe that the town offers greater opportunities) for employment.

They migrated to town, but only to become tenants on house sites.

Upon settlement in the kampung they would turn to relatives or friends who could 'negotiate' for wage labour employment. This is simply because their main concern was security of income. After a while, either because their jobs paid too little or because they did not provide avenues for increasing their daily income (for example, the fixed daily wage labour employment in the sawmills or the factories), they turned to self-employment like vending, pedalling trishaws or being a middleman. As indicated earlier, they seem nowadays to believe that they are able to manipulate if not increase their daily income by exerting more energy or by working longer hours in such sef-empoyment. The main characteristics of employment among this category of rural migrants is that they are very prone to changing it every few years. Obviously some are able to improve themselves economically in the process, as implied by the number who are now employed in 'middle range' employment shown in Table 33. This however does not change their status of being tenants in the kampung.

In order to illustrate the pattern which creates economic differences among settlers from rural areas in the kampung, let us examine four cases which I believe are typical of these processes.

i) Pa'man came from a fishing village in the district of Pasir Puteh about forty miles from the town, where he owns a fishing boat and nets which are operated mostly by his kinsmen. His main task was to take charge of distributing the catch to the market in Kota Bharu. Subsequently, he purchased a small truck to transport and distribute not only the catch from his boat but also from other independent fishermen in the manner of a middleman. He latter expanded his operation to include trading in fruit, chiefly bananas. In 1960, he purchased a house site in the kampung which soon became his headquarters for trading operations.

ii) Hj. Pa'min came from a fishing village about fourteen miles from the town in 1958. He started as a labourer with the match factory and lived in quarters provided which were subsequently demolished due to their unpopularity among the workers. Due to his piety in religious practics, he was invited by the royal persons in the kampung to lead the nightly prayers at the prayer house in the kampung. This also provided him with the opportuity to rent a house site. In the early 1960's however, with the help of royal persons in the kampung, he was able to secure employment with the nearby sawmill and later was given the position as an overseer (*mandor*).

iii) Hamid came from one of the 'islands' (*pulau*) in the estuary of Sungai Kelantan. He had been pedalling a rented trishaw in between harvesting coconuts as a share-cropper. In 1968 he settled in the kampung by purchasing a house on a rented house site and devoted himself to full time trishaw pedalling. Dissatisfied with it, he started a street stall selling food and drinks in 1972.

iv) Pa'lah came from the same fishing village as Hj. Pa'min (case ii above) where 'being a member of a fishing crew was not a profitable employment'. As a result, he became an itinerant batik cloth seller, which took him to different parts of the Peninsula. After a time he settled as a labourer with a sawmill in the district town of Pasir Mas about twelve miles from Kota Bharu town. This was followed by a wage labour employment at a sawmill near the kampung — he had settled in the kampung in the early 1960's. These two actions were largely attributed to the help of Hj. Pa'min, a fellow-villager. Subsequently, he changed his employment to pedalling a rented trishaw and in 1972, he again changed his employment to vending bread.

These cases show that rural origins are not important in determining the types and forms of employment and the economic differentiation among new settlers. It is, rather, their economic position prior to their migration. As shown by these four cases, an already privileged person (case i) seemed to face no difficulties in the new environment of the town. In fact the town offers greater opportunities to accumulate more wealth. In contrast, those people who were already poor in rural areas came to town only to share the poverty of the poor townsmen as shown in case iv. While the town offers economic opportunities or employment for rural settlers, at the same time it maintains if not increases for rural settlers, at the same time it maintains if not increases their inherent economic differences in the new context.

However, it is not to be denied that there are opportunities of economic mobility inherant in their settlement in the kampung. As shown by case iii, personal dedication and enterprise has a place in the capitalist economic structure of the town. As I have indicated earlier, this has been the main attraction for migration to the town, i.e. the contrast between rural poverty and a vision of better economic opportunities in the town. In favourable circumstances therefore, this seems to compensate for the migrant's lack of secular education.

As a cautionary note, the question of 'personal contact' for 'negotiation' is also important (as shown in case ii). The proportion of those able to improve their economic position is small. Out of the total of 30 rural settlers, 25 can be classified as poor, of these only 9 have been able to shift from 'toilsome' to 'middle range' employment.

Economic differences prior to their settlement in the kampung, then, seem to affect present employment and economic positions. In fact they came to town for different reasons: the rich peasants migrated to town with the idea of increasing their wealth, as shown in the cases of the entrepreneurs, while the poor peasants migrated to town mainly with the hope of alleviating their poverty and economic insecurity.

Recapitulation

From the foregoing discussion, it is possible to suggest that the economic differentiation among the people in the kampung is largely determined by their socio-economic backgrounds. These may be stated as follows: regardless of the place of origin, employment and economic differences among people in the kampung seem to be largely determined by the level of their secular education and possession of 'proper contacts' to 'negotiate' for employment. There is some advantage in being royal or knowing royal persons because some of them hold positions of influence. It also follows that more poor people who only associate among themselves are encapsulated within the poor circle.

Thus rich peasants and advantaged urban dwellers constitute the rich class of the kampung. Their employment is much more stable, and more economically viable. They are more likely to be followed by their children who have the advantage of secular education. Their women are employed, if at all, in jobs which are relatively well rewarded.

People in this group clearly differ from poor migrant peasants and poor townsmen, who are uneducated and illiterate. Their income is low and variable. This leads to frequent changes in employment in order to fulfill their hope of earning more than their present income. This also forces their women into low income, dirtying employment, and their children are often recruited into similar types of work.

In between the two extremes, however, fall people who are in the intermediate economic situation which, from the above discussion, is evident by those who are employed in the 'middle range' employment. This class consists of local born people and settlers from the vicinity and from rural areas. The majority of people consists of those who have been able to improve economically through factors other than education, i.e. either the 'proper contacts' or personal energy. This class also includes women who enjoy the choice of being employed or of remaining housewives, and children who may or may not climb the economic ladder through education.

In essence, therefore, the economic differentiation between people on the basis of their objective positions in the productive system characterises the economic structure of the kampung. It is founded on the fact that the kampung is an urban ward where the economic differences between people takes the form of classes distinguishable into petty bourgeois and bureaucrats, an intermediate class who have established a stake in the town's economy, and the urban proletariat class. A privileged person then — one who has rich parents, high secular education or skills, and proper contacts, may achieve superior economic status regardless of his origin. Even royal persons, have to incorporate or recognise these new elements to supplement their royal birth. Otherwise, both the royal persons and the commoners would be forced into the state of poverty with few opportunities for improvement.

Footnotes

1. This is the case of the itinerant seller (*batik*) who was previously employed as a driver with the Malayan Tobacco Company. The case is however different from the rest of those employed in the 'toilsome' employment. For his change of employment from driving to an itinerant seller was not a matter of choice nor was it instigated by the desire to increase his income, simply because driving gives a higher income than such selling. He was rather dismissed from being a driver when the company ceased operation in Kelantan in 1971.

2. To cite one such case seems here necessary. On the death of his father, Nik Par who is working as a clerk found that he was not officially a share-owner of the inherited land. When a quarrel broke out with the members of his family, he chose not to remain on the land which is about one mile away, and rented a house site in the kampung.

CHAPTER SEVEN

STATUS IDENTIFICATION AND CLASSES

From our discussion so far, it is clear that social categories in the kampung overlap and cross-cut class differences. This would appear to dislocate expressive social relationships from relations of production. The former appear to be determined by subjective evaluation dominated by the notion of 'honoured' (*mulia*), whereas the latter are located within the new capitalist relations of production in the town. Expressive social relationships are also conceived differently: royal persons emphasise the persistence of '*daulat*' relations while commoners place greater importance on the ideology *mulia*. In this chapter, we will examine what this apparent disjunction between expressive social relationships and class relations means to the people concerned.

Expressive social relatioships are subjective in nature, and we may begin with Weber's notions of 'styles of life' and 'status honour' to form an analytical framework. 'Styles of life' is the 'ethos' of a group which is characterised by a particular manner of consumption, this goes hand in hand with 'opinions and attitudes and principles'. 'Status honour', on the one hand is the expression of differences in relative prestige between 'styles of life' which depend entirely on the 'positive or negative social estimation of honour' where "honour may be connected with any (non-economic) quality that is shared by a plurality". (Weber 1930, 47–48; Bendix 1960, 257–281; Gerth and Mills 1948, 180–195). An individual or group endowed with such 'quality' is therefore held in high esteem. In contrast, a person or a group lacking 'quality' is regarded as having low prestige. This then lead to differences, in terms of prestige, between individuals or groups. They may be seen, therefore, as being differentiated into distinct 'status groups'. One such group should then be exclusive from another and should relate to that of the other not only through 'distance' but also in terms of dominant and subordinate relationships. They are thus ordered hierarchically within a system of status stratification.

How is the central notion of 'honour' (*mulia*) meaningful to individuals in the kampung? It may be recalled that the 'honour' ideology emphasises such things as religiousness (feasting ad observing daily rituals), the use of proper language, including court language as necessary, proper manners and behaviour and abstention from coffee shops. Obviously the classification of individuals into categories which we call the feasting circle, individualists (land owning and tenants) and raft-users rests on this ideology. The feasting circle is distinguished from raft-users by being *mulia* rather than 'non-honoured' (*ta'guna*). Individualists are distinguished as people 'who take no notice of other people', they show no respect to the 'honoured' feasting circle (unlike the raft-users) and they are not placed into a definite category on the basis of the 'honour' ideology. In the kampung at least they seem to fall outside such an ideology. Instead, they constitute a homeless social category which is possible in the urban social milieu. So the notions of 'honour' and 'styles of life' as the principle underlying status group formation excludes the individualists. They shall be explained separately.

The Feasting Circle and Raft-Users

In suggesting that the feasting circle and raft-users are dominated by the *mulia* ideology, we may, following Weber, consider how far these two social categories form separate and discrete status groups. The characteristics which, according to Weber, constitute elements of their styles of life would be their patterns of consumption, their social behaviour and their ideas and principles they associate with it.

Let us examine their patterns of social behaviour. We have seen how members of the feasting circle regularly attend the prayer house, participate in the religious ritual of feasting, use 'court language' (*bahasa raja*) when it is proper to do so and refrain from 'conversing' and using vulgar language at coffee shops. In short they show a particular way of behaving and acting and this is described by the raft-users as 'proper and good behaviour'.

The raft-users however, show an opposite pattern of behaviour while regarding the pattern of behaviour of the feasting circle as 'good'. Specifically they are irregular in their attendance at the prayer house, do not participate in the feasting, and converse and use vulgar language at the coffee shops. They also gamble on cock-fights. This kind of behaviour is regarded as 'improper' or as 'bad behaviour' by people of the feasting circle, since gambling is abhorred by Islam.

What all this seems to imply is that there are clear cut ideas of what 'proper' and 'improper' behaviour entails. 'Proper' behaviour falls into the ideological sphere or the cultural-normative order, i.e. being a Malay and a Muslim. An individual in the kampung is expected to know and observe the kind of behaviour that Islamic religion requires, 'improper' behaviour, on the other hand, seems to be interpreted as defiance to the teachings of Islam. 'Proper' behaviour is held in high esteem, and individuals who exhibit such behaviour, like people of the feasting circle, are regarded as *mulia.* In contrast, individuals who overtly fail to comply with such principles as the raft-users are regarded as 'worthless' (*ta'guna*). Mutual evaluation between the two categories therefore places the feasting circle in the higher status position.

These ideas and principles governing their social behaviour are incongruent with their patterns of consumption. This contradition may be shown as follows:

Table 34
PATTERNS OF CONSUMPTION OF THE FEASTING CIRCLE AND THE RAFT-USERS

Categories	*Houses:* *Big Houses*	*Tiled Houses*	*Huts*
Feasting circle	9	3	—
Raft-users	—	7	25

	Ownership of Prestige Goods:				
	Motor-cars	*Television Sets*	*Motor-cycles*	*Bicycles*	*Transistor Radios*
Feasting circle	3	11	1	4	12
Raft-users	—	—	—	7	3

Even though the general pattern suggests that the high and varied consumption pattern is dominated by the feasting circle, there are significant variations within each category of people. For instance, unlike nine others in the category, three people of the feasting circle owned 'tiled houses' and so do seven raft-users who differ from others in the category who own 'huts'. The distribution of 11 bicycles and transistor radios also shows cross-cutting ownership of the goods between categories remarkably. The boundaries of consumption between the categories are unclear and the categories certainly do not constitute exclusive consumption groups.

Their pattern of consumption, indeed, is independent of the ideology governing their social behaviour. This however does not discount the fact that there are people within the feasting circle who own 'big houses' as well as prestige goods. They are the bureaucrats and petty bourgeois in the category identified earlier. Likewise there are poor raft-users who own 'huts' and do not possess any prestige goods. It is the middle subsistence class of the kampung which creates the discrepancy between social behaviour and consumption. The social behaviour of some of them is similar to some high consumption bureaucrats and petty bourgeois while others behave like poor raft-users. By generating the incongruence between social behaviour and consumption, they forestall the formation of status groups in the kampung.

We have shown in an earlier chapter that consumption is the function of household economic status. The consumption of bureaucrats and petty bourgeois therefore are not only high but appear to be exclusive, because their positions in the capitalist production of the town are the most rewarding. Other people in the kampung are employed in less rewarding employment. Being the poor of the town, these proletariat and poor self-employed seldom own expensive houses or superfluous prestige goods. Therefore, rather than the ideology of 'honoured' and the ideas and principles associated with it, it is their class positions which governs their patterns of consumption. This is further shown by employment of women and children as may be summarised in the following table:

Table 35
EMPLOYMENT OF WOMEN AND CHILDREN OF THE FEASTING CIRCLE AND THE RAFT-USERS

	Employment of Wives:		
Categories	*Working Wives*		*Not Working Wives*
Feasting circle	dyeing batik cloth	(3)	5
	teaching	(1)	
	shop keeping	(2)	
Raft-users	dyeing batik cloth	(15)	3
	labouring in factory	(3)	
	selling at market	(1)	
	traditional masseuse	(1)	

	Employment of Children:			
	White-Collar	*Labourer*	*Labourer in Singapore*	*Unemployed*
Feasting circle	3	2	2	2
Raft-users	2	8	1	20

The table shows that there are three women of the feasting circle employed in the same employment as most raft-users' women — dyeing batik cloth. There are also three raft-users women who are not working, resembling five women of the feasting circle. These latter group of women either belong to the rich households of bureaucrats and petty bourgeois or to households which are not so poor as to force their women into employment. These women would be employed only if employment is economically rewarding or if they have appropriate education to qualify them for employment in a white-collar job. Otherwise they remain 'not working'. Household economic status certainly determine the pattern of employment of these women.

In fact it extends to govern the employment of children as well. As shown in Table 35, the children of the poor raft-users constitute the majority of those who are unemployed. As discussed earlier, this is largely because poor parents are unable to finance the education of the children sufficiently and being poor, they also lack access to the right persons who are capable of 'negotiating' an employment, especially the white collar employment.

It is true that each element of 'styles of life' is independently evaluated; for instance social behaviour depends on whether one is considered to have 'proper behaviour', that of consumption depends on whether one shows a high pattern of consumption; that of employment depends on the nature of work and the income derived therefrom; women are evaluated in terms of ideal employment for women; and the children are evaluated in terms of their employment in desired white collar jobs. All these result in the conception of an ideal, prestigious style of life, where all the desired elements are present, in polar contrast to a style of life in which the desired elements are absent. Consequently, the most valued and the most prestigious style of life is one which is expressive of 'proper social behaviour', comfortable employment, a high level of consumption with the wife either not working or working in high income and non-dirtying employment, and with the children showing success in achieving the desired white collar employment (cf. Syed Husin Alatas, 1968), somewhat idealising the mode of living characteristic of the indigenous ruling class.

Paradoxically however, their ideal mode of living fails to take place among people other than bureaucrats and petty bourgeois because their class positions do not allow their consumption to coincide with the ideal patterns of social behaviour. Class difference cuts across categories thus denying the social categories to form status groups. To put it in Weberian terms, these two categories lack the 'ethos' which is essential to define social categories as 'status groups; leading different styles of life.

To describe the feasting circle and raft-users as two 'status groups' in a pure Weberian sense is therefore misleading if not erroneous. A description of the categories as classes is similarly untenable and unacceptable to the people concerned. The ideology of *mulia* as the ideal principle of social relations is conceived to be real and effective. People see themselves as ordered in status groups rather than their respective objective class position. The latter has become unreal, and may well exist only in the minds of the people concerned. Corollarily their expressive social relationships are dislocated from their social relations. In other words, their subjective evaluation (ideology of *mulia*) undermines their objective class relations, distorts images of class in the kampung and subverts class consciousness as a whole.

Status Identification

Classifying themselves into the honoured and non-honoured rather than the rich and poor, the people of the kampung generate a system of inequality which may be called status identification. This seems to be expressed in several ways.

The first of these lies in the subjective meaning of the expressive social relationships between the feasting circle and raft-users. As we noted earlier, the two categories relate to each other in the manner of what we have termed the 'deferential greeting' relationship. Following Goodenough (1965), we can distinguish two basic properties of such a relationship: one is the 'rights' (over), and the other is 'duty' (owed); the 'rights' being the claim of a superior position in the particular interaction, and 'duty' is essentially the acceptance of the inferior position.

When people of the feasting circle elicit deference from the raft-users whenever and wherever the two meet, we may suggest that the raft-users owe 'duty' to the feasting circle who is return claim 'rights' over the raft-users. This exchange of 'rights' and 'duty' implies that there is an exchange of social estimation of each other, i.e. while the feasting circle regards the raft-users as being in the lower 'status' position, the latter accepts such a position and in return gives recognition to the superior 'status' position of the feasting circle.

Such a relationship shows that both categories of people have definite claims to certain status identities. The raft-users identify themselves as the 'non-honoured' status group, inferior to the feasting circle, and likewise, the feasting circle identify themselves as the higher 'honoured' status group which makes them superior to the raft-users. The manner through which one group relates to the other therefore shows how the individual of each category expresses not only his identification to different 'status' position, but this also shows that the very way of relating they adopt is in turn determined by such identification.

This 'status' identification is further expressed by individuals' *choice* of meeting places for leisure. As we mentioned earlier, the people of the feasting circle congregate nightly at the prayer house, and raft-users gather at coffee shops. Attendance at the prayer house is regarded as an element of the 'honoured' position, and 'conversing' at coffee shops is associated with the 'non-honoured' position.

Given this identification to two different 'status' positions, the people of the feasting circle are therefore differentiated from the raft-users and vice versa. What separates them from each other is their conscious identification to different 'status' as it is expressed in their daily behaviour: while the feasting circle chooses to observe the attributes of religiousness and consciously conform to the general ideology of proper behaviour, the raft-users prefers to abstain from doing so.

To put it in their own way, this is expressed in the notion of 'compatibility' (*padan*). For instance, the people of the feasting circle seem to believe that 'proper behaviour' is 'compatible' with 'our way', and similarly the raft-users seem to regard that (sinful) gambling, 'conversing' at coffee shops and absence from nightly prayers at the prayer house are 'compatible' with 'our way'. What is identified as being 'compatible' by people of one category as their way then becomes 'incompatible' for people of the other category. This 'opposition of compatibilities' shows that people of each category see themselves as belonging to a definite 'status' group. Thus when people of the feasting circle wear clean and to some extent smart clothing, the raft-users do not; and when people of the feasting circle converse with one another in polite expressions to talk to one another. What people of each category see as 'compatible' with their 'status' positions essentially orders their daily behaviour. As 'compatibility' in this sense is defined in terms of opposing 'honoured' and 'non-honoured', it therefore suggests that the notion 'compatibility' is a direct expression of individuals' identification with a particular 'status'.

As an illustration, I observed that on many occasions, the raft-users behaved differently when they are outside the kampung social environment. To cite one particular case, a raft-user was observed to wear a set of clothing different from what he normally wore when he was going to the town centre for an appointment with a dentist. This particular pattern of behaviour expresses the fact that outside the kampung social environment, the ideology of the kampung cease to be a coercive force on the behaviour of the individual, that is his behaviour is no more governed by the notion of 'compatibility'. Therefore he does not have to behave in the manner in which he behaves in the kampung while he is in the town centre. To put it in other terms, the behaviour of any individual of the two categories in places other than the kampung need not necessarily express his 'status' identity.

The fact that the behaviour of an individual in places outside the kampung is different from his behaviour in the kampung strengthens the suggestion that the latter is essentially an expression of his identification with a particular 'status' position. It determines his daily behaviour, and necessarily differentiates the individuals in the kampung into two supposedly different 'status' groups of the feasting circle and the raft-users. It is so real to the people concerned that it separates the two categories from each other in daily social life.

Identification and Class

In suggesting that the two categories are mutually exclusive in social terms due to their identification were two different 'status' positions, it is also possible to argue that class positions and likewise class relations become confused and at any rate unreal. I see this as shown in the individual's choice whether or not to feast.

As I have indicated above, the middle class of the kampung consists of some people from the feasting circle as well as some raft-users. The former include those people who are employed as the overseer, drivers, a firewood retailer and two retired individuals who are on a monthly pension from the government. On the count of their monthly income and their employment they are then economically similar to some raft-users who are employed as drivers, middlemen, stall operators, night guards and labourers in Singapore. In fact some of them show a striking similarity in their pattern of consumption in that they own 'tiled houses' similar to houses owned by some of these raft-users.

However, people of the feasting circle in this class choose to feast, while raft-users do not. This implies that the two categories of people choose to identify to two different status positions. As I have indicated earlier, feasting involves an expenditure of a certain level of surplus wealth or a form of public display of wealth possible only among the rich in high status group. For it is only the wealthy who would choose to expend their economic surplus in this economically unrewarding manner. But when there are few middle class individuals of the raft-users category choose not to feast, we may argue that the choice to feast among the middle class is not more than mere expression of identification to the wealthy and supposedly high status position. They consciously differentiate themselves from the rest of the middle class who do not feast and who seem to choose to identify themselves with the poor supposedly low status raft-users. There is thus an opposing identification and differentiation of the middle class into two supposedly different status positions. They are both recognised and regarded as real by people of the kampung, and this fact significantly distorts the reality of classes and relations in the kampung.

Social Inequality and Social Mobility

In essence, therefore, we may suggest that people of the feasting circle identify to the higher and dominant status position, while at the same time the raft-users seem to express subordinate and inferior status position. This determines their lines of social intercourse, their manner of relating, their association with others in the kampung and it demarcates their places for leisure activities. In short, the identification affects the social life of the two categories of people as a whole.

The positions of these categories may be seen as subjectively arranged in a hierarchy of perceived status positions with the feasting circle superior to and dominating the raft-users. The only thing which separates them is the subjective acceptance of their relative positions as manifested by their subscription to the belief that they are 'compatible' to particular patterns of activities and behaviour which are different for each category. By this very fact there is mutual recognition of each other's status position in a non-antogonistic and interdependent manner, sonewhat refurbishing the indigenous '*daulat*' class relations. To revive the indigenous class relations supported by the ruling class dichotomy of '*daulat*' and 'non-*daulat*' is however impossible. The productive system of the town has changed and now denies the persistence of such class division. Capital has introduced capitalist relations of production and people in the kampung have been slotted into one position or the other within a capitalist mode of production. Incorporation of these people into capitalits relations of production however is highly selective. There are some who are directly and completely proletarianised and there are others who exist on the fringes of capitalist production like the service workers and petty traders. But like the proletariat, they are also important to capital.

It is this incomplete capitalisation of the town which allows indigenous class relations to persist in the minds of people in the kampung. Instead of pure '*daulat*' relations however, ideas about social relations have been modified to centre on the ideology of 'honoured' where religiousness is a strong determinant. This process incorporates and makes social relations generated by the new mode of production meaningful to the people concerned. It does not constitute a challenge to capital, and so it is condoned, if not promoted by capital.

The inequality system which arises is however, not a rigid one. As I have been suggesting throughout this chapter, it is essentially based on individual choice, that is one has the choice to feast, to attend to nightly prayers, to abstain from congregating at coffee shops and ideally to show a high level of consumption. In other words there seems to be a strong possibility of mobility into the dominant positions if one chooses to adhere to 'honoured' characteristics. Individuals who show a high level of wealth, but do not subscribe to the patterns of behaviour which are regarded as 'proper', as for instance the wealthy individualists (below), are not regarded as 'honoured' in the context of the ideology prevailing in the kampung. Similarly individuals who show a pattern of social behaviour equal to the members of the feasting circle, but without displaying the requisite possession of economic surplus through feasting, would be excluded from the group of 'honoured' people. As an illustration of the latter case, let us discuss the position of Pa'mud who sometimes acts as the prayer caller (*bilal*) at the prayer house of the kampung.

Pa'mud is a night guard and lives in a 'tiled house' which he shares with one of his married daughters. He sometimes acts as the prayer caller and is always present at the nightly prayers before he goes to work. He abstains completely from attending the coffee shops. However, he does not feast and only acts as a helper at the feasts given by some people of the feasting circle. To both people of the feasting circle and the raft-pusers Pa'mud is therefore regarded as a pious (*lebai*) person but not an 'honoured' one. It seems that he is not accepted as an equal by the people of the feasting circle. At the same time, however, he does not spend his leisure time with the raft-users.

From this case, it is possible to generalise that the people who are able to identify to the 'honoured' position are those who can afford to display economic surplus and adhere to 'proper behaviour'. This combination is hardly separable, in fact, since prior to the social recognition of being 'honoured' one has to feast where expenditure of economic surplus is inevitable. Thus neither the class criterion alone, nor 'proper behaviour' in itself qualifies an individual to the dominant position; but while both are required for social recognition to the dominant position, the economic surplus is still the stronger determinant.

In other words, though the identification system is open and it is partly dependent on the individual's choice, the economic condition of relative economic security shown by surplus expended at feasting on top of the individual's conformity to the ideology of 'honoured' (religiousness and proper behaviour) determines social mobility in the present case. Being able to adhere to either one of these two general conditions would only leave an individual in an anomalous position, if not in the position as adjunct to the individuals in the dominant position as in the case of Pa'mud above. This, I believe is one of the characteristics of inequality system where capital dominates without disolving pre-capitalist relations.

As it is perceived by people within it, status groups then form non-discrete social groups, and class becomes merely an indicator of employment and income. In this situation, it is possible for a worker to be thoroughly exploited by capital, but any traits of alienation and proletarianisation of his life resulting therefrom are cushioned by the imagined persistence of indigenous social relations where the objective economic position within the productive system is legitimised and dominated by the prevailing bourgeois ideology of 'honoured'. Class position and exploitation of workers in the town are then regarded by all the people concerned as irrelevant to their daily social life. Classes and class relations are secondary issues as far as they are concerned. Likewise, the emerging pattern of inequality is not explained in class terms. Instead the ideology of 'honoured' (mainly religiousness and proper behaviour) and the system of inequality it generates is regarded as real, effective and legitimate. In short, even though class relations dominate and order their everyday existence, the people of the kampung still regard them as alien and foreign.

Identification and Marriage

To illustrate how real and effective the inequality system is in the kampung, let us examine the pattern of marriage. I believe this is one area of social life in the kampung where identification to a particular status is most clearly and pervasively expressed.

During the period of observation, there was one case of marriage and one case of a rejected marriage proposal in the kampung. These may be described as follows:

a) Mail is the son of an individualist who is a firewood retailer. He has been employed as a driver with a Chinese biscuit wholesaler since the beginning of 1975, and has been secretly courting a daughter of a person of the feasting circle, Hj. Pa'min. With the security of a steady income, he expressed his desire to marry the girl to his parents who, on his behalf, proposed the marriage to Hj. Pa'min. The latter however, rejected the marriage proposal mainly on the grounds that Mail does not behave 'properly'. For one, Mail does not attend nightly prayers.

b) Din came from a rural village about 8 miles away from the town in

February 1975 to work in a batik printing factory in the kampung. At night time he spends most of his time at the coffee shops conversing and playing cards with most of the raft-users including Derome whose niece is a young eligible woman. By May 1975, Din was observed to be courting the niece of Derome and on 26th July, the two were married. The marriage ceremony however, took place in the rural village where the girl came from.

What seems important from these two cases is that the pattern of marriage in the kampung is significantly determined by the notion of 'compatibility' of perceived status identity, that is when the status positions of the two potential allies are regarded as being 'compatible' by the two parties concerned, the marriage proposal is accepted and marriage occurs. Otherwise, the marriage proposal is rejected. In order to generalise further however, I believe it is necessary to examine 17 cases of marriage which occurred in 1970–1975 which were investigated. This may be shown as follows:

Table 36
MARRIAGE BETWEEN CATEGORIES

i) Marriage within the Kampung:

Group I (male)		*Group II (female)* F/C	*Ind.*	*R/U*	*Relative*
Feasting circle	2(1r)	1	—	1*	—
Raft-users	2	—	1	1	—

ii) Marriage with persons outside the Kampung:

Categories	*People in kampung:* Male	*Female*	*Origin of Spouse: Rural* M	*Rural* F	*Vicinity* M	*Vicinity* F	*Employment Male Spouse*	*Relative*
Feasting circle	2(1r)	3(1r)	3	1	—	1-(r)	teacher (1) drivers (2)	4
Individualists	—	2	1	—	1	—	teacher/clerk	1
Raft-users	1(r)	5	5	—	—	1	stall operators soldiers night guards labourers (2)	—
Total	3(2r)	10(1r)	9	1	1	2		5

Key: i. F/C, Ind. and R/U indicate the feasting circle, individualists and the raft-users groups respectively.
ii. (r) indicates the number of persons who are royal by origin.
iii. * asterisk indicates disapproved marriage.

The tables show us that marriage proposals within the kampung seem to be accepted and exchanged within the confines of perceived status groups. As may be seen from Table 36(i), the people of the feasting circle exchange children only with another feasting circle just as the raft-users exchange children among themselves. Marriage proposals between supposedly different status groups, if any, are therefore rejected. The rejection however, is done by the members of the supposedly higher status group, as in the case of Hj. Pa'min above.

However, it may also be noted that marriage between the two categories of feasting circle and raft-users may in certain circumstances occur.[1] In particular, this occurs when the male children of the feasting circle choose to marry women from a supposedly lower status group like the raft-users. As shown in Table 36(i), there is one such case in the kampung. However, the marriage is seen as improper and incompatible by the feasting circle, in which case he expressed strong disapproval of the marriage to the effect that the married couple had to 'run away' or settle away from the kampung. Marriage which occurred in such circumstances does not create alliances nor does it amount to an exchange of children between two families.

Marriage patterns in the kampung therefore show a strong tendency for the feasting circle group to be endogamous. Marrying down for females seems to be prevented through rejection of marriage proposals, and it seems to be strongly discouraged for males to do so by expressing disapproval.

Marriage with persons from outside the kampung follows a somewhat similar pattern. As may be seen from Table 36(ii), both the feasting circle and the raft-users receive 'in-laws' (*menantu*) who supposedly share the same status positions. In particular, the people of the feasting circle concerned seem to receive male 'in-laws' who show evidences of similarities in terms of their employment as teachers and drivers. They also seem to create alliances within their kinship group as shown by the fact that all but one royal (female) cases of marriage among children of the feasting circle occur with outsiders who are relatives.

Similarly, the children of the raft-users tend to marry people supposedly from the same status group. As shown in Table 36(ii), save for one case of the female who married a soldier (a private in the Armed Forces), all other 4 female raft-users married rural people who had migrated to town to find employment and who are not relatives. The same is true for the males; for instance the male royal person in the category married a labourer who came from an area in the vicinity. In any case, and disregarding the endogamous (kinship) nature of marriage with people from outside the kampung among the children of the feasting circle, we may suggest that the marriage patterns among the feasting circle and the raft-users seem to emphasis their perceived status identity.

Such patterns of marriage within the kampung and with persons from outside the kampung tend to disregard both the kind of birth (royal and commoner) as well as the place of origin of the individuals concerned. As may be seen from the tables above, the royal persons (males and females) marry royal persons and commoners alike, or there seems to be little significance in whether one is rural or town by origin. For instance, two royal males of the feasting circle marry a commoner female within the same circle (Table 36(i)) and a royal female in an area in the vicinity (Table 36(ii)). Likewise a royal female of the feasting circle married a commoner male teacher from a rural area (Table 36(ii), and the royal male raft-user married a commoner female who is a labourer (Table 36(ii)). The significant fact here is that perceived status considerations seem to take precedence over royal birth or place of birth. In short, marriage patterns for the people in the kampung seem to be horizontal exchange of marriage proposals within the confines of perceived status boundaries.

One reason for such patterns of marriage, we may argue, is that it is one sphere of social life in the kampung in which people express 'compatibility' of their perceived status identity, i.e. unless the two potential partners in marriage are regarded to be within more or less the same status position, the marriage and consequently the alliance between their families would not occur. Even if a marriage occurs as a result of an independent act of the males, such marriage would be disapproved, and no alliance would occur.

In other words, marriage in the kampung tends to be endogamous along perceived status lines and also, alliances in these cases are no more than an expression of similarity in identity. What this amounts to, therefore, is that marriage is the most real manifestation of the expression of identification to a particular status by the people of the feasting circle as well as by the raft-users.

However, it is important to note that to a large extent this expression of similarities in the identity perceived or alliances through marriage is possible because the institution of marriage persists largely in the traditional manner of 'arranged marriage' (Swift 1963) or marriage which occurs only after a period of negotiation between two parents concerned. Marriage proposals are therefore subjected to detailed investigation by both parents as regards the behaviour, employment and ancestors' behaviour, and employment of the prospective 'in-law' (*manantu*). It is only when such investigation proves positive in the sense that there are evidences of 'compatibility' of perceived status between the two households concerned that marriage and alliance occur.

The Individualists

Let us now turn to the group in the kampung whom we have described as individualists. We suggested earlier in the chapter that these people from outside the ideological system of the kampung and that their social life is located in the wider town or Kota Bharu. I see this conclusion as supported by several considerations.

Firstly, as we have noted, the individualists are distiguishable as a social category on the grounds that they relate to people of the other categories through mutual greetings. These greetings, we suggested, imply mutual exchange of non-recognition of each other's superior position between two interacting individuals, i.e. the relationship neither signifies claims to 'rights' over the greeted party, nor does it imply an owing of 'duty' by the greeted party.

As such the individualists show us respect towards the feasting circle and demand no respect from the raft-users. Likewise they are regarded neither as equals nor subordinates by the feasting circle, and neither as superiors nor equals by the raft-users. The individualists as a social category in the kampung, therefore, are made up of people who do not subscribe to the ideology of the kampung and consequently they do not seem to have a definite position in its system of social inequality.

There are also differences in terms of social behaviour among the individualists themselves. One person of the category feasts, for example, but the feasting is neither complemented by his attendance at the prayer house nor does it involve invitees from the kampung. There are people in the category who very rarely attend the prayers at the prayer house, and at the same time there are people who 'converse' at coffee shops, but the chatting is restricted only to fellow workers and at coffee shops outside the kampung. Apart from this diversity in social behaviour, they also relate to one another (if they are not relatives) in the same manner as they relate to people of the other two categories in the kampung, i.e through mutual greetings.

In terms of social behaviour, the individualists as a social category are neither exclusive nor homogeneous. Out of such diversity however, the individualists tend to show one common characteristic: that on the whole, their behaviour is oriented outside the social life of the kampung.

We may also recall that individualists are distinguishable in terms of their economic status as rich, intermediate and poor individualists as shown in Chapter 5. What this amounts to is that some of these people, especially those who are wealthy, are in a position to claim high positions within the status system of the kampung. Instead of doing so, however, they choose to show a high level of consumption which is expressive of high wealth or a crude expression of their class position. In addition, some choose to feast without inviting people from the kampung and, more importantly, without showing the traits of 'proper behaviour' as these are defined by the ideology of the kampung. This again seems to be another direct expression of high class position typical of wealthy individuals in the town, and perhaps of the urban areas of Malaysia generally.

On the one hand, wealthy bureaucrats and petty bourgeois individualists seem to disregard the 'honoured' ideology of the kampung by not advancing claims to any position in its system of social inequality. On the other, they are expressing a challenge to indigenous social relations existing in the kampung by emphasising class attribute of wealth, or the capitalist relations of production.

Given the fact that the kampung is located with the contexts of Kota Bharu and urban Malaysia as a whole, the individualists' emphasis on their class position seems to show that their points of reference lie outside the social boundary of the kampung. In short, their residence in the kampung need not necessarily mean their subjugation to the local ideology and its attendant distortions of social relations.

Recapitulation

In essence therefore, we suggest that social relations in the kampung today are distorted because of incomplete capitalisation which allows indigenous relations of production in somewhat modified form to persist, at least in the minds of the people. The relations are meaningfully and legitimately conceived (by the people concerned) in the form of the 'honoured' ideology determined largely by the notions of religiousness and proper behaviour which supposedly sort people into high and low status groups. Of course the real determinant of such a subjective classification is mainly class, or the objective position of a person within the productive system of the town, but the people deny this and make such considerations subject to the dominance of the honoured ideology. This gives way for the not so rich and the not so poor to identify themselves subjectively with the supposedly high or low status groups respectively. This distortion of class and its relations in this manner is characteristics of social relations in this underdeveloped town where ideas about indigenous relations of production persist strongly but not to the disadvantage of capital.

Footnotes

1. This is possible due to the provision in the Muslim law that males need not necessarily have approval from parents in order to marry, and this seems to be augmented by the choice of partners from 'love affairs'.

CHAPTER EIGHT

FROM *DAULAT* TO URBAN RELATIONS

Kampung Bendahara is a ward of Kota Bharu town. In spite of some strong claims made by some of its residents as regards to its exclusiveness as a kampung in the Malay sense of a villiage, it is neither an autonomous social unit, nor is it an isolated urban villiage. It is in fact part of the wider urban milieu of the town with the residents forming a small proportion of the urban population in contrast to the mass of rural peasants of the state. The patterns of social life and social dynamics of the kampung are therefore reflections of the overall social relations operating in the urban formation as a whole. In the same way, the implications of change which may be drawn from the present study of the kampung would reflect the process of change occurring in the bigger social formation of the town generally.

I have stated at the outset that the aim of this study is to outline the changes in the social relations of Kota Bharu town. More specifically, I posed the problem of changes in the patterns of social formations in the town following the shift in its mode of production from an indigenous one to present day Western capitalism. In the light of the preceding discussion, it is now possible to suggest the implications of historical change which has taken place in the town.

i. Urban expansion changed the physical character of the conglomeration from the walled estates of the royal families into urban wards around a town centre.

From the inception of British interests in Kelantan in the late 19th century, and the subsequent bureaucratic changes associated with colonial political control, Kota Bharu town started slowly to centralise the political, economic and social life of Kelantan in the sense of becoming the seat of capital in the state as it is today.

For the peasants in the rural areas, the town has become the centre of attraction; for the rich peasants, it offers opportunities to accumulate and expand their wealth; while for the majority of the poor, especially the landless peasants, the town promises alternate forms of subsistance. The town has become the symbol of everything western if not modern. Consequently, there is an influx of rural peasants, especially males, into the town (Statistics Department 1971, 19). However, just like any other town in Malaysia, such migration leads to settlement in the already predominantly Malay residential areas (McGee 1968, 225; Hamzah Sendut 1962). This is either because poor migrant peasants are able to seek help from relatives and friends who have migrated earlier in order to survive in the new and different envinment, or because rich peasants are able to buy house sites from the original owners who are also Malays. Within the context of the general increase in the population, Kota Bharu has become the most densly populated town in Kelantan, and in the geographical sense, the most urbanised area in the state (Hamzah Sendut *op. cit.,* 122; Dobby 1951).

Physically, each town ward therefore consists of migrant peasants and townsmen living close together, either on their own land or on land rented from original land holders, who are mostly royal persons. They live in houses which range from expensive brick and high quality timber houses, to less expensive medium quality timber houses, and finally to cheap and low quality timber houses or 'huts'. In other words, the various classes live alongside one another within the same ward, instead of being segregated into high or low class zones (cf. Neil 1966). In effect each town ward (kampung) which emerged from indigenous fort settlement is a residential area which is distinguishable from another only on the basis of residential classification or their different names.

In short, the nucleated 'fort' settlement or the estates of the royal families of Kota Bharu are now subdivided into house lots or house sites, and these are again compartmentalised into residential units by crosscutting road patterns.

ii. The emergence of the town as the centre of capitalism in the state gives rise to distinct classes of people based on their types of employment.

One of the most important changes following the expansion of the town is the dominance of capitalist mode of production. In particular, the changes in the political system from the absolute domination by the *'daulat'* class to colonial rule was followed by the rise of commerce and industry. While the political change gives rise to a class of bureaucrats, the rise of commerce and industry creates various classes of merchants, businessmen, petty traders, service and transport workers (cf. Nash *op. cit.* 117-118). In short, the people of the town are now distinguished from one another mainly on the bases of their types of employment which are locally classified into 'comfortable', 'middle range' and 'toilsome' employment. These emphasise leisure and high esteem at one extreme and lowly regarded heavy physical labour at the other. The scheme of classification is also congruent with the division of people into wealthy bureaucrats and petty bourgeois, less wealthy semi-manual workers and exploited wage labourers, poor petty traders.

One of the most important charactaristics of these classes is the employment of women and children: the wives of the high class individuals are either employed in high income, non dirtying employment or remain as housewives; the wives of the middle class have the option to be employed or to remain as housewives; and the wives of the poor class individuals are compelled to work in any available form of employment in order to supplement the incomes of their husbands. In addition, the rate of success in achieving the desired white-collar employment among the children of these classes varies from high in the rich class to extremely low in the poor class, in which case the children as a whole are generally employed, if at all, in types of employment, similar to those of their parents.

McGee has argued that a certain proportion of the poor class whom he calls the 'proto-proletariat' is characterised by subsistance. They are migrant peasants who are employed in low capital employment, and this he argues further is attributable to their peasantry characteristics (1973 *op. cit.*). In fact McGee assumes that petty trading and the like self-employments are part and parcel of the bazaar economic system which characterised the traditional Malay world (1968 *op. cit.*). The description is certainly true for some subsistence[1] townsmen who are employed in middle range employment either in wage labour or in self-employment. Their type of employment is sufficiently rewarding to meet their daily requirement and needs. In short, they have enough to exist from day to day.

It is however doubtful whether the poor self-employed class may be included in the same category as the proto-proletariat. Far from being subsistence, they are poor and hardly able to reproduce their labour power. They are the urban poor who are created by capital and form the potential labour force for further exploitation and expansion of capital. They may not be seen as directly related to capital as the wage labourers, but one must take into account that the productive system of the town is structured (by capital) in such a way that this form of employment is the only opportunity open to some of the urban poor. A member of the urban poor who does not sell his labour to become a wage labourer is forced into self-employment but without a significant difference in the amount of income he would have received as a wage labourer. The former only allows a member of the poor to manipulate the flow of his daily income. However, whenever wage labour employment offers a higher income, there is a tendency for the urban poor to opt for it even if it means travelling to distant places like Singapore and Kuala Lumpur.

To a large extent, therefore, it is the lowly paid wage labour employment in Kota Bharu which promotes petty trading, trishaw pedalling and the like forms of self-employments in the town.

In other words, these self-employeds are the potential industrial labour force of the town who in fact presently help to keep the wages of wage labourers low. So together with the wage labourers, they constitute the poor class who may be simply described as poor. This also emphasises the process of improverishment which operates to create what they are today. For instance, the poor as a whole describe their employment as 'toilsome' employment regardless of whether they are wage labourers or self-employed. All they possess is their labour (*modal reng*) which may be utilised independently on their own in self-employment or to be sold to the capitalists in the town.

So while the life of wealthy class individuals (bureaucrats and petty bourgeois) is marked by a certain degree of leisure, some townsmen exist at the level of subsistence, the bulk of the population who may be classed as the urban poor are all struggling to make a living within the capitalist mode of production. Regardless of whether one is rural or town-born, *daulat* or commoner, the capitalist relations of production which emphasise ownership of capital, exploitation of cheap labour, secular education and the important factor of personal contact to 'negotiate' for an employment inevitably create different classes of people. In short, Kota Bharu town has now changed from being a centre serving the *daulat* class into a centre where capital dominates to effect a class formation mainly based on types of employment.

iii. The new physical and productive system of the town forms the basis for a distinct pattern of social life characteristic of the urban Kota Bharu.

The people of Kota Bharu may subjectively see themselves as urban townsmen and consider themselves different from other Malays in Kelantan. Though this may be true and they are in return classified by other people as the most urbanised (*hilir*), we are not going to dwell at this point on the futile argument about the rural-urban diachotomy (McGee 1968, *op. cit.,* 146) and the artificial problems associated with the so-called dual economic structure (Stavenhagen 1968: Griffin 1973). Our immediate concern is to consider the objective state of social life which the new productive system generates.

Types and forms of employment which concern direct cash income in the forms of salaries, wages and earnings from services rendered are important to each and every townsmen, especially the poor. Economic differentiation and the division of labour in the new productive system affect the operation of social institution and practices which are traditionally associated with the Malay community. For instance, the institution of economic co-operation (*gotong royong*) in the kampung now takes a different form from what it is understood and practices by the Malays. Rather than forced by communal spirit of self-help and neighbourling feeling (Swift 1965, *op. cit.,* 164; Firth 1966, *op. cit.,* 4), participation in co-operative work as in making and mending the raft is more akin to membership in a voluntary association where individuals who are too poor to buy individual water pumps or to erect indoor sanitation facilities are forced to co-operate with one another. It is their basic daily requirements and needs which bought about such co-operation. The traditional communal co-operative spirit persists, if at all, in the minds of the people as a ready-made framework which may be utilised when the occasion and the time requires it.

The uneven operation of social institutions in the kampung is also observable in the case of the prayer house (*madrasah*) as the centre of Malay community. Traditionally, it is the principle institution around which village life persists (Firth 1966, *op. cit.,* 19). But is is observed that the *madrasah* in the kampung is only meaningful to a certain proportion of the population. The fact that the kampung is located within the bigger capitalist framework of the town, the country and the capitalist world as a whole, the capitalist relations of production have thrown some people into the 'anonymity and self-seeking of the town' (Swift 1965, *op. cit.,* 150). Others remain alien to it. The ideology prevailing in the kampung is therefore non-encompassing and segmental. It is real and meaningful only to those who choose to be subjected to it.

This uneven subjection of the prevailing ideology is the reverse side of the coin to uneven subsumption of capital and the consequent dislocation within the social formation (Taylor 1979). Some people are completely absorbed into capitalist relations of production; therefore they are freed from the confines of the indigenous ideology, when they choose to do so. Some others may be economically dependent on capitalist production, either directly or indirectly, but this does not mean that they are automatically subjected to the ideology of capitalism, i.e. one may be a capitalist or a worker but at the same time remain ideologically a Malay in the real sense of the word. The co-existence of capitalist production and indigenous ideology thus confuses the reality of social life. In particular the real economic issues or the capitalist relations of the town is denied and rejected as unreal in favour of non-existent indigenous relations. This is observable for instance in the case of tenure of house sites in the kampung. Those who have land rent out small portions of it for house sites at the rate of \$60.00 per year. The rate, of course, varies according to the actual size and locality of the land. The landowners are usually royal persons or richer residents who claim the tenancy system as the altruistic provision of accommodation to the poor and the landless in the manner of being responsible for the welfare of personal followers carried out by the traditional wealthy class. Though the system is loose in that the tenants are free to move to any house sites in the town, the social insubordination of the tenants is inevitable. This is especially the case when the landlord is again a wealthy, religious and honoured bureaucrat or petty bourgeois. The good deeds and the consequent high estimation of the wealthy and the concordant submission effected among the tenants offsets economic differences and any injustice the wealthy may have caused. The fact that house sites are becoming increasingly scarce strengthens the position of the wealthy.

Economic differences, exploitation and impoverishment of the poor are therefore justified by the prevailing ideology, especially among those who are convinced of its legitimacy. It dampens class consciousness and avoids class issues altogether. All it takes to maintain the status quo and to strengthen the present dominance of capital in the town is therefore simply an invigoration of the popular bourgeois ideology (including religiousness or the popular bourgeois interpretation of religion). This, I believe is one of the main requirements for capital to reproduce the socio-economic structure or the underdevelopment of Kota Bharu (Djurfeldt and Lindberg 1976, 208). In fact it is necessary for capital to promote the present bourgeois ideology, especially religiousness as it is popularly understood by the population because the increasing dominance of capital and improverishment of the people may tip the precarious balance between capital and the indigenous ideology in favour of the former.

The relation between the promotion of indigenous bourgeois ideology, the parallel expansion of capital and the increasing improvishment of the population is, I believe, the foundation upon which social life in Kota Bharu persists.

> iv. The social relations emerging from the articulation between the indigenous bourgeois ideology and the capitalist relations of production distorts the class position and pushes the subjective evaluation of status to the foreground.

However, the important consideration in the present study is to examine how the present structure of social relations differs from the previous one. I have argued that this is shown by the contrast between the *daulat* model and that of the present structure of status identification.

As I have shown in Chapter Seven, the structure of the inequality system represents a conjuncture of indigenous and capitalist relations of production. It may be objectively defined by individuals' economic position within the productive system of the town. There are pure class differentiation between people, but there are also individuals, especially the middle class of the kampung, who manipulate the ideology of 'honoured' to deny the class structure and class relations and instate, instead a system of inequality based on individuals' identification to conceived status positions.

The inequality system is not only acceptable but it is as real to the people concerned as any subjective, particularly religious, phenomenon (cf. Kessler *op. cit.,* 223 ff). It orders their daily social life and more important, it seems to make their class difference or social relations meaningful. It absorbs the alien class relations into the Malay community. In this way class relations are not only distorted and condemned, but are dismissed as unreal, or as insignificant to the social life of the town.

However, it must be noted that the system of inequality rests primarily on an individual's choice either, given the necessary economic and non-economic conditions to identify to a particular conceived status groups, or to deny the legitimacy of the system completely as is done by people whom I have called the individualists. By this very fact, the inequality system is therefore open and penetrable by any aspiring individuals who, regardless of their origin and kind of birth have sufficient economic and non-economic resources to do so.

The system of inequality is therefore a complex one. Though the basic structure more or less remains the same in that people are stratified and arranged in a hierarchy, the traditionally dominant *daulat* class is now dismembered into various classes and distributed unevenly into various 'status groups' of the kampung. The system of inequality is no longer defined and dictated by the *daulat* class. It is rather governed by the ideology of the 'honoured' which is almost coterminous with religiousness as it is understood to the kampung. This however does not discount the important dominance of the economic instance on the inequality scheme. As we have noted earlier, a relatively secure economic position provides the necessary condition for an individual to choose to identify with a particular position within the 'status hierarchy'. Under normal circumstances, a poor person will not be able to identify with a higher 'status' position because he would not possess the necessary economic surplus required to perform the rituals of the position such as feasting. The point to be emphasised here is that the emergence of the new inequality scheme has weakened the monopoly of wealth, power and prestige of the traditional *daulat* class. The importance of an individual's *daulat* heritage has changed into a formal term of address for greetings and conversation. This also means that the commoners in the town today are now able to penetrate into the high 'status groups' with all the social implication it entails.

This preoccupation with the indigenous class structure — that is, the *daulat* model which is now expressed in the form of bourgeois 'honoured' ideology — suppresses the reality of class relations in the town. This is perhaps attributable to the fact that the capitalisation of Kota Bharu is incomplete or uneven. While it creates local capitalists and bureacrats in the service of capital, and accordingly a class of poor townsmen directly or indirectly exploited by capital, it has not changed Kota Bharu into a capitalist town. It may have changed the economic infrastructure and tied Kota Bharu to wider networks of capital, but the pre-capitalist superstructure (the bourgeois ideology) is not retained and strengthened. In fact capital strengthens the position of some *daulat* individuals in the new bureaucracy and turns only a small proportion of townsmen into wage labourers. The bulk of the population is allowed to carry on independently exploiting any economic opportunities which may have been generated by capital in the town. They are absorbed to serve capital directly only when necessary. Otherwise they are set loose to exist on the fringes of capitalist production in such forms of employment providing services, petty trading and vending. This gives them the illusion of independence and unwarranted visions of economic mobility.

The illusion of economic independence and the deceptive yet effective control by capital are the main reasons why real class relations in Kota Bharu are disguised, misunderstood, falsified and replaced by the subjective identification to conceived status positions.

v. The reality of the inequality system is, however, marked by some degree of competition among those in the so-called high status group, subordination and egalitarianism among the 'low status group' and the legitimacy of the system as a whole appears to be constantly challenged by class relations.

To some extent however, the so-called high status group appears to consist of people who are competing with one another to confirm their place within the group. Some individuals justify their claims to the position through showing high economic surplus while others use their religiousness to compensate for lesser wealth. There is also a strong competition between individuals who are the descendants of traditional *daulat* class and the commoners. *Daulat* people appear to struggle to defend their traditionally dominant position against penetration by those commoners who possess sufficient economic resources to do so. The competition is intense and is manifested, in part, by feasting.

Excluded from such competition, the so-called low status group appears to develop an egalitarian ideology to redress any signs of disparity among them. Built into this ideology is their submission to the so-called high status group. This is expressed in their adherence to certain etiquettes and patterns of behaviour which are not practiced by individuals in the so-called high status group. It may be argued, in fact, that individuals in the so-called low status group have developed a subordinate ideology in which any form of behaviour held as 'incompatible' by people of the so-called high status is considered permissible. Some of them defy the formality of prayers, subscribe to a particular pattern of behaviour which may be described as 'coffee shop behaviour', tend to be involved in 'sinful' gambling, and to some extent, some of the women tend to be involved in prostitution. All these may be attributable to the fact that they are, in the majority of cases, poor.

However, the people themselves do not explain their ideology or patterns of behaviour as the way of the poor. Rather, they explain them as 'non-honoured'. Class explanation is consciously avoided. Even their classification of employment is toilsome (*susah*), emphasising difficulties and hardships of living, rather than pointing to the cause of such hardship which is the direct or the indirect exploitation by capital in the town.

The submissive egalitariansim of the poor also appears to have dispensed with muddles over the rights of birth. The descendants of the traditional *daulat* class have forfeited the higher position which their birth formerly would have given them. If at all, such birth is now important as a historical fact and points for reminiscence. They are however, constantly reminded of their birth when their *daulat* title is used as a formal term of address. It appears that these displaced *daulat* persons find accommodation within the poor, submissive and egalitarian class of people.

Such a system of inequality is by no means static. While the relationships between the high and low status groups reinforce the system, the system as a whole faces a threat from the anonymity and individuation of the urban social life. The *daulat* model of social relations was challenged and succumbed to the dominance of capital. Similarly the existence of the 'individualists' in the kampung appears to perpetuate the challenge to the present system of social inequality. As we have seen, the 'individualists' propogate an idea of class differentiation and relations.

The dominance of capitalism in the town has changed the social formation considerably. Differences in the ownership of wealth, type and forms of employment, level of secular education, skill to manipulate capital and 'proper contacts' have largely contributed to economic differentiation and class formation. However, this operates within a context which emphasises the ideology of 'honoured', a modified form of the traditional bourgeois ideology of the *daulat*. The persistence of this ideology inhibits, neutralises and cripples the capitalist relations of production in the town.

The net effect is therefore the rise of a form of social relations which is determined by capitalist production, but operates within the effective indigenous system of ideas and meaning. In fact it is the articulation between these two forces which forms the present pattern of social relations. Consequently it makes a combination of alien division of labour and indigenous social institutions and relationships, i.e. social life, meaningful to the people concerned. More importantly however, this allows capital to expand and accumulate freely without creating any serious social dislocation among the population. What are usually referred to as the 'custom', 'tradition', 'belief' and the popular religion of the Malays have therefore been manipulated to promote capital, underdevelop their economy and impoverish many of them.

Footnotes

1. I am here taking 'subsistence' to mean the 'struggle to make a living' in the Malay sense of *cukup mahan*.

APPENDIX 1
PROCESS OF SETTLEMENT IN KAMPONG TENGKU BENDAHARA

Year	*Rural migrants*	*Settlers from areas in vicinity*
1949	—	1
1950–55	—	6
1956–60	7	5
1961–65	8	6
1966–70	10	4
1971–75	5	2
Total	30	24

Reason and method of settling:

a) People from rural areas:

Reasons	*No. of settlers*	*Help of relatives*
Buying house sites	4	1
Work around and in Kampong	4	4
Work in Kota Bharu	16	12
Marriage	5	—
Rent a house	1	—
Total	30	17

b) People from areas in the vicinity:

Reasons	*No. of settlers*	*Help of relatives*
Making and buying house	3	2
Buying house site	11	—
Work in and around Kampong	7	4
Marriage	2	2
Rent a house	1	—
Total	24	8

APPENDIX 2 : CASES

Origin: LB(r) = local born (royal); LB(c) = local born (commoner); V = areas in vicinity; R = rural area

Ownership of land: R = rentier; OH = owner of house site; FS = free settler; T = tenant

Groups and Cases	*Ownership of land*	*Origin*	*Occupation*	*Estimates of monthly income (M$)*	*Occupation of wives*	*Children (living in Kampong)* Occupation	*No. in school*	*Pre-school*
I. Feasting Circle:								
1. Che Hassan	OH	V	Driver	200.00	Shop keeper	—	1	—
2. Hj.Mat	OH	V	Officer in Customs Dept.	400.00	not working	Shop assistant	4	1
3. Hj.Mohd	OH	LB(c)	Retired clerk	150.00	Dyeing batik cloth	Labourer in Singapore. 2 unemployeds.	3	—
4.Hj.Pa'min	T	R	Overseer in sawmill	250.00	Dyeing batik cloth	2 labourers. Labourer in Singapore	3	1
5. Kumat	FS	LB(r)	Sergeant in Armed Forces	not working	—	—	1	—
6. Kunor	OH	LB(r)	Chief clerk	400.00	not working	2 clerks	1	—
7. Kupar	R	LB(r)	Retired clerk	200.00	not working	Clerk. Instructor of motor-car repair	1	—
8. Kusah	R	LB(r)	Retired	80.00 (rent) dependent of children	—	Owner of barn to cure tobacco leaves. Owner of batik factory. School teacher. Sergeant in Armed Forces. 2 civil servants.	2	—

Groups and Cases	Ownership of land	Origin	Occupation	Estimates of monthly income (M$)	Occupation of wives	Children (living in Kampong)		
						Occupation	No. in school	Pre-school
9. Kusin	FS	LB(r)	Owner of batik factory	300.00	Shop keeper	—	2	—
10. Kuya	R	LB(r)	Chief clerk	500.00	School teacher (ustazah)	—	—	2
11. Pa'man	OH	R	'towkay' dealing in fish/fruit	300.00	not working	Driver	—	2
12. Pa'su Din	T	R	Firewood retailer	150.00	Dyeing batik cloth	—	2	—
II. Raft-users:								
1. Bidah	T	R	Seller at	60.00	—	—	—	—
2. Che Lah	T	R	Driver	200.00	Dyeing batik cloth	Unemployed	4	1
3. Daud	T	R	Carpenter	150.00	Labourer in factory	—	2	—
4. Derome	T	V	Trishaw pedaller	150.00	Dyeing batik cloth	—	1	1
5.Dollah	T	R	Batik printer	150.00	Seller at market	2 unemployeds.	—	—
6. Esah	T	R	Labourer in factory	90.00	—	Labourer. Dyeing batik cloth	—	—
7. Ghani	FS	LB(c)	Driver	180.00	Dyeing batik cloth	—	2	1
8. Hamid	T	R	Stall operator	200.00	Dyeing batik cloth	—	2	1
9. Hj.W.Minah	T	R	Retired (dependent of children)	—	—	—	—	—

Groups and Cases	Ownership of land	Origin	Occupation	Estimates of monthly income (M$)	Occupation of wives	Children (living in Kampong) Occupation	No. in school	Pre-school
10. Idris	T	R	Labourer in Singapore	300.00	Dyeing batik cloth	Labourer. Unemployed	1	—
11. KuDaud	T	R	Vendor	150.00	Dyeing batik cloth	Office boy	2	2
12. Kuman	FS	lb(r)	Night guard	150.00	—	—	1	—
13. Latif	T	V	Labourer	90.00	Dyeing batik cloth	Labourer	1	2
14. Mamat	FS	LB(c)	Labourer in Singapore	300.00	Dyeing batik	—	2	—
15. Meknab	T	R	Seller at market	60.00	—	Labourer. Dye-ing batik cloth. Unemployed.	2	—
16. Minah	FS	V	Seller at market	60.00	—	—	—	—
17. Pa'Lah	T	R	Vendor	120.00	Traditional masseuse	Unemployed	—	—
18. Pa'mud	T	V	Night guard	150.00	Dyeing batik cloth	Labourer. Labourer in Singapore.	—	—
19. Pa'soh	T	V	Vendor	120.00	Labourer in factory	Unemployed	2	1
20. Razak	T	R	Trishaw pedaller	100.00	Dyeing batik	—	—	1
21. Said	T	V	Itinerant batik seller	130.00	Dyeing batik cloth	3 unemployeds	—	—
22. Salleh	T(share house)	R	Night guard	150.00	not working	—	—	—
23. Sohok	T	R	Trishaw pedaller	150.00	Dyeing batik cloth	Carpenter Labourer.	2	2

Groups and Cases	Ownership of land	Origin	Occupation	Estimates of monthly income (M$)	Occupation of wives	Children (living in Kampong) Occupation	No. in school	Pre-school
24. Som	T	R	Seller at market	80.00 Dyeing batik cloth.	—	Seller at market	1	1
25. Stopa	T	R	Labourer	150.00	Dyeing batik cloth	—	3	1
26. Sudin	T	R	Tailor	90.00	Dyeing batik	—	—	—
27. Timah	T	V	Seller at market	60.00	—	—	—	—
28. Wan Ali	T	V	Seller at market	150.00	—	Clerk 2 unemployeds.	1	1
Wan Husin	FS	R	Labourer	100.00	not working	—	—	1
30. W.Sin	T	V	Trishaw	100.00	Dyeing batik	—	2	—
31. W.Timah	T	V	Domestic servant	50.00	—	Labourer Unemployed	—	1
32. W.Ya	T	R	Stall operator	250.00	Labourer in factory	Unemployed	3	2
33. Ya'akob	T	R	Driver	200.00	not working	Unemployed	2	1
III. Individualists:								
1. Berehim	OH	LB)c)	Driver	250.00	not working	—	4	2
2. Che gu him	OH	V	School teacher	400.00	not working	—	4	2
3. Che Hamid	OH	R	'towkay' dealing in fish	300.00	not working	—	3	2
4. Che mud	OH	R	Taxi driver	300.00	not working	—	—	2
5. Che Osman	OH	V	Driver	250.00	Seller at market	Typist	2	1
6. Che Saudah	OH	LB(c)	Tailor	40.00	—	2 clerks	1	—
7. Hj.W.mah	OH	V	Retired (dependant of child)	—	—	School teacher	—	—

Groups and Cases	*Ownership of land*	*Origin*	*Occupation*	*Estimates of monthly income (M$)*	*Occupation of wives*	*Children (living in Kampong)* Occupation	*No. in school*	*Pre-school*
8. Hj.Zain	OH	R	Retired clerk	100.00	not working	—	—	—
9. Ismail	OH	V	Carpenter	150.00	Seller at market	—	—	—
10. Ja'afar	OH	LB(c)	Driver	200.00	Dyeing batik cloth	Clerk	2	3
11. Malek	OH	V	School teacher	500.00	not working	School teacher	3	—
12. Mohd	OH	V	Driver	200.00	Dyeing batik cloth	—	3	2
13. W.Aziz	OH	V	Retired teacher	150.00	Seller at market	Unemployed	1	—
14. W.Yusof	(share house)	V	Clerk	250.00	not working	—	—	—
15. Kunawi	FS	LB(r)	Driver	200.00	Dyeing batik cloth	Labourer in Kuala Lumpur. Labourer in Singapore.	2	2
16. Che Amat	T	V	Firewood retailer	150.00	Seller at market	Driver. Unemployed. 2 dyeing batik cloth.	2	3
17. Che Man	T	R	Labourer	150.00	Dyeing batik cloth	—	—	—
18. Husin	T	V	Labourer	150.00	Dyeing batik	—	—	—
19. Mail	T	R	Labourer	120.00	Dyeing batik cloth	—	5	2
20. Mustapha	T	R	Driver	200.00	Dyeing batik cloth	—	—	1
21. Nik par	T	V	Clerk	300.00	Dyeing batik cloth	Unemployed	3	1
22. Nik sin	T	R	Driver	180.00	not working	—	—	
23. Ranik	T	R	Middleman	200.00	Dyeing batik cloth	—	2	2

APPENDIX 3a

(I) Licenced Premises in the town of Kota Bharu in 1949

Type and use of premises	*Number*
Coffee Shops	80
Eating Shops	41
Lodging Houses	14
Bakery Shops	18
Milk Vendors	13
Dhobby Shops	26
Barber Shops	6
Tinsmiths Shops	7
Blacksmiths Shops	15
Carpenter Shops	15
Soap Works	1
Cinema Halls	5
Motor repair premises	7
Lime Kilns	1
Painters Shops	4
Vulcanising Tyres	3
Timber Stores	18
Sawmills	3
Smoke Houses	3
Street Stalls	9
Coffee Stalls	21
Itinerant Hawkers	108
Safety Match	1
Copra Store	9
Coconut oil Mills	3
Daun Rokok Stores	2
Treating Skins	1
Goldsmith Shops	22
Batik Printing	5
Calcium carbine Stores	2
Printing Presses	6
Rice Mill	1
Rubber Factory	1
Bottling acetic acid	1

(II) Registration of non-mechanical vehicles in 1949:

Type of License	*Number*
Cycle trishaws	850
Handcarts	294
Bullock carts	78
Trishaw drivers License	615

(Source: Annual Report 1949, Town Board, Kota Bharu.)

APPENDIX 3b

TYPES OF LICENCES ISSUED BY TOWN BOARD, 1968–1972

Year	*coffee shops*	*bakery*	*restaurants*	*hotels*	*stalls*	*vendors*	*sellers of foodstuffs*	*petrol stations*	*dhobby*	*car park*	*motor-car repairs*	*factory*	*cinema halls*
1968	172	24	86	26	72	73	57	32	9	4	50	7	4
1969	159	27	77	25	69	94	48	35	8	7	51	7	4
1970	160	27	75	24	67	97	56	37	8	10	58	7	4
1971	168	32	96	25	69	104	157	35	11	14	65	7	4
1972	175	30	86	28	166	51	149	60	9	19	62	8	4

(Source: Adbul Aziz Bin Talib, 'Lapuran Kemajuan Majlis/Lembaga Bandaran, Kota Bharu bagi tempoh lima tahun 1.1.1968 hingga 31.12.1972.)

APPENDIX 4

HING BING SAWMILL

The sawmill was established in 1940 by Tuan Haji from Telok Anson in Perak and it is claimed to be one of the earliest sawmills in Kelantan. It was confiscated by the Japanese during World War II and afterwards it was reopened and enlarged by a Chinese entrepreneur, Hing Bing, who obtained a lease on the land belonging to Tengku Bendahara.

In the 1950's the sawmill employed 70 to 80 workers, many of whom were Chinese labourers from outside of Kelantan. Local Malay labourers were regarded as inefficient due to the fact that they were absent from work for 2 or 3 days after each payment of wages.

In 1970 the sawmill was again employing labourers from outside of Kelantan, but many of them were Malay labourers from the state of Trengganu. The daily wage was then M$1.50.

However, there was an increase of Kelantan Malay labourers working in the sawmill after 1970 with the majority of the workers coming from rural areas. In 1973 there was a large proportion of Kelantan Malay workers working there at wages of M$2.00 to M$3.00 per day. In the same year, the workers threatened to strike for higher wages. Since they were not organised into any Workers Union, the leaders of the strike were dismissed. The wage, however, was increased to M$3.40/M$3.70/M$4.70 per day.

In 1975 the sawmill employed a total of 36 workers; as follows:

Clerical	2
Semi-manual workers (2 drivers, 1 night guard and 1 overseer)	4
Contract workers who on the average are earning M$3.00 to M$4.00 per day	20
Daily wage labourers who are earning M$3.40 to M$4.70 per day	10

The majority of the workers come from rural areas and commute about 5–6 miles daily to Kota Bharu town. There are a few who live in the town and there are also three who live in 3 out of the 8 workers' quarters provided by the management. The workers are however less permanent; in most cases, they do not work in the sawmill for more than one year.

APPENDIX 5

GAI HING ENGINEERING WORKSHOP

It is claimed as one of the earliest Engineering Workshops in the State. It was established in the early 1950's and was involved in the contract of servicing and maintaining the port of Tumpat from which iron ore was exported mainly to Japan. At the time, the Workshop was employing more than 100 workers. However, when the iron ore export trade ceased in the 1960's, the Workshop turned mainly to servicing industrial machines.

At present (1975), the Workshop employs 34 workers consisting of the following:

Clerical workers	3
Semi-manual (night guard) workers	1
Labourers	30

Wages:

The clerical and semi-manual workers are paid monthly, while the labourers are paid daily, with skilled workers receiving M$7.00 to 8.00 per day and unskilled workers M$3.50 to 5.00 per day, depending on experience.

APPENDIX 6

BATIK PRINTING FACTORY

The batik printing factory of Kusin is one of several in the kampung.

Organization:
The factory was established in 1974 as an agent of Batik Malaysia which is an organization dealing in batik production run by MARA. Batik Malaysia allocates specific quota of production for each individual agent or factory and it provides monetary loans and subsidies for purchase of raw materials (white cloth, dyes and chemical), and collects the finished product. There are three labourers and one printer in the factory.

Process of production:

Type I, e.g. 'sarong':
At the beginning of the process, the white cloth is waxed with the floral pattern (*pukul*) after which the cloth is distributed to workers (mostly women) to be dyed in various colours (*choteng*). Each piece of cloth costs M20¢ for dyeing and a further M5¢ for waxing over the dyed parts (*tutup*). This dyed and waxed cloth is sent back to the factory for dyeing the background dye (*chelop*). When it is dry, the process is completed by boiling in water to get rid of the wax, after which the cloth is washed and left to dry.

Type II, one colour batik in rolls:
The process begins with waxing the pattern (*pukul*) after which the uncut cloth is dyed (*chelop*). After dyeing, the cloth is dipped into wax and when it is dry, it is treaded so that the wax is cracked into fine cross-cutting lines. This is followed by dyeing into the same colour dye thus giving darker dye on the previous dyed spaces and lighter dye on the fine lines in between. When it is dry, the cloth is boiled in water to get rid of the wax and this is completed by washing. It is then left to dry.

Cost of production:
The average cost per yard is M$4.30.
The average time for production for type II is 3 days.

Wages:
The printer (pemukul) is paid M$5.00 per day and the labourers are paid M$3.00 per day. On the average the entrepreneur nets about M80¢ per piece of Type I.

APPENDIX 7a

MARRIAGE AND DIVORCE IN MUKIM MISJID MUHAMMADI, 1973 and 1974

Year	*Marriage*	*Divorce*	*% of divorce from total marriage*
18.5.1973 – 31.12.1973	104	33	31.73
26.8.1974 – 31.12.1974	69	22	31.88

(Source: Compiled from records of marriage and divorce, Office of Chief Kadhi of Kelantan, Kota Bharu, Kelantan.)

APPENDIX 7b

MARRIAGE, DIVORCE AND REVOCATION OF DIVORCE IN KELANTAN, 1970–1974

I = total number of marriages
II = total number of divorces
III = total number of revocations
%II = percentage of divorce from total number of marriages
%III = percentage of revocation from total number of divorces

Districts		*1970*			*1971*			*1972*			*1973*			*1974*		
		I	*II*	*III*	*I*	*II*	*III*	*I*	*II*	*III*	*I*	*II*	*III*	*I*	*II*	*III*
Kota Bharu		2311	1267	123	2461	1257	186	2127	1082	129	2333	1161	179	2263	1282	150
	%		*54.82*	*9.71*		*51.08*	*14.8*		*50.87*	*11.9*		*49.76*	*7.67*		*56.65*	*11.7*
Pasir Puteh		1050	631	60	1075	622	78	1041	574	86	1057	597	83	1054	614	67
	%		*60.09*	*9.51*		*57.86*	*6.11*		*55.14*	*14.98*		*56.48*	*13.90*		*58.25*	*10.91*
Bachok		838	527	59	919	502	60	957	531	54	932	509	41	890	516	74
	%		*62.89*	*11.20*		*54.62*	*11.95*		*55.49*	*10.16*		*54.61*	*8.05*		*57.98*	*14.34*
Tumpat		805	383	38	908	381	40	944	408	37	859	385	66	796	287	41
	%		*47.58*	*9.92*		*41.96*	*10.50*		*43.22*	*9.06*		*44.82*	*17.14*		*36.05*	*14.28*
Pasir Mas		1311	660	66	1294	635	54	1221	569	68	1253	564	65	1299	571	59
	%		*50.34*	*10.00*		*49.07*	*8.50*		*46.60*	*11.95*		*45.01*	*11.52*		*43.95*	*10.33*
Machang		686	391	61	695	377	51	696	404	54	767	373	58	657	375	59
	%		*56.99*	*15.60*		*54.24*	*13.53*		*58.05*	*13.36*		*46.63*	*15.54*		*57.07*	*15.73*
Tanah Merah		677	478	61	711	405	55	683	426	43	848	469	48	875	492	54
	%		*70.60*	*12.76*		*52.53*	*13.58*		*62.51*	*10.09*		*55.31*	*10.23*		*56.22*	*10.97*
Kuala Kerai		490	364	92	504	331	55	556	376	59	626	392	67	748	713	63
	%		*74.28*	*25.27*		*65.67*	*16.62*		*67.63*	*15.69*		*62.62*	*17.09*		*95.32*	*8.83*
Total		8168	4701	560	8627	4510	579	8225	4370	476	8675	4450	607	8582	4850	567
	%		*57.55*	*11.91*		*52.28*	*12.84*		*53.13*	*10.90*		*51.30*	*13.64*		*56.51*	*11.70*

(Source: Compiled from records of marriage and divorce, Office of Chief Kadhi of Kelantan, Kota Bharu, Kelantan.)

APPENDIX 8

A NOTE ON KELANTAN BIBLIOGRAPHY

To uncover and integrate all the work on Kelantan in a single study is almost impossible. In order to facilitate further studies, especially in the issues and problems raised in the text, a short note on the existing bibliography seems in order. However, this does not pretend to be exhaustive.

1. General

Apart from references cited in the text, there is voluminous work in various forms available in English and Malay. A great number of these are housed in the Library of University of Malaya, Kuala Lumpur, where the collection has been classified and compiled by Zainab Awang Ngah as *Kelantania di Perpustakaan Universiti Malaya,* Library, University of Malaya, June 1979. Almost all known work on Kelantan, including books, theses, articles, journals, novels, magazines and articles in newspapers concerning all aspects of life are included in this volume. This is the bibliography on Kelantan which no student should be without.

Studies with specific emphasis on inequality and underdevelopment are scanty. One may cite Syed Husin Ali, *Kelaparan Tanah di Kelantan,* 1978 and Kessler, *Islam and Politics in a Malay State* as two main examples. The former emphasises the raw facts of inequality expressed in terms of landownship, and the latter is an expression of the politics of inequality. A team mainly from Social Sciences, Universiti Sains Malaysia, Pulau Pinang, Malaysia tried to locate for policy recommendation the process of underdevelopment of Kelantan in 1977 and 1978, but the study was conducted only in rural areas and treated within the wider processes of underdevelopment of Northern Peninsular Malaysia as a whole *in Rural–Urban Transformation and Regional Underdevelopment; The case of Malaysia,* United Nations Centre for Regional Development, Nagoya, Japan 1978. Generally speaking therefore, the study on Kelantan underdevelopment and its manifestations is underdeveloped itself, partly because of the dominance of 'modernisation' studies, and the current tendency for technocratic policy studies undertaken by local and foreign consultants and organisations sponsored usually by Government Departments and/or Aid Agencies. Government Departments have always been interested in policy studies as the basis to map out plans and strategies for development. The consultants on the other hand provide information, reports and recommendation which are desired and expected by Government Departments concerned. Consequently, the scholarly content of studies are increasingly questionable, and in any case reports are dominantly quantitative. There is also a tendency for scholars to be appointed as consultants and mobilised for such technocratic studies following the conscious effort by the Government to do away with foreigners and to develop and depend more on local expertise and local consultants. To some extent, it is the confrontation between scholars, technocrats and the emerging scholar-cum-technocrats which now defines the state of studies and research not only in Kelantan but in Malaysia as a whole.

2. History

The importance of historical perspective in socio-anthropological research and studies is now recognized. As far as Kelantan historical materials are concerned, Kessler's *Islam and Politics in a Malay State, Appendix I* indicates most of the known historical work on Kelantan. There is also a comprehensive recent work by Rhamat Saripan, *Politik Melayu Tradisional Kelantan 1776–1842,* Dewan Bahasa dan Pustaka, Kuala Lumpur 1979. Talking about historical documents, however, it must be emphasised that the Arkib Negara (The National Archives) in Kuala Lumpur is an indispensable collection of historical records and information. In this regard, it is worth mentioning that *Kelantan British Advisors Annual Report 1909–1940* is now accessible in Microfilm.

3. Government Publication and Research

Government Printers has come out in 1979 with *Kelantan Tinjauan Ekonomi dan Rancangan Perlaksanaan.* This is the Kelantan version of development plans in the tradition of Malaysian Five-Year Plans and forms an important manifesto on development proposed by the State Government. The Malaysian Government, through the Kota Bharu Branch of the Malaysia centre for Development Studies, Prime Minister's Department, has also been involved in studying issues and problems of Kelantan development. Of particular relevance to issues raised in the text are the studies on small-scale industries and small businesses in town centres in Kelantan. To this effect, it has produced two relevant reports, namely, i) *Kejian Awal Terhadap Empat Bidang Perusahaan di Kelantan,* 1976 and ii), *Lapuran Akhir Kajian Penyertaan Bumiputra dalam Bidang Perniagaan dan Perusahaan,* 1976.

The Government, through the Economic Planning Unit has also contracted out policy research on socio-economic issues and problems in Kelantan. Examples in this case are i) Robert Nathan Associate Inc., *Kelantan Regional Planning and Development Study,* 1973 and ii), SGV-Kassim Chan Sdn. Bhd., *Study on the Rehabilitation of the Schemes of the Lembaga Kemajuan Tanah Negeri Kelantan,* 1979. In this context, it may also be noted that the Town Council of Kota Bharu has nominated consultants to carry out a Master Plan Study of Kota Bharu as the basis for future development of the town.

4. Scholars and Research on Kelantan

It has to be stated that all research, especially those conducted by foreigners is usually screened and recorded by the Socio-economic Research Unit, Prime Minister's Departmenr of Malaysia. It is also usual for the department to request local researches to furnish the Department with a copy of their research reports. The Department is therefore the biggest reservoir of previous studies conducted in the State.

Up to 1979, most of the known scholarly work, except Beaglehole, *The District,* Oxford University Press 1976, and theses on Kelantan, especially those submitted to University of Malaya, have been included in the *Kelantania di Perpustakaan Universiti Malaya* mentioned above. However, of the seven Ph.D. theses recorded in the volume, only one is directly related to social life in Kota Bharu town. This is Mohamad Fauzi Yaakob, *Peniaga dan Perniagaan Melayu di Kota Bharu, Kelantan,* University of Malaya, 1978, which is also the only known Ph.D. thesis on Kelantan social life submitted to a local University.

The exact number of Master of Arts theses is difficult to determine. This is because, together with other people, Kelantan students enrolled in various Universities around the world usually 'go home' to conduct Master of Arts research without being recorded in any centralised agency or institution. Referring only to those submitted to local Universities, there are only 12 Master of Arts theses on Kelantan submitted to University of Malaya and one thesis submitted to Universiti Kebangsaan Malaysia. The latter has been published as Rahmat Saripan, *Perkembangan Politik Melayu Tradisional Kelantan 1776–1842,* noted earlier. From these there are two theses submitted to University of Malaya which are related to Kota Bharu social life raised in the text. These are i) Karimah Zainab bt. Hj. Abdul Karim, *Wanita Melayu Dalam Konteks Perubahan Ekonomi dan Politik; Satu Kes Studi di Kota Bharu,* 1975 and ii), Abdul Rashid Bin Haji Ahmad, Bureaucracy Negeri Kelantan; Satu Kajian Perubahan dan Perkembangan, 1969.

5. Academic Exercises

It has been the tradition in the Faculty of Economics and Administration and the Faculty of Arts, University of Malaya to produce graduation exercises involving primary and original data collection. This has been followed by Universiti Kebangsaan Malysia and possibly other universities in the country in the near future. In this case, it is usual for students to choose their own social environment (usually their immediate kampung, mukim, towns and districts) to carry out surveys and interviews for such exercises. Up to date there have been 96 and 84 such exercises produced by University of Malaya and Universiti Kebangsaan Malaysia respectively. While the former may be found in the *Kelantania di Perpustakaan Universiti Malaya* noted earlier, the latter is classified and compiled by Library, Universiti Kebangsaan Malaysia in *Theses and Academic Exercises, Universiti Kebangsaan Malaysia 1973–1979,* 1980. Among those which raised issues about social life in Kota Bharu from the collection in Universiti Kebangsaan Malaysia include Wan Aminah Wan Yusoff, *Pembangunan Semula Bandar, Satu Kajian Kes Bandar Kota Bharu,* 1975, and Nik Hasnah Nik Li, *Sejarah Bandar Kota Bharu 1900–1940,* 1977. The academic exercises with the similar theme at University of Malaya are Aziz Yusoff, *Perusahaan Batik di Kota Bharu Kelantan,* 1967, Roszehan bt. Mohd. Idrus, *Pemilikan Tanah di Bandar Kota Bharu,* 1974–74, Aini Abdul Rahman, *Kaum Bawahan Melayu Buruh Kota Bharu, Satu Kajian Kes,* 1975, Rosmah bt. Mansor, *Perniagaan Kecil Orang-orang Melayu yang dijalankan di Kubang Krian, Kelanta,* 1973–74, and Azizah Abdul Rahman, *Peranan Wanita dalam Politik dan Agama di Kubang Pasu,* 1974–75.

To conduct further research into the problems and issues raised in the text one will probably have to begin with records and reports on Kelantan held by Government Departments in the State as well as in Kuala Lumpur, and of course researchers inevitably would have to be equipped with three indispensable bibliographies prepared by the Libraries in both Universiti Kebangsaan Malaysia and University of Malaya. These are namely, i) *Problems and Prospects of Bumiputra Economy,* Library, Universiti Kebangsaan Malaysia, 1978, ii), *Kelantania di Perpustakaan Universiti Malaya,* Library, University of Malaya, 1979 and iii) *Theses and Academic Exercises,* Library, Universiti Kebangsaan Malaysia, 1980.

BIBLIOGRAPHY

Abbreviations:
JRASSB: *Journal of the Royal Asiatic Society, Straits Branch.*
JMBRAS: *Journal of the Royal Asiatic Society, Malayan Branch.*

The bibliography differentiates Government Enactments and Records into a separate section at the end.

Allen, D.F., *Report on minor ports of Malaya,* Government Printer, Singapore 1953.

Amin, S., *Accumulation on a world scale: A critique of the theory of underdevelopment,* Volume 1, Monthly Review Press, London 1974.

Annandale, N., 'Siamese Malay States', *Scottish Geographical Magazine,* 16, 1900; 505–523.

Banaji, J., 'For a Theory of Colonial Modes of Production', *Economic and Political Weekly,* Vol. 7 No. 52, 1972; 2498–2502.

Bendix, R., *Max Weber; An Intellectual Portrait,* Methuen & Co. Ltd. 1960 (University Paperback, Great Britain 1966).

Bradbym B., 'The destruction of natural economy', *Economy and Society,* Vol. 4, No. 2 1975; 125–161.

Bukharin, N., 'Imperialism and the Accumulation of Capital', in Luxemburg, R. and Bukharin, N., *Imperialism and the Accumulation of Capital,* Allen Lane The Penguin Press, London 1972: 153–270.

Chan Su-Ming, 'Kelantan and Trengganu 1909–1939' *JMBRAS* 38, pt. I, 1965: 159–198.

Clifford, H., *In Court and Kampong; being tales and sketches in the Malay Peninsula,* The Richards Press Ltd., London, 1897.

—— *Expedition to Trengganu and Kelantan: a report,* Kuala Lumpur, 1938.

Crawford, H.A., 'The birth of the Duff Company in Kelantan 1900–1912', *Malaysia in History,* 13, 2, 1970: 2–10.

Dakers, C.H., 'The Malay Coins of Malacca', *JMBRAS,* 17, pt. I, 1939: 1–12.

Djamour, J., *Malay kinship and marriage in Singapore,* London School of Economics Monographs on Social Anthropology No. 21, The Athlone Press, London 1965.

Djurfeldt, G. and Lindberg, S., *Behind Poverty: The Social Formation in a Tamil Village,* Scandinavian Institute of Asian Studies, Monograph series no. 22, Oxford and IBH Publishing Co., New Delhi, 1976.

Dobby, E.H., 'Kelantan Delta' *Geographical Review,* 41. 1951; 226–255.

Downs, R., 'Kelantanese Village' in Steward, J. (ed.), *Contemporary Change in Traditional Societies,* Vol. 2, University of Illinois Press, U.S.A., 1967; 107–186.

Emerson, R., *Malaysia; a study in direct and indirect rule,* University of Malaya Press, Kuala Lumpur, 1964.

Evers, Hans-Dieter (ed.), *Modernization in South-East Asia,* Oxford University Press, Kuala Lumpur 1973.

Evers, Hans-Dieter and Goh Ban Lee, *Urban Landownship in Kota Bharu and Jeli, Kelantan,* project paper series no. 5, Centre for Policy Research, Universiti Sains Malaysia, 1976.

Firth, Raymond, *Malay fishermen: their peasant economy,* 2nd edition, Routledge and Kegan Paul, London 1966.

Firth, Rosemary, *House-keeping Among Malay Peasants,* London School of Economics Monographs on Social Anthropology No. 7, The Athlone Press, London 1966.

Foster, G., 'Peasant Character and Personality', in Potter, J.M., Diaz, M.N., Foster, G. (ed.), *Peasant Society: A Reader,* Little Brown & Co., Boston 1967: 296–300.

Foster-Carter, A., 'The Modes of Production Controversy', *New Left Review,* 107, 1978; 47–77.

Fowler, J.A., *Netherlands East Indies and British Malaya: a commercial and industrial handbook,* Government Printing Office, Washington, 1923.

Geertz, C., *A Social History of an Indonesian Town,* M.I.T. Press, Cambridge Massachusetts, 1965.

Gerth, H.H. and Mills, C.W. (eds.), *From Max Weber: Essays in Sociology,* Routledge and Kegan Paul, Great Britain, 1948.

Giddens, A., *The Class Structure of the Advanced Societies,* Hutchinson and Co. Ltd., London, 1973.

Goffman, E., *Interaction Ritual: Essays on Face-to-Face Behaviour,* Penguin University Books, Great Britain, 1967.

Goodenough, W.H., 'Rethinking status and role' in Banton M. (ed.), *Relevance of Models in Social Anthropology,* Association of Social Anthropologist Monographs No. 1, Tavistock Publication, London 1965; 1–24.

Graham, W.A., *Kelantan: a state of Malay Peninsula,* James Maclehose & Sons, Glasgow, 1908.

Griffin, K., 'Underdevelopment in Theory' in Wilber, K. (ed.), *The Political Economy of Development and Underdevelopment,* Random House, New York, 1973, 15–25.

Gullick, J.M., *Indigenous political systems of Western Malaya,* London School of Economics Monographs on Social Anthropology No. 17, The Athlone Press, London, 1958.

Hamzah Sendut, 'Patterns of Urbanisation in Malaya', *Journal of Tropical Geography,* 16, 1962; 114–130.

Heine-Geldern, R., 'Conception of State and Kingship in Southeast Asia', *Far Eastern Quarterly,* 2, 1942; 15–30.

Ismail Bakti, 'Bunga Emas, Golden Flowers, Gift or Tribute', *Malaysia in History,* 6, No. I, 1960; 40–42.

Kahar Bador, 'Social rank, status-honour and social class consciousness amongst the Malays' in Evers, Hans-Dieter (ed.), *Modernization in South East Asia,* Oxford University Press, Kuala Lumpur, 1973; 132–149.

Kassim Ahmad, *Kesah pelayaran Abdullah,* Kuala Lumpur, 1960.

Kelantan, *Tinjauan Ekonomi dan Rancangan Perlaksanaan,* Government Printer, Kuala Lumpur, 1979.

Kessler, C.S., *Islam and Politics in a Malay State,* Cornell University Press, London, 1978.

Khoo Khay Kim, 'Malay Society 1874-1920's', *Journal of Southeast Asian Studies,* 5, No. 2, 1974; 179-198.

Laclau, E., 'Feudalism and Capitalism in Latin America', *New Left Review* 67, 1971; 19-38.

Laidlaw, F.F., 'Travels in Kelantan, Trengganu and Upper Perak', *JMBRAS,* 26 pt. 4, 1953; 148-165.

Lenin, V.I., *Imperialism, the Highest Stage of Capitalism,* Foreign Language Press, Peking 1970.

Lim Teck Ghee, *Peasants and Their Agricultural Economy in Colonial Malaya 1874-1941,* Oxford University Press, Kuala Lumpur 1977.

Luxemburg, R., *The Accumulation of Capital,* Routledge to Kegan Paul Ltd., Great Britain, 1951.

Mandel, E., *Marxist Economic Theory,* Merlin Press, London, 1962.

Marx, K., *Capital volume I,* International Publishers Co., Inc. New York, 1967.

McGee, T.G., *Malays in Kuala Lumpur City: a geographical study of the process of urbanisation,* Ph.D. thesis, Victoria University of Wellington, 1968.

—— 'Peasants in Cities: A paradox, a paradox and most ingenious paradox', *Human Organisation,* 32, No. 2, 1973; 131-141.

Mohd. Noor Bin Mohamed, 'Masalah pemilikan tanah di Mukim Gunong;, *Journal Antropoloji dan Sosiologi,* jil. III, 1974; 41-47.

Moore Jr., Barrington, *Social origins of Dictatorship and Democracy,* A Peregrine Book, Great Britain, 1966.

Murad bin Mohd. Nor (Chairman), *Jawatan Kuasa Diatas kajian mengenai pelajaran dan masyarakat (kajian keciciran),* Bahagian Perancang dan penyelidik pelajaran, Kementerian Pelajaran dan Jabatan Perangkaan, Kuala Lumpur 1973.

Nash, M., *Peasant Citizen: politics, religion and modernization in Kelantan, Malaysia,* Papers in International Studies, South East Asia series no. 31, Centre for International Studies, Ohio University 1974.

Neil, C.C., *Kuala Trengganu: a case study of economic and non-economic rationalities as determinants of urban behaviour,* M.A. Thesis, Australian National University, Canberra 1966.

Nik Mohamad bin Nik Mohd. Salleh, 'Kelantan in Transition' in Roff W.R. (ed.) *Kelantan; Religion, Society and Politics in a Malay State,* Oxford University Press, Kuala Lumpur 1974.

Parkin, F., *Class Inequality and Political Order,* Paladin, Great Britain 1971.

Peppys, W.E., 'Kelantan during World War I', *Malaysia in History,* 6, No. I, 1960; 36-39.

Population Census 1921, *The census of British Malaya: the Straits Settlements, Federated Malay States of Johore, Kedah, Perlis, Kelantan, Trengganu and Brunei, 1921,* by J.E. Nathan.

Reid, J., *Kota Bharu Advisory Board Meeting: a report* 1932.

Roberts, L., 'The Duff Syndicate in Kelantan 1900–1902', *JMBRAS,* 45, pt. I, 1972; 81–110.

—— *Kelantan in 1890–1939,* M.A. Thesis, University of Malaya, Kuala Lumpur 1973.

Roff, W.R. (ed.) *Kelantan: Religion, Society and Politics in a Malay State,* Oxford University Press, Kuala Lumpur 1974.

Rydberg, P., Jonsson, G., Elmquist, A., and Langemar, A.M., *The History Book* (translated by Carol Baum Schmoleitz), Peace Press Incorporation, California 1974.

Sa'ad Shukri bin Haji Muda, Detik Sejarah Kelantan, Pustaka Aman Press, Kota Bharu 1971.

Sheppard, Mubin, 'Traditional Malay House forms in Trengganu and Kelantan', *JMBRAS,* 42, pt. 2, 1969: 1–9.

Simmel, G., *Sociology of George Simmel,* Wolff, Kurt (tr. ed.), The Free Press, Glencoe, Illinois, 1950.

Skeat, W.W., 'Reminiscences of the expedition', *JMBRAS,* 26, pt. 4, 1953, 9–147.

Skinner, C., *Civil War in Kelantan in 1839,* Monographs of the Malaysian Branch, Royal Asiatic Society No. 2, Kuala Lumpur, 1965.

—— 'Abdullah's voyage to the East Coast seen through contemporary eyes', *JMBRAS,* 39, pt. 2, 1966; 24–33.

Statistics Department, *1970 Population and Housing Census: urban connurbations — population and households in ten gazetted towns and their adjoining built up areas,* Kuala Lumpur, 1971.

Statistics Department (Kelantan AD, 02), *Occupations and Community and Sex: Kota Bharu, Peringat, Pangkal Kalong,* Kuala Lumpur, 1970.

Stavenhagen, R., 'Seven fallacies about Latin America' in Petras, J. and Zeitlin (eds.), *Latin America Reform or Revolution? A Reader,* Fawcett Publications, U.S.A. 1968; 13–31.

Swift, M.G., 'Indigenous political systems of Western Malaya and Malay kinship and marriage in Singapore; a review; *Journal of Southeast Asian History,* I, 1960; 90–94.

—— 'Men and women in Malay Society' in Ward, B.E. (ed.), *Women in New Asia,* UNESCO, Paris, 1963; 268–286.

—— *Malay Peasant Society in Jelebu,* London School of Economics Monographs on Social Anthropology No. 29, The Athlone Press, London 1965.

—— 'Economic concentration and Malay peasant society' in Freedman, M., (ed.), *Social Organisation,* Frank Cass and Co. Ltd., London, 1967; 241–269.

Syed Hussein Atatas, 'The Grading of Occupational Prestige Among Malays in Malaysia', *JMBRAS,* 14, pt. I, 1968; 146–156.

—— *The myth of the Lazy Natives,* Frank Case, London, 1977.

Syed Husin Ali, 'Land concentration and poverty among the rural Malays', *Nusantara,* vol. I, 1972; 100–113.

—— *Kemiskinan dan Kelaparan Tanah di Kelantan,* Dinamika Karangraf Sym Ber Had, Kuala Lumpur, 1978.

Taylor, J.G., *From Modernisation to Modes of Production,* Mcmillan Press Ltd., Great Britain, 1979.

Tham Seong Chee, *Malays and Modernization: A Sociological Interpretation,* Singapore University Press Ptd. Ltd., 1977.

Town Board, *Annual Report 1949.*

Tregoning, K.G., *Home Port Singapore: a History of Straits Steamship Co. Ltd. 1890 -1965,* Oxford University Press, Singapore 1967.

Tweedie, M.W.F., 'An early account of Kelantan', *JRASSB,* 26, 1923; 216–219.

Van Leur, Jacob, C., *Indonesian Trade and Society; Essays in Asian Social and Economic History,* The Hague, 1955.

Wang Gung Wu, 'An early Chinese visitor to Kelantan', *Malaysia in History,* 6, No. I, 1960' 31-35.

Weber, M., *Basic Concepts in Sociology,* tr. by Secher, H.R. Citadel Press, New Jersey, 1972.

—— *Protestant Ethic and the Spirit of Capitalism,* George Allen and Unwin Ltd., Great Britain, 1930; (12th impression Unwin University Books, 1974).

Wertheim, W.F., *Dawning of an Asian Dream,* Publikatie nr. 20, Afdeling Zuid-en Zuidoost Azie Anthropologisch — Sociologisch Centrum, Universteit van Amsterdam, 1973.

Winstedt, R.O., 'Kinship and enthronement in Malaya', *JMBRAS,* 20 pt. I, 1947; 129-138.

Wong, D., *Tenure and Land Dealings in the Malay States,* Singapore University Press, 1975.

Zaharah Hj. Mahmood, 'The period and nature of traditional settlement in Malay peninsula', *JMBRAS,* 43, pt. 2, 1970; 82–113.

Government Enactments and Records

Government of Kelantan, Enactment No. 28, 1938.
—— Enactment No. 6, 1972.
—— Shariah Courts and Matrimonial Causes Enactment, 1966 and Kelantan Council of Religion and Malay Custom Enactment, 1966, Kuala Trengganu, 1974.

B.A. (Kelantan) Letter to editor Straits Times, September 1931.
" " files 183/31.
" " files 162/31.
" " memo K168/1931.
" " memo 29/8/1931.

